Code Generation in Action

JACK HERRINGTON

MANNING

Greenwich
(74° w. long.)

For online information and ordering of this and other Manning books, visit
http://www.manning.com. The publisher offers discounts on this book when
ordered in quantity. For more information, please contact:

Special Sales Department
Manning Publications Co.
209 Bruce Park Avenue   Fax: (203) 661-9018
Greenwich, CT 06830   email: orders@manning.com

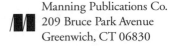
Manning Publications Co.   Copyeditor: Elizabeth Welch
209 Bruce Park Avenue   Typesetter: Aleksandra Sikora
Greenwich, CT 06830   Cover designer: Leslie Haimes

ISBN 1-930110-97-9

Printed in the United States of America
1 2 3 4 5 6 7 8 9 10 – VHG – 06 05 04 03

This book is dedicated to my wife, Lori, and my daughter, Megan,
whose support and sacrifice made the book possible.
The lesson I've learned from this experience
is that writing a great book is important—
but appreciating family is even more important.

Lieben und arbeiten.
—Sigmund Freud

brief contents

contents

Part II   Code generation solutions   97

preface

The two main constants in software engineering are:

- Programmers' time is valuable.
- Programmers don't like repetitive, boring tasks.

Code generation takes over the task of writing repetitive infrastructure code, leaving more time for engineers to concentrate on the interesting programming challenges that they do enjoy.

Code generation doesn't just eliminate grunt work; it provides benefits to the software engineering lifecycle in these four broad categories:

- *Productivity*—Using code generation, you can realize productivity levels that are impossible to attain via hand-coding. Code generators can build hundreds of classes in seconds. And when you need to modify your code, your changes can be propagated across the system quickly.

- *Quality*—Generated code has a uniform quality across the entire code base. When you find a bug, you can fix it across the code base with a single generation cycle. Code generation also supports the use of unit testing, the bedrock of quality assurance in a software system.

- *Consistency*—APIs built using code generation techniques are consistent in both signatures and variable naming. This makes the systems easier to hand-code later, if necessary, and makes building layers of functionality on top of the APIs equally straightforward.

- *Abstraction*—Some code generators take an abstract model of the target system as input. This abstract model represents the high-level business rules of the target system. In this way, the rules are visible to both analysts and engineers; by contrast, rules are hidden in the implementation minutiae of hand-built code. In addition, the abstract model makes the system portable because you can target the templates used by the generator to different languages, technologies, or frameworks.

This book presents six code generation models, ranging in complexity from simple ones that perform small tasks to generators capable of maintaining the code base for an entire tier of an n-tier system. You can draw on these models to create solutions that will work for your application. We describe each model using real-world case studies, which provide a starting point for your development.

acknowledgments

It takes a lot of effort to write a book, and that doesn't happen on one's own. My thanks go to Eric Rollins for his contribution to chapter 10, "Creating database access generators." I'd also like to thank Marjan Bace, Lori Piquet, and the Manning team for their valuable insight and support. My thanks to technical editor Joe Kleinschmidt for his assistance and advice, and to the following reviewers who took the time to read the manuscript as it was being developed and send in their comments: Wai-Sun Chia, Jeff Cohen, Joel Farley, Clifford Heath, Bruce Ikin, Mark Probert, Norman Richards, Dan Sugalski, and Austin Ziegler.

And finally, I'd like to thank the 2001–2002 Miami Hurricanes football team for providing an example of excellence that I can only hope to achieve.

about this book

This book is designed for technical professionals involved in building and shipping computer software. Our intended audience includes anyone involved in the technical development process, from front-line engineers, to architects, to technical team leaders. The code generator examples are written using the Ruby programming language. Although you may be unfamiliar with Ruby, you should be able to read and understand the code if you know any modern imperative programming languages (e.g., C, C++, C#, Java, Perl, or Python). In addition, the chapters contain target code in a variety of languages, including C, Java, and SQL. Some familiarity with these languages is required.

The term *code generation* is often used to refer to the back end of a compiler, but this is not how it is used in this book. We use the term to refer to the building of high-level code (e.g., C, C++, Java, Perl, Ruby, HTML) using generators that read definitions stored in code or files.

Code generation has a wide variety of applications, but compilation is not one of them. If you are looking for ways to use code generation in a compiler, I suggest you read *Compilers: Principles, Techniques, and Tools*, by Alfred Aho, Ravi Sethi, and Jeffrey D. Ullman (Addison-Wesley, 1986).

Chapter roadmap

This book is organized into two parts. The first part introduces the basics of code generation and shows some simple examples of the various models we present. The second part applies the code generation models to common coding cases, such as documentation, test cases, database access, and so forth.

Chapter 1: Introducing code generation

The introductory chapter provides an overview of the problem-solving capabilities of code generators, and also examines cultural concerns.

Chapter 2: Code generation basics

In this chapter we provide a foundation of code generation models that we will use throughout the book.

Chapter 3: Code generation tools

This chapter covers the tools we use in this book and the skills you need to be able to develop your own generators.

Chapter 4: Building simple generators

The last chapter in part 1 shows a number of simple generators that solve small but realistic engineering problems. You can use these simple generators as starting points to build more elaborate generators.

Chapter 5: Generating user interfaces

Building high-quality and consistent user interfaces quickly is a problem to which we apply the code generation technique in this chapter. The case study provides a complete component-based generator for building JSP interfaces from an abstract definition of the interface requirements.

Chapter 6: Generating documentation

JavaDoc is an example of using code generation to build documentation from source code. In this chapter, we discuss how JavaDoc works and then apply it to SQL documentation.

Chapter 7: Generating unit tests

This chapter applies code generation techniques to building and maintaining unit test code. This makes it easy to build quality test cases and keep them updated as the code changes.

Chapter 8: Embedding SQL with generators

Simplifying SQL work has been a goal of a number of commercial products, such as Pro*C and SQLJ, which embed SQL in C and Java, respectively, and then use a generator to build production C and Java code. This chapter describes how these generators are built and used.

Chapter 9: Handling data

Reading, writing, importing, exporting, and converting data are common engineering problems. This chapter provides code generation solutions for all of these problems.

Chapter 10: Creating database access generators

Database access code is the most commonly generated code because of the primary importance of database code and the ease with which it can be generated. This chapter covers both custom and off-the-shelf generation solutions for several implementation languages.

Chapter 11: Generating web services layers

Providing web services layers for applications is a growing field. In this chapter, we apply code generation to building high-quality web services layers.

Chapter 12: Generating business logic

Business logic isn't usually a generation target, but with some creativity you can go a long way with generating business logic code. This chapter applies that creativity to provide pragmatic generation solutions to building stronger business logic layers.

Chapter 13: More generator ideas

This final chapter in the solutions portion of the book provides several examples of small generators applied to specific problems, such as generating firewall configurations, DLL wrappers, lookup tables, lookup functions, and more.

Appendix A: A brief introduction to Ruby

The generators in this book are written in Ruby. This appendix offers a brief introduction to the Ruby syntax as well as some more advanced concepts.

Appendix B: The simple system test framework

Testing your generator is the key to confidently maintaining and extending the generator. This appendix describes the system test framework that we use on all of the generators in the book.

Appendix C: EJBGen code and templates

This appendix provides the code for the case study generator described in chapter 10.

Appendix D: Integrating code generation into your IDE

Ease of use is critical to ensuring that your generators are used. This appendix shows how you can integrate your generator into some of the popular IDEs to make it easy for other engineers to use.

Appendix E: Simple templating

Sometimes using a text template tool like XSLT, JSP, ASP, or HTML::Mason is too much for a small project. This appendix provides powerful text-templating tools that you can implement in just a few lines of code.

Appendix F: Patterns for regular expressions

Code generators use a lot of text processing, so regular expressions are key. This appendix offers information on using regular expressions in all of the popular languages.

Source code and errata

Source code for our examples, as well as some source code not shown directly in the book, is available at the book's web site, www.manning.com/herrington or at www.codegeneration.net/cgia. The latter is a site managed by the author and there you will find additional articles, interviews, and downloads of interest.

We purposely reduced the number of comments in the source code; the markup around the code acts as documentation. This is not to say that your generator code has to look like the code in the book; you should follow your commenting standards. Fully commented source is available on both web sites.

We have been thorough in our editing, but some errors may have made it to the printer's press. You can check for errata for this book at www.manning.com/herrington or www.codegeneration.net/cgia/errata. You can also submit any errors you might find in this book.

Conventions

In the text, `Courier` typeface is used to denote code. In a concession to the unique nature of code generators, text that is destined to go to generated output is shown in `italic Courier`. This makes reading code embedded within code a little simpler. In the example

```
print "for( int x=0;x<20;x++) {\n";
```

the `for` loop is going to the output file, so it is shown in italics. Because the host `print` operation is part of the generator, it is presented in regular Courier font. Despite the typographic differentiation, discriminating between output code and the code that generates it is not usually an issue because the generator is often written in a language different from that of the output code.

When an important new term is introduced, we use *italics*.

Author Online

Code Generation in Action is supported by an Internet forum, where you may interact with the author and other readers of this book. To access the forum and subscribe to it, point your web browser to www.manning.com/herrington or www.codegenerationi-naction.com. There you will find a link to the forum and registration instructions.

Community support is vital for building and encouraging the adoption of code generation techniques. If you find the ideas presented in the book valuable, we would love to hear about it. If you are having trouble with the concepts, we want to hear that as well.

About the author

Jack Herrington is a senior software engineer who has been developing business and scientific applications for 21 years. He has used code generation throughout his development work. In 2002 he started www.codegeneration.net to provide educational materials and support for code generation techniques in software development. He lives in Union City, California, with Lori, his wife of 10 years, and his baby daughter, Megan Michele. He is a proud Miami Hurricane.

about the title

By combining introductions, overviews, and how-to examples, the *In Action* books are designed to help learning *and* remembering. According to research in cognitive science, the things people remember are things they discover during self-motivated exploration.

Although no one at Manning is a cognitive scientist, we are convinced that for learning to become permanent it must pass through stages of exploration, play, and, interestingly, retelling of what is being learned. People understand and remember new things, which is to say they master them, only after actively exploring them. Humans learn *in action*. An essential part of an *In Action* guide is that it is example-driven. It encourages the reader to try things out, to play with new code, and explore new ideas.

There is another, more mundane, reason for the title of this book: our readers are busy. They use books to do a job or to solve a problem. They need books that allow them to jump in and jump out easily and learn just what they want just when they want it. They need books that aid them *in action*. The books in this series are designed for such readers.

about the cover illustration

The figure on the cover of *Code Generation in Action* is a "Beduino Armado," an armed Bedouin taken from a Spanish compendium of regional dress customs first published in Madrid in 1799. Nomadic Bedouin tribes roamed the Arabian desert on horseback for many hundreds of years until their decline in the twentieth century. The adventure and freedom of their lifestyle continue to captivate the modern imagination.

The Bedouin on the cover certainly depended on his horse to get him where he needed to go. Replacing "horse" with "code generator," the words of the Bedouin legend might still apply to the adventuresome developer of today: "God took a handful of southerly wind, blew His breath over it and created the horse." Code generators are trusted companions that will help you ride in the desert and save you in many a tough spot.

The title page of the Spanish compendium states:

> *Coleccion general de los Trages que usan actualmente todas las Nacionas del Mundo desubierto, dibujados y grabados con la mayor exactitud por R.M.V.A.R. Obra muy util y en special para los que tienen la del viajero universal.*

which we translate, as literally as possible, thus:

> *General collection of costumes currently used in the nations of the known world, designed and printed with great exactitude by R.M.V.A.R. This work is very useful especially for those who hold themselves to be universal travelers.*

Although nothing is known of the designers, engravers, and workers who colored this illustration by hand, the "exactitude" of their execution is evident in this drawing. The "Beduino Armado" is just one of many figures in this colorful collection. Their diversity speaks vividly of the uniqueness and individuality of the world's towns and regions just 200 years ago. This was a time when the dress codes of two regions separated by a few dozen miles identified people uniquely as belonging to one or the other. The collection brings to life a sense of isolation and distance of that period—and of every other historic period except our own hyperkinetic present.

Dress codes have changed since then and the diversity by region, so rich at the time, has faded away. It is now often hard to tell the inhabitant of one continent from another. Perhaps, trying to view it optimistically, we have traded a cultural and visual diversity for a more varied personal life. Or a more varied and interesting intellectual and technical life.

In spite of the current downturn, we at Manning celebrate the inventiveness, the initiative, and, yes, the fun of the computer business with book covers based on the rich diversity of regional life of two centuries ago, brought back to life by the pictures from this collection.

Code generation fundamentals

Part I lays the foundation for understanding code generation techniques and their applications. We cover the various types of code generators and provide simple examples that illustrate their construction and use. We also examine the important, and often overlooked, cultural and procedural aspects of code generation.

In part II, we provide code generation solutions to common software engineering tasks, such as establishing database access layers, developing user interfaces, and creating unit test systems. Part I gives you the background you need to get the most out of the solutions chapters in part II.

C H A P T E R   1

Overview

Code generation is about writing programs that write programs. With today's complex code-intensive frameworks, such as Java 2 Enterprise Edition (J2EE), Microsoft's .NET, and Microsoft Foundation Classes (MFC), it's becoming increasingly important that we use our skills to build programs which aid us in building our applications. Generally speaking, the more complex your framework, the more appealing you will find a code generation solution.

This book is the first to cover the breadth of high-level code generation at the theory level. As we drill down into implementation, we show you how to create generators ranging from very simple coding helpers that you can write in an hour or two, to complex generators that build and manage large portions of your application from abstract models. The book will also aid you in using generators which you can find on the shelf—we explain not only how to find the generators appropriate to your task, but also how to customize and deploy them.

To understand why generators are so valuable, let's start with a hypothetical case study illustrating the building of applications using generation.

1.1 A GENERATION CASE STUDY

In this section, we examine a case study that shows the potential for code generation in modern application development. Our case study examines a corporate accounting application. Because of the complex nature of the accounting work, the initial schema has 150 database tables. By any estimation, it is a massive effort. The requirements specify that the application work in both a client/server mode as well as over HTTP using a web interface.

We chose Java and Enterprise JavaBeans (EJB) as our back-end database access layer, JavaServer Pages (JSP) for the web pages, and Swing for the client portion of the client/server model. This is a standard J2EE architecture. Figure 1.1 shows the block diagram for the accounting application.

The design is simple and standard. The web client comes in through the Tomcat/JSP layer, and the desktop client comes in through a Swing interface that will talk directly (over Remote Method Invocation, or RMI) to the database access layer. This common database access layer encapsulates both database persistence and business logic. The database access layer, in turn, talks directly to the database.

1.1.1 Step 1: generating the database access layer

The code generation portion of the story starts with the building of the database access layer. We establish two teams: one for the database access layer and one for the user interface. We'll start with the database access team.

Our implementation of the EJB architecture specifies five classes and two interfaces per table. This is not a usual object/relational mapping in the EJB model. Each class or interface is in its own file. These seven files make up a single EJB "entity." Seven files multiplied by 150 tables tells us that we are already looking at 1,050 files for the EJB entities. It's a big number, but it is not unusual for a J2EE system with this many tables.

We build from scratch four EJB entities all the way to completion. These entities provide a cross section of the various table structures we have in our schema. Building just these files takes four man-weeks.

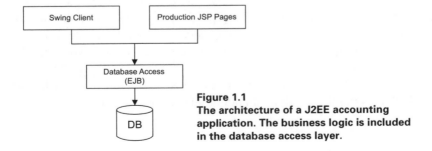

Figure 1.1
The architecture of a J2EE accounting application. The business logic is included in the database access layer.

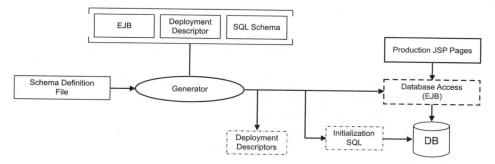

Figure 1.2   The database generator builds the database access classes.

At this point, the schedule looks bad, with only four tables built in four weeks. By extrapolating this timetable, we calculate that the database access layer alone will take three man-years of effort. We must reduce that schedule significantly.

The first thing we notice about the EJB code is that it is pretty standardized, which means it is going to entail a lot of monotonous work. We've had some experience with generators in the past and think that a code generator can be successful in this case. Our previous experience tells us that the first version of the generator will take about two weeks to build. We decide to take the risk and spend two weeks building a generator to create the EJBs.

Using the four example EJBs we have already built, we create templates for a template-based generator. As you'd expect, a template-based generator uses a page-template language (e.g., JSP, ASP, or PHP) to build code. Instead of creating web pages dynamically, we build class implementation files or Extensible Markup Language (XML) deployment descriptors. Figure 1.2 shows the processing flow of our database access layer generator.

The generator takes an XML file as input. This file defines the tables and fields of the database and feeds this input to a series of templates—one template per output file type—and stores the output of the template in the target files. These target files include the database access EJBs (all seven files per table), the Structured Query Language (SQL) for the database, and the deployment descriptors.

This technique is known as *model-driven generation*. The model of the system is abstracted into the schema definition file, which is used to build large portions of the production system. The model can be generated by hand or by using a tool such as Rational Rose, which can export Unified Modeling Language (UML) in XML form.

Our first pass of the generator builds the EJB files, the deployment descriptors, and the schema file for the database. Rather than start with all 150 tables, we pick 10 that together provide a solid test set of the various table types.

The initial results are encouraging. The SQL for the first 10 database tables is built properly on the first try. The EJB classes have some initial problems, but we are able

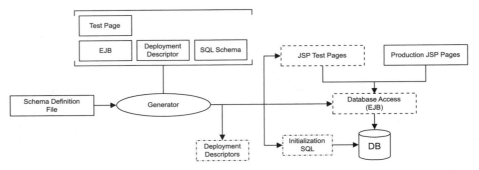

Figure 1.3   The generator builds the JSP test pages as well as all the previous output files.

to debug the classes and then alter the templates accordingly. Running the generator fixes bug occurrences across all the EJBs.

This is a good start, but we want an end-to-end test—one that will show the system working through a web server. We decide to upgrade the generator to have it also build a set of simple JSP test pages that will work through the EJB layer. This will not be the finished interface, but it will allow us to create a simple unit test of our database access layer. At this point the generator block diagram looks like the one shown in figure 1.3.

Again the results are encouraging. The generator builds test pages that will test the EJB session beans to make sure the whole system works from end to end. To make it simple, our test pages map one to one with the session beans. We know that there will be a more complex mapping between entities and production pages because of the requirements of the user interface.

Now we are able to make some observations about the code generation workflow and its benefits:

- Our work on the generator itself is both interesting and motivating. It also broadens our engineering experience.

- We are moving much more quickly toward completion than we would have if we had been hand-coding.

- We are pushing our understanding of both EJB and JSP and finding issues early that we believe we would not otherwise have found until much later.

- We experiment with various types of EJB implementation styles to spot performance or deployment issues. Having the generator means we can write the code one way and try it, and then change the template to try another approach.

Code generation for the database access layer is no longer an option; it is now the implementation model. The next step is to complete the schema definition XML file, which we accomplish with the aid of an XML editing tool such as Altova's XMLSpy.

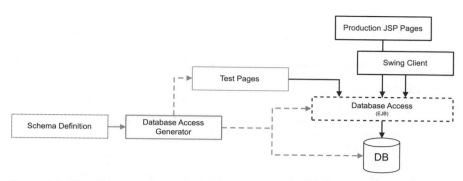

Figure 1.4   How the database generator fits into the accounting application architecture

Figure 1.4 shows how the database generator builds portions of the complete system. In the figure, the production units have a solid black border and the generator has a dark-gray border. A light-gray border indicates an output file, and user-editable files have a dotted light-gray border.

An accounting application is not just schema; it also includes business logic that defines how the schema is used. The schema definition file shown in figure 1.4 is a combination of files that includes the schema and extensions for custom business logic. These are merged together during the construction of the database access classes. We find that putting the business logic and the schema together in a single place makes maintenance and synchronization much easier.

In total, the generator for the database access layer takes four weeks to design, implement, and test—a little longer than the anticipated two weeks, but we can deal with that given the productivity gains. (This timeframe is somewhat misleading because the generator and its templates are software and, as such, require long-term maintenance as the project evolves.)

Some initial project metrics

Our estimation of how long it would have taken to hand-code all 1,050 classes is three man-years; it takes us one man-month to build the generator. This represents a significant reduction in our schedule. The resulting EJBs are much more consistent than any we would have handwritten, and they contain all of the functionality we could want. In addition, if large-scale changes are required we can alter the templates and roll them out across the entire code base in seconds.

It's not all about schedule time, though; there are other metrics to analyze. Table 1.1 compares hand-coding and code generation for the database access layer.

Table 1.1 A comparison of hand-coding and code generation for the database access layer

Hand-Coding	Code Generation
Each new class slightly increases on the quality of the previous one. There is a lot of copy-and-pasted code. The code base is of inconsistent quality across the entities.	The code quality is consistent across all of the entities.
Making additions means altering every entity one by one.	When mass changes are required, the templates are updated with the new code and the generator is rerun.
Bugs are fixed one by one across the entities. When a bug affects more than one class, each must be hand-fixed and verified. Some changes made in base classes do not suffer from this problem.	Bugs in the classes are fixed by changes to the templates. When the generator is rerun, all of the classes get the fixes automatically.
Each class has a corresponding unit test that fits within the unit test framework.	Unit tests are critical. We use text differencing to make sure that the generator is still creating the proper implementations. We compare the latest generation against the known goods. In addition we can author or generate classical unit tests as we would by hand-coding.
A compatibility layer is required underneath the code to move it to a different framework.	Because the schema and business logic are stored in a meta description, the generator and templates can be altered to build code for a different language or framework.
The maintenance of the schema is a separate task from the maintenance of the corresponding EJB entity. It is likely that the field definitions in the database will diverge from the corresponding variable definitions in the EJB entities and cause aberrant behavior.	The schema and the entity classes are created at the same time by the same mechanism. Synchronization is automatic. If there is a synchronization problem it is the fault of the generator, so the issue can be addressed easily by fixing and rerunning the generator.

1.1.2 Step 2: generating the user interface

While the database access layer team is busy building the generator, the front-end team is hard at work designing the user interface for our application.

Once the database access team has finished with the first four EJB entities, the user interface team develops all of the necessary pages to support them by hand. For each table, it takes one man-week.

After this prototype phase, we take account of where we are. We know that the engineers will improve their speed over time, but with padding, the schedule for the web user interface is projected to take three man-years to cover all 150 tables with JSP pages.

We decide to use generation for the user interface as well. Given our success with a template-based generator for the database access layer, we decide to use a similar

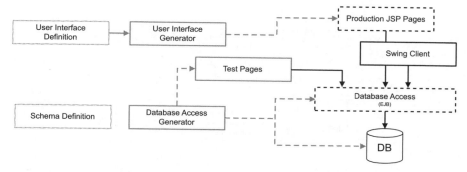

Figure 1.5   The user interface generator building the production JSPs as shown in relation to the database generator

technique for the user interface. We use the pages we built to cover the four database access EJB entities as the basis of the templates. Then we build a user interface generator that takes an XML definition file containing all of the information about the beans and use the templates to generate JSP pages. Figure 1.5 adds the user interface generator to our diagram.

The generator takes six man-weeks to design, build, and test. Even with the first version complete, we make sure that everyone understands that the user interface generator is an ongoing project that will require constant maintenance.

The user interface definition is actually a combination of raw field data and custom options that can be set on a page-by-page basis. That allows for some customizations to be made to the interface on a case-by-case basis.

We hand-code the user interface definition for our four prototype EJBs and use the generator to build the pages. It takes four seconds to build the pages.

That's great, but we still have to create the definitions for all 150 EJB entities. That would be a pain. Instead, the front-end team works with the back-end team to alter the database access generator so that it builds the entity definitions for the user interface.

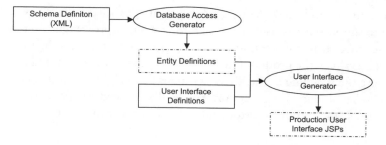

Figure 1.6   The database generator building entity definitions, which are used by the user interface generator in the process of building the JSPs for the production interface

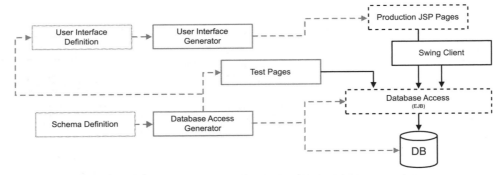

Figure 1.7   The user interface generator now gets part of its information from the database generator. All of the other generator components remain the same.

The two generators now cascade. The output of the database generator is fed into the user interface generator that created the production web interface. Together the two generators build all 150 entities and page sets in four minutes. Figure 1.6 illustrates this cascading architecture. Figure 1.7 shows the linkage between the database access generator and the user interface generator.

Once again, we've turned several man-years of effort into a couple of man-months.

1.1.3   Step 3: building the client interface

Our success with the database and user interface generators make it an easy decision to build a Swing generator. Our experience with building the user interface generator helps us when we work with the graphic designer to simplify the interface to make it easy to generate.

To build the Swing generator, we alter the interface generator to build both JSP and Swing interface code. Developing the templates and altering the generator takes another four weeks. Figure 1.8 shows the addition of the Swing client outputs to the user interface generator.

Our original estimate for building Swing for each entity was two to three days, which meant one and a half man-years for the entire process. Our four weeks of development to support Swing using the generator is a big improvement over that estimate.

These schedule impacts sound almost too good to be true, and in a sense, they are. When you evaluate the productivity benefit of a generator, you should always attempt to compare the schedule of the direct coding tasks against the time taken to develop, deploy, and maintain the generator. You will still need to spend time debugging, building tests, and building custom code that can't be generated.

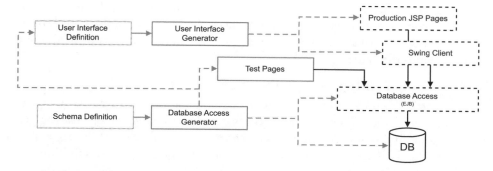

Figure 1.8   The user interface generator builds both the Swing and the JSP code.

1.1.4   Step 4: building unit tests

At this point, the power that the generators hold over our project is a bit intimidating—one small glitch in the templates could invalidate almost every class or page in the system. We need unit tests to ensure that the system runs as expected after the generators are run.

First we need a test data set. The QA group uses an automated tool to preload the data set from the user interface. Now that the database is populated, we can extract the data from the database into a set of test data files. We can then use a generator to build a data loader that will load the test data files through the EJB layer and check the output. This becomes our first unit test tool. Figure 1.9 shows our system with the addition of the unit test generator.

Now whenever the generator is run, we can run a unit-test pass on the output to ensure that the interfaces perform properly.

One enterprising engineer takes it a step further. Because the JSPs built by the generator are so consistent, he is able to build a *user agent* robot using Perl and LWP::Simple that will automatically log into the site, virtually walk around the site

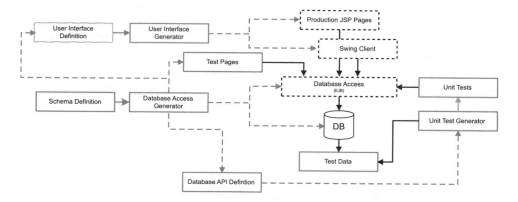

Figure 1.9   The addition of the unit test generator, which tests the database access layer

as if it were a user, and load the test data through the JSP interface. This provides a convenient system test that will check the entire technology stack from end to end. Figure 1.10 shows how the user agent generator connects through the user interface into the system.

1.1.5 Step 5: integrating a technical change

After two weeks of testing, we discover a bug that involves the storage and display of very large numeric values. After some direct debugging against the generated code, we find that the fix requires a change to the definition of 90 percent of the fields in the database, as well as changes to the corresponding type definitions in the majority of the Java classes.

Altering the templates within the generator takes a day. Running the generators requires four minutes. Unit and manual testing consumes two more days.

We calculate that manually making these fixes across all of the Java classes and across the database schema definition would take six months of work and that the code we would have at the end of the process would be of questionable quality.

As you can guess, we are pleased with the difference in outcomes between code generation and hand-coding when it comes to altering the entire code base.

1.1.6 Step 6: integrating a design change

Using code generators has accelerated development to the point where we are able to show some reasonably useful demos early in the process. The demos give both the engineering team and the product marketing group insight into the shortcomings with the original application specification. It is obvious that extra functionality is necessary, to the tune of about 20 new tables. Substantial changes are also required in the structure of some of the existing tables.

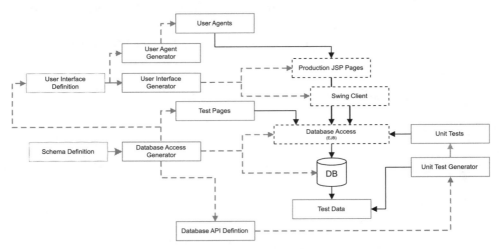

Figure 1.10   The user agent generator builds robots that test the application using the JSP interface.

We are able to react to these changing business requirements by altering our schema definition files and regenerating. After a few iterations and some alterations to the templates, we are able to demo the rudiments of the new schema and refine the feature set even further.

It's almost impossible to calculate how far we would have progressed toward project completion if we had been hand-coding. Discovering the flaws in the design would have necessitated making a serious business decision: either rewrite major portions or maintain the faults in the design. Using code generation, we are able to quickly react to customer demands and make large-scale changes to the structure of the software.

1.1.7   Step 7: building an RPC layer

One of the items on the "wish list" for the project is a Remote Procedure Call (RPC) layer. This had originally fallen off the list because of schedule pressures. Now that we are ahead of schedule, we decide on the fly to take the next step of building a Simple Object Access Protocol (SOAP) layer on top of our application. The RPC layer will go on top of our database access layer. Using the API definitions file that is already being generated for the user interface generator, we create another RPC generator that builds not only the server side of the SOAP layer but also client adapters for Visual Basic and C++, which makes it easy for our customers to use our APIs.

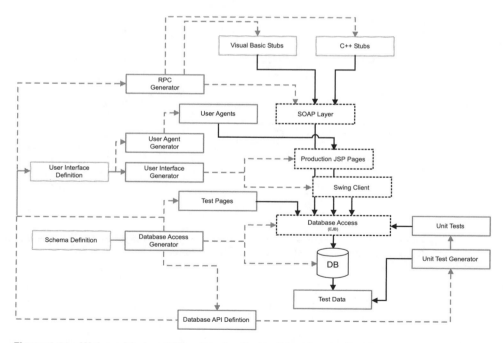

Figure 1.11   We've added an RPC generator that builds not only the server code but the client stub code for both Visual Basic and C++.

Figure 1.11 shows the entire RPC layer. This includes the RPC generator, which in turn builds the SOAP layer, the Visual Basic code, and the C++ stubs.

To test the RPC layer, we use a derivative of the user agent test system. This new robot uses Perl and `SOAP::Lite` to talk to the SOAP layer to implement the test data-loading.

1.1.8   Step 8: building documentation

The final engineering task before deployment is to build documentation both for the RPC layer as an external resource and for the internal APIs as a programmer reference. Using a documentation generator, we build RPC documentation using a definition file that is output as part of the RPC layer generation. The internal API documentation is built using standard JavaDoc tools. Figure 1.12 shows our completed system (the JavaDoc output is implied in this figure).

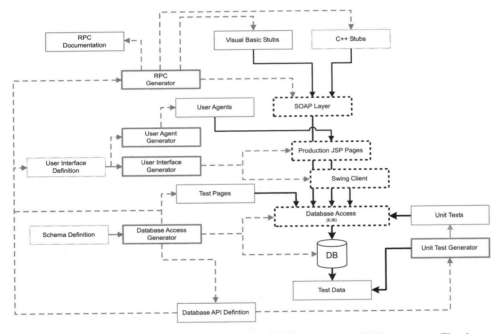

Figure 1.12   The documentation generated for the RPC layer by the RPC generator. The Java-Doc output for the other layers is not shown here.

1.1.9   Case study conclusions

We can make several assertions from this hypothetical case study:

- Code generation has a dramatic impact on development time and engineering productivity.
- The application is amenable to change on a large scale.
- The business rules are abstracted into files that are free of language or framework details that would hinder portability.
- The code for the application is of consistently high quality across the code base.

In the chapters that follow, we describe the techniques we used in this case study in detail.

The case study uses a lot of generation. You may find that your application doesn't need to use that much. Not to worry—this book covers both small and large code generation implementations.

1.2   BENEFITS OF CODE GENERATION FOR ENGINEERS

As the case study shows, code generation techniques provide substantial benefits to software engineers at all levels. These benefits include:

- *Quality*—Large volumes of handwritten code tend to have inconsistent quality because engineers find newer or better approaches as they work. Code generation from templates creates a consistent code base instantly, and when the templates are changed and the generator is run, the bug fixes or coding improvements are applied consistently throughout the code base.
- *Consistency*—The code that is built by a code generator is consistent in the design of the APIs and the use of variable naming. This results in a no-surprises interface that is easy to understand and use.
- *A single point of knowledge*—Using the case study as an example, a change in the schema file percolates through all of the cascading generators to implement the change across the system. Even in the best hand-coded systems, a table name change would involve individual manual changes to the physical schema, the object layer and its documentation, and the test bed. A code generation architecture allows you to change a table name in a single location and then regenerate the schema, the object layer, the documentation, and the test bed to match the new naming requirement.
- *More design time*—The schedule for a code generation project is significantly different than for a hand-coded project. In the schedule for hand-coding large sections, little room exists for analyzing the best use of the system and the APIs. When faulty assumptions are made about use of the framework APIs, then either those decisions are retained or large sections of code have to be

rewritten to use the API appropriately. With code generation, engineers can rewrite the templates to modify how APIs are used and then run the generator to produce the fixed code.

In addition, because code generation compresses time on certain projects, more time can be spent doing adequate design and prototype testing to avoid downstream rework.

- *Design decisions that stand out*—High-level business rules are lost in the minutiae of implementation code. Code generators use abstract definition files to specify the design of the code to be generated. These files are much shorter and more specific than the resulting code. Small exceptions stand out much more clearly in a five-line definition file than in the resulting five hundred lines of implementation code.

To sum up, when you can work *smarter* rather than *harder* and use the computer to offload some of your work, your project will be better off.

1.3   *BENEFITS OF CODE GENERATION FOR MANAGERS*

Many of the advantages to the engineer should be important to engineering management, such as increased productivity and quality. There are certain aspects, however, that are uniquely important at the business level. Let's take a look at these business-level advantages:

- *Architectural consistency*—The code generator used for a project is the realization of the architecture decisions made upfront in the development cycle. This has three advantages:

  - The generator encourages programmers to work within the architecture.
  - When it is difficult to "get the generator to do what I want it to do," it is a good indication that the new feature does not work within the existing architecture.
  - A well-documented and -maintained code generator provides a consistent structure and approach, even as team members leave the project.

- *Abstraction*—The architectures of the code generators presented in this book have the application logic (business logic, database schema definition, user interface definition, etc.) in language-independent definition files. This abstraction of the semantics of the application from the code that implements the semantics has profound benefits:

  - Engineers will be able to build new templates that translate the logic into other languages, or onto other platforms, much more easily than the equivalent port of handwritten code.
  - Business analysts can review and validate the design in the abstract.

- Capturing the application semantics at the abstract level can aid in the development of work products outside implementation code. These can include various forms of documentation, test cases, product support materials, and so forth.

- *High morale*—Long projects can be tough on teams, and long projects with large amounts of tedious coding can be even worse. Code generation reduces project schedules and keeps the engineers focused on the interesting, unique work, as opposed to grinding through large volumes of tedious code. In addition, because the quality of generated code is uniformly high, the engineering team will have confidence and pride in the code base.

- *Agile development*—A key feature of generated code bases is their malleability. We discussed this topic at a technical level earlier; at the business level, this means that the software will be easier to change and upgrade over the long run.

1.4   THE CODE GENERATION PROCESS

In upcoming chapters, we discuss the development lifecycle and how to build a generator. In this section, we provide a roadmap for the development and deployment of a generator within the engineering organization.

The sections that follow outline the entire lifecycle of the generator—from assessing the need, to development, to maintenance.

1.4.1   Assessing the need

The first step in getting help is admitting you have a problem. So it is with code generation. You first need to see the problem you have at hand and then decide if code generation is the right solution to that problem.

In the case study, the first clue that we needed a code generation solution was the schedule impact of writing 1,050 Java files. The second clue was the monotony of the task of writing the Java code. Both of these are strong indicators for using code generation. If you need a lot of Java files, and writing them is monotonous work, you will want to generate those files.

Once you have assessed the need, you must decide for yourself how you want to present the case to engineering and management. You can choose from three basic strategies: the formal method, the Skunkworks method, and the "my own tool" method.

The formal method

This method involves turning the generator into a full-fledged project from the beginning and following whatever process your company has for the design and implementation of software engineering projects.

The first phase of software design is the requirements phase, in which you gather information about what the generator needs to do. In this phase, you want to agree on the scope of the work handled by the generator. In particular, you must clarify these issues:

- How much will the generator do in the first release? The scope should be very clear on this issue.
- How much will the generator do in the subsequent releases? This will help define the long-term architecture of the generator.
- For what is the generator responsible? Having clear lines of responsibility will allow you to ensure that key features are implemented and that extraneous features are left out.
- For what is the generator not responsible? Going through the exercise of cataloging what a piece of software is and is not responsible for is very valuable.
- From an outside perspective, is there anything unusual about what it covers or does not cover? Make sure you catalog the areas of responsibility that could be considered unusual to someone just coming into the project.

In addition to clarifying the scope of the project, make sure you establish some basic goals about the development process for the generator. Here are some points you may want to clarify:

- How will the generator fit into the development cycle?
- Will the generator go to the customer or stay in-house?
- What style of generation will it use? It's important to get a consensus on what type of generator to build. This book will present many types of generators as we go along.
- How and when will an engineer use the generator?
- Is it a permanent or temporary solution?
- Who will maintain the generator?
- Who is the arbiter of features for the generator?
- Is the first release of the generator prototype code or production code?
- What development tools will be used?

These types of questions have to be answered in addition to the standard feature specifications.

The advantage of the formal method is that if the project goes forward, it has everyone's blessing. The disadvantage is that the generator project may fail through bad project management, or by having too many features, or by having too little clarity around the feature set.

The Skunkworks method

The term Skunkworks is used when an engineer goes off on her own time and implements a solution and then returns with it to the team. At this point the question of deployment and maintenance becomes an issue for the team to resolve.

The value of this technique is the elimination of all external influences from the process. You think up the project and then build it. If the generator project fails, then nobody knows but you.

Of course, the disadvantage is that you can frighten or alienate other engineers or managers, and you may lose your work if they decide not to use your generator.

The "my own tool" method

The directive comes down on high that all your methods must now have X by next week to conform to the new architectural standard. What do you do? You can either get typing, or you can make a tool to do the work for you. This is the type of scenario that breeds the "my own tool" generator.

The my-own-tool method is the same as the Skunkworks model except that, at the end, the tool remains yours. You don't present it to the team, because they might say it shouldn't be used. As long as the tool is yours, you can use it as you wish, and nobody will be the wiser.

You may find that you have a perception problem if people find out. It's not good being "that nut with that tool nobody understands."

That being said, there is nothing stopping the my-own-tool generator from becoming a Skunkworks generator or being promoted to a formal method generator. All you need to do is tell people about it and do a little educating.

1.4.2 Laying down the infrastructure

After figuring out what problem you are solving and how you are going to solve it, the next step is to get your tools ready. This process involves several steps. The most important is to control and track versioning across the development team. You will also need to set up a test environment, select the full suite of tools that your team will use, and communicate those choices clearly.

Ensure source-code control

Source-code control is so important that I will mention it many times. Source-code control is vital when working with code generators because large blocks of code are rewritten in the blink of an eye.

Make sure that you are familiar with the command-line interface of your source-code control system. Also, be familiar with any check-in or checkout automation facility the system may have. Using the automation facility may be an easy way to integrate your generator into the development workflow. For example, you could have your documentation generator automatically build documentation upon source code check-in.

You should also check the Internet to see if a wrapper is available for your source-code control system. Perforce, for example, has Perl modules on CPAN that give you access to all of the Perforce functionality through convenient Perl functions.

Build your sandbox

You should use your source-code control system to build a sandbox for the generator and the code it creates—particularly when integrating a generator into an existing system to replace existing code. This allows you to run and test the generator in isolation without worrying about corrupting the main branch and interrupting anyone else's work.

Standardize your development tools

If you are using different development tools for the generator than you are for the application, you will want to spend a little time preparing those tools for deployment. In particular, you should take the time to create an installation kit with just the executables and extra modules required to support the generator. Be sure to document the installation procedure; nothing kills the enthusiasm of an engineering tool deployment quite like installation problems.

This also means locking in the version of the development tool you use. You should look at the versioning of these tools with the same skepticism that you would an update to your C, C++, or Java compiler. Each compiler, interpreter, or plug-in module you use should be frozen at the deployment version and then upgraded with care.

Buy it or build it

At this point, you've laid the groundwork for the development. Now you need to decide whether to buy or build the generator.

Buying a generator is not the end of the game; it is just the beginning. First, you must test and customize the generator against the code you would like to build. Remember, the generator is just a tool. Because you must assume complete responsibility for the code that it generates in production, you should feel completely confident about the behavior of the generator and the code that it creates. Also, standardize the installation of the base package and any customizations that you have made—just as you would with any development tool you use.

The emphasis of this book is on building generators. This approach provides you with full control and also allows you to understand what an off-the-shelf generator is doing for you.

1.4.3   Documenting it

Once the generator is finished with its first release, you should concentrate on documentation. You have to create this documentation regardless of whether you buy or build the generator.

Two basic forms of documentation go along with the generator. The first is the architectural document and will be used by the maintainers of the generator. This document should include:

- The design goal of the generator
- Pros and cons of the generator approach as it applies to the problem at hand
- The block architecture diagram for the generator (see figure 1.5 for example)
- Information about the tools used (e.g., versions, links, installation guidelines, good resources)
- The directory organization
- The format of any input files
- The purpose of every file associated with the generator
- The unit test process
- The installer build process
- Information required to explain the special cases covered by the generator
- Behaviors of the generator that would not be apparent at first glance to someone unfamiliar with the generator
- Contact information for the current maintainers
- Known bugs

The second document is aimed at the end user. It describes how the system is to be used and should address the following:

- What the generator does and does not do
- Installing the generator
- Testing the installation
- Running the generator
- Deciding who should run it
- Determining when it should be run

You should also include:

- A warning about altering the output of the generator by hand
- A graphic that shows the input and output files and the flow of the generation process

- An illustration of possible problems (for example, if a runtime error occurs, describe what that error looks like and what it might mean)
- Contact information for the current maintainers

If the end users of the generator are also the maintainers, then you can merge these documents.

Buy it and alter it

If the third-party code is close enough to your ideal but not quite there, you should consider building a code munger to alter the code to your specifications post-generation. Building and maintaining a custom code generator is no small effort, and anything that can spare your company that expense is worth considering.

1.4.4 Deploying it

Deployment is the most critical phase—and often the most overlooked. Does a tree fall in the forest if nobody is there to hear it? The same applies to programs. A program is of no use to anyone if it is never used. You'll want to concentrate on two areas during deployment: creating installation tools and educating your users.

Making the installers

Your generator will go nowhere if it can't be reliably installed or easily used. You should spend the time building and documenting an installation tool for the components required for the generator. In addition, you need a facility for testing the installation without running the generator. This will make it easier for people who are nervous about running the generator to ensure that it is able to run when they want it to.

Educating the users

Software tools, particularly ones built in-house, need evangelism and support. As the builder, buyer, or maintainer of a generator, it falls on you to educate your fellow engineers and managers on the use and the value of the generator.

An easy way to educate a large group of people is to give a seminar. The seminar should be brief, but should at least cover this information:

- Describe what the generator does.
- Describe what the generator does not do.
- Emphasize the value of the target code and its impact on the project. Emphasize that the code that the engineers write is important, and that the generated code is also important. An architectural decision was made to build the code that is output from the generator; you should support this decision.
- Show the architecture. Explain at a high level how it does its job, but leave the gory details to a question-and-answer session.

- Show how the generator is run. Ideally, you should run the generator during the session so that people get a feel for the code generation cycle and how it integrates into their workflow.

- Show the generated code in action.

- Address fears. Fear of the unknown is natural. At this point you will have been working with the generator for a while, so it will be familiar to you. This will not be the case with others. It is important that you address their natural fears about this new tool. It is also important that you do not attempt to teach them every little detail of implementation of the tool. If you drill down to a low level, then your audience won't know if what you are telling them is important information about how to use it, or just self-aggrandizing trivia about how you built the generator.

- Show the future potential without looking like a zealot. This is a tricky balancing act. You want to appear enthusiastic about the potential of the generator without looking like a megalomaniac. The last thing you want is a room full of people who interpret your words about the generator doing this and that in the future as "It will do your job, and your job..."

- Point people to the documentation.

For more information on how to give an excellent lecture, you should read the books of Edward Tufte: *Visual Explanations, Envisioning Information* (both from Graphics Press, 1998), and *The Visual Display of Quantitative Information* (also from Graphics Press, 1999).

1.4.5 Maintaining it

Any successful software needs to be maintained. If you are the key implementer, you should maintain the project for a while until a suitable replacement can be found to take over the next maintenance period. In addition, you should strive to ensure that you have access to architectural discussions and decisions that might affect the generator.

1.5 THE BUY/BUILD DECISION

The case study spent no time at all on the buy-or-build decision—and that was intentional. This book is primarily about the design and implementation of code generators, and the introductory chapter should talk to the value of the custom solution. In real life, the buy/build decision is a serious one.

To start, there are more options than just buying or building. Several excellent open source code generators are available on the Internet. For purposes of this section, the decision to use an open source code generator will be coupled with the decision to buy, which brings us back to buy and build. If you like, you can say that the decision is to either develop or to use "off the shelf."

The cost of developing and maintaining software is high, so the decision to develop something internally should not be taken lightly. Often the long-term maintenance costs of software are ignored. This is a mistake; maintenance of an existing successful software tool always outstrips the initial development cost.

You and your company will have to decide for yourselves, but we can offer some pros and cons in both directions.

Advantages of building:

- You own the solution outright.
- You control completely the evolution of the tool.

Disadvantages of building:

- Your company must train engineers to use the tool.
- You must maintain the code base long term.
- You must keep the tool reasonably current with the development tools that were used—tools whose version cycles may conflict with your own release schedule.
- The cost of a developer is very high—much higher than the price of an off-the-shelf package.

Advantages of buying:

- There is no upfront developer time building the foundation elements of the tool.
- You may inherit a user community around the tool.
- You can use the documentation provided with the tool to train new engineers.

Disadvantages of buying:

- The deployment cycle needs to account for the time required to customize the tool to the requirements of the application; this could be significant.
- The tool may not work within your development environment the way you would like.
- The long-term evolution of the tool is out of your hands.

We have made every effort to discover the generators that are available both for purchase and from the open source community. We have put references to these tools in the sections that best relate to their function in all of the code generation solution chapters.

1.6   CODE GENERATION AT ITS BEST

With all of the great things we have said about code generation, why not use it for everything?

- Code generation has a large initial schedule overhead for developing the generator before any useful output is created. Code generation becomes genuinely useful only when it is used to create a reasonably significant volume of work.

- You must consider the stability of the design and the feature set. Code generators are ideal for well-known large-scale problems—for example, database access layers, stored procedures, or RPC layers. When the feature set is not particularly stable, or the design for the implementation is shifting, you should consider some hand-coded functional prototypes before implementing a full solution using generation.

- A single tool is not a panacea. Effective solutions are derived by using a number of heterogeneous tools that are well suited to their specific tasks. Code generation is powerful when used appropriately—and laborious when used in the wrong circumstance.

1.7   TOP TEN CODE-GENERATION RULES

Here is a handy set of rules that you can use when you are designing, developing, deploying, and maintaining your code generator:

1 *Give the proper respect to hand-coding*—You should both respect and loathe hand-written code. You should respect it because there are often special cases integrated into code that are overlooked with a cursory inspection. When replacing code you've written by hand, you need to make sure you have the special cases accounted for. You should loathe hand-code because engineering time is extremely valuable, and to waste it on repetitive tasks is nearly criminal. The goal of your generator should always be to optimize the organization's most valuable assets—the creativity and enthusiasm of the engineering team.

2 *Handwrite the code first*—You must fully understand your framework before generating code. Ideally, you should handwrite a significantly broad spectrum of code within the framework first and then use that code as the basis of the templates for the generator.

3 *Control the source code*—I can't stress enough the importance of having a robust source-code control system. This is critical to a successful code-generation project. If your generator works directly on implementation files that contain some hand-written code, make sure you have a versioning system running that can protect your work.

4 *Make a considered decision about the implementation language*—The tools you use to build the generator do not have to be the same tools you use to write the application. The problem that the generator is trying to solve is completely different

from the problem being solved by the application. For that reason, you should look at the generator as an independent project and pick your tools accordingly.

5 *Integrate the generator into the development process*—The generator is a tool to be used by engineers; thus, it should fit cleanly within their development process. If it is appropriate, it can integrate with the integrated development environment (IDE), or in the build process or check-in process. For examples of how to integrate a generator with an IDE, refer to appendix D.

6 *Include warnings*—Your generator should always place warnings around code that it generates so that people do not hand-tweak the code. If they hand-tweak the code and rerun the generator, they will lose their revisions. In addition, your first response to people ignoring the warnings should be to help them and not to berate them. The fact that they are using your tool is a big step. Learn why they needed to ignore the warnings and improve the generator or the documentation. You are the emissary of your tool.

7 *Make it friendly*—Just because a generator is a tool for programmers doesn't mean it gets to be rude. The generator should tell the engineer what it's doing, and what files it has altered or created, and handle its errors with a reasonable amount of decorum. It may sound silly, but a tool that is difficult to use or that's flaky will be ignored and your efforts will be wasted.

8 *Include documentation*—Good documentation is a selling point for the generator. Your documentation should be thorough but not overwhelming, and should highlight the key points: what the generator does, how it is installed, how it is run, and what files it affects.

9 *Keep in mind that generation is a cultural issue*—Educating your colleagues through documentation, seminars, and one-on-one meetings is critical to successfully deploying the generator. People are skeptical of new things, and a good programmer is twice as skeptical as the average person. You need to break through those concerns and doubts and emphasize that you designed the generator for their benefit.

10 *Maintain the generator*—Unless the generator is just a temporary measure, it will need to be maintained long term. If the generator manages a large portion of code, treat it just as you would an engineer maintaining that same piece of code. Your budget should include dedicated time and money for maintaining and upgrading that resource.

1.8 GENERATORS YOU ARE USING TODAY

Understanding that tools that we use every day are code generators can help ease adoption of code generation techniques. Compilers are the most common form of code generators. Compilers generate assembler or virtual machine operands from a high-level language (e.g., C, C++, Java, or Perl).

The C preprocessor is a code generator that is commonly used. The preprocessor handles the `#include`, `#define`, `#if`, and `#ifdef` precompiler directives. Another common generator is a resource compiler that takes a text definition of application resources and builds binary versions of those resources for inclusion in the application.

1.9 SUMMARY

Code generation is an extremely valuable tool that can have a stunning impact on productivity and quality in software engineering projects. It is my hope that through the rest of this book you'll gain a solid understanding in the principles, design, construction, and maintenance of code generators.

In the next chapter, we introduce the basic forms of code generation.

CHAPTER 2

Code generation basics

This chapter introduces you to the range of code generation models that are used throughout the book. Code generators are separated into two high-level categories: active and passive. In the passive model, the code generator builds a set of code, which the engineer is then free to edit and alter at will. The passive generator maintains no responsibility for the code either in the short or long term. The "wizards" in integrated development environments (IDEs) are often passive generators.

Active generators maintain responsibility for the code long term by allowing the generator to be run multiple times over the same output. As changes to the code become necessary, team members can input parameters to the generator and run the generator again to update the code. All of the generators shown in this book follow the active generation model.

In this chapter we look at the various types of active code generators so you can select the one that best works for you. We examine the abstract process flow for a generator so you can understand what goes on under the covers. You'll likely encounter many arguments against code generation, so we talk about what those concerns are and how to evaluate any risk they might present. Finally, we list the various skills you need on your team in order to succeed with code generation.

2.1 THE VARIOUS FORMS OF ACTIVE CODE GENERATION

Within active code generation are several types of models that encompass a range of solutions—from the very simple and small to the large and complex. There are many ways to categorize generators. You can differentiate them by their complexity, by usage, or by their output. We chose to distinguish the generators by their input and output, arriving at six discrete types. This works well because the models tend to have vastly different architectures and are used for different problems and in different ways. By defining various models we can describe how these models are built and used, and then concentrate on their application later in the code generation solutions portion of the book (part 2).

In the sections that follow we examine these six models.

2.1.1 Code munging

Munging is slang for twisting and shaping something from one form into another form.

Given some input code, the munger picks out important features and uses them to create one or more output files of varying types. As you can see in figure 2.1, the process flow is simple. The code munger inputs source code files, most likely using regular expressions or simple source parsing, and then uses built-in or external templates to build output files.

A code *munger* has many possible uses; you could use it to create documentation or to read constants or function prototypes from a file. In chapter 4, "Building simple generators," we discuss seven code mungers. In addition, chapters 6 ("Generating documentation") and 11 ("Generating web services layers") present case studies based on the code munger model.

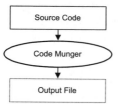

Figure 2.1
The input and output flow pattern for a code munging generator

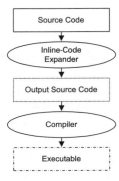

Figure 2.2
The input and output flow pattern
for an inline-code expander

2.1.2 The inline-code expander

An *inline-code expander* takes source code as input and creates production code as output. The input file contains special markup that the expander replaces with production code when it creates the output code. Figure 2.2 illustrates this flow.

Inline-code expanders are commonly used to embed SQL into a source code file. Developers annotate the SQL code with distinguishing marks designed to be cues for the expander. The expander reads the code and, where it finds these cues, inserts the code that implements the SQL query or command. The idea is to keep the development code free of the infrastructure required to manage the query.

See chapter 4 for an example of an inline-code expander. Also, the case study in chapter 8, "Embedding SQL with generators," provides a complete example implementation.

2.1.3 Mixed-code generation

A mixed-code generator reads a source code file and then modifies and replaces the file in place. This is different from inline-code expansion because the mixed-code generator puts the output of the generator back into the input file. This type of generator looks for specially formatted comments, and when it finds them, fills the comment area with some new source code required for production. The process is shown in figure 2.3.

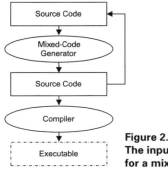

Figure 2.3
The input and output flow pattern
for a mixed-code generator

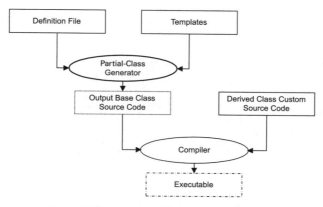

Figure 2.4   The input and output flow for a partial-class generator, including the compiler and the code that uses the generated base classes

Mixed-code generation has a lot of uses. One common use is to build the marshalling code that will move information between dialog controls and their representative variables in a data structure. The comments in the code specify the mapping between data elements and controls, and the mixed-code generator adds an implementation that matches the specification to the comment.

Chapter 4 introduces the mixed-code generator. In addition, chapter 7, "Generating unit tests," describes a case study that illustrates a practical use of the mixed-code generation model to augment C++ code with unit tests.

2.1.4   Partial-class generation

A partial-class generator reads an abstract definition file that contains enough information to build a set of classes. Next, it uses templates to build the output base class libraries. These classes are then compiled with classes built by the engineers to complete the production set of classes. Figure 2.4 shows the flow of input to and output from the partial-class generator. Figure 2.5 contains an example of the process.

Figure 2.5 illustrates how the output code of a partial class generator fits into a three-tier web server architecture. The data access layer beans are based on two classes. Once the partial-class generator builds the base class, the engineer adds the final touches in a derived class to create the production bean.

A partial-class generator is a good starting point for building a generator that creates an entire tier of code. You can start with building just the base class; then as the generator handles more of the special cases, you can transition to having the generator build all of the code for the tier.

Chapter 4 describes a partial-class generator, and chapter 9, "Handling data," also uses a partial-class generator model.

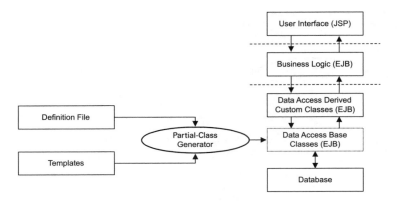

Figure 2.5   A partial-class generator can be used in a web application architecture.

2.1.5   Tier or layer generation

In this model, the generator takes responsibility for building one complete tier of an n-tier system. The case study in chapter 1 included examples of tier generators.

An example of tier generation is *model-driven generation*, wherein a UML authoring application is used in conjunction with a generator and an input definition file (often in XML) to output one or more tiers of a system.

As figure 2.6 shows, the input and output flow of a tier generator is the same as with a partial-class generator. The tier generator reads a definition file and then uses templates to build output classes to implement the specifications in the definition file. Figure 2.7 shows a tier generator building the data access layer for a three-tier web application.

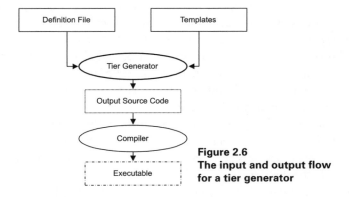

Figure 2.6
The input and output flow
for a tier generator

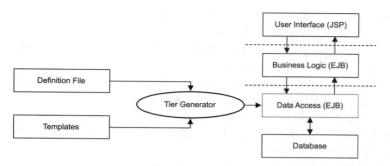

Figure 2.7 A tier generator builds a full tier of an n-tier web application.

The big difference between tier and partial-class generation is that in the tier model the generator builds all of the code for a tier. In the partial-class model, the generator builds the base classes but derived classes are still required to finish off the code for the tier.

The primary advantage of partial-class generation is speed of implementation. The most common difficulty in building a tier generator is designing for special cases, but with a partial-class generator, you can build a relatively simple generator and then implement the special cases with custom code. You should think of moving from partial-class generation to tier generation as a migration path. When the requirements and design are loose, you may still be able to develop a partial-class generator; after the problem space is well known—by the second or third release—you can upgrade the partial generator to a tier generator by migrating the special cases and custom code.

In chapter 4 we describe a simple tier generator, and chapters 6 and 9 present complete examples.

2.1.6   Full-domain language

A *full-domain language* is a Turing complete language customized to allow engineers to represent the concepts in the domain more easily. A *Turing complete language* is a general-purpose computer language that supports all of the variable management, logic, branching, functional, and object decomposition abilities included with today's programming languages.

Code generation, as the term is used in this book, is about generating large amounts of high-level language production code based on descriptive requirements. The end of the spectrum of descriptive requirements is a Turing complete language. So it follows that the end of the spectrum of code generation is a Turing complete domain-specific language.

It is outside the scope of this book to describe the implementation of a domain-specific language. However, let's look at the pros and cons of taking this route.

The advantage is that you have a very high-level functional description of the semantics of your solution that can be compiled into almost any high-level language. As for disadvantages, your team is buying into supporting a new language that you must maintain and document. In addition, you must train your colleagues in the use of this language. Also, with a fully functional language it is difficult to generate derived products (e.g., documentation or test cases). With a tier or partial-class model, the generator understands the structure and purpose of the class being built from the abstract definition. With a Turing complete language, the generator will not understand the semantics of the code at a high level, so automatically generating documentation or test cases will not be possible.

The case study in chapter 12, "Generating business logic," presents a limited example of a full-domain language.

An example of Turing complete domain-specific language is the math language used by Mathematica, a language that supports matrix math in a simple manner. Using matrix math is difficult in traditional languages such as C, C++, or Java. Having a domain-specific language in a product like Mathematica allows the language users to spend more time concentrating on their problem by enabling them to present their code in familiar domain-specific terms.

2.2 CODE GENERATION WORKFLOW

As shown in figure 2.8, the classic workflow for developing and debugging code is "edit, compile, and test." Figure 2.8 shows the edit, compile, and test workflow that cycles between the three states. Code generation adds a few new workflow elements, as shown in figure 2.9. The edit, compile, and test phase still applies for all of the custom code that is either used by or makes use of the generated code.

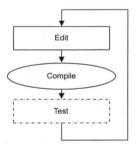

Figure 2.8   The edit, compile, and test workflow

CHAPTER 2   CODE GENERATION BASICS

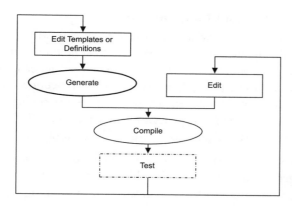

Figure 2.9
The coding workflow when
a code generator is involved

The left-hand side of figure 2.9 shows the generation workflow. First, you edit the templates and definition files (or the generator itself) and then run the generator to create the output files. The output files are then compiled along with the custom code and the application is tested.

If your target language is not a compiled language, then simply disregard the compile phase in the diagrams.

2.2.1 Editing generated code

Unless you are using the inline-code expander model (in which the output files are used in the generation cycle), you should never edit the output files of the generator directly. Generators completely replace the output files so that any revisions to the output files created by the previous generation will be lost. For this reason, we recommend that you bracket in comments the implementation files that are output, to specifically warn the user not to edit them.

There is one exception to this rule. When you are debugging the code in the templates it is easier to edit the output files, diagnose the problem, and then integrate the fix back into the templates.

2.3 CODE GENERATION CONCERNS

No technique is without drawbacks, and code generation is no different. In the following sections, we describe some of the issues you may encounter when proposing, building, and deploying code generators.

Some of these are fear of the unknown, others are an unwillingness to change, and still others are well-founded technical concerns. All of these issues will need to be addressed at some level and at some time during the deployment of a generator. We list them here to help you with some counterpoints to the criticism.

2.3.1 Nobody on my team will accept a generator

Creating a tool that builds in minutes what would take months to write by hand will have a dramatic effect on the development team, particularly if no one on the team has experience with automatic code generation. With a small engineering team or one that has had generator experience, there probably won't be any reticence toward adopting generation. With larger teams you may experience problems. Some engineers may dig in their heels and swear that they won't use generators; they may try to influence other team members as well. Here are suggestions for handling these problems:

- *Start small*—Take a small section of the code base that requires maintenance and replace it with a generated version. Ideally, this will be a section of code that could become larger over time so that the investment in building the generator has a high payoff. Start with a small section of code so that engineers and management can see how code generation works and understand the benefits for the organization.

- *Integrate with the architecture*—When building a new generator, people often suggest changing the architecture of the application in conjunction with building the generator. The idea is to kill two birds with one stone. The first goal is to fix the architecture and the second is to speed up the development process. These findings are welcome of course, but coding more quickly and changing to a better architecture are two separate issues. Our recommendation for your first code generation project is to tackle building code in the existing framework. Once you've finished the generator and tested and stabilized the output code, you can alter the templates to move to a new architectural model.

- *Solve one problem*—The ideal generator can solve a number of problems in the architecture and the implementation of a product, as well as accelerate the schedule. If this is the first generator going into a project, you should concentrate on the schedule issue alone. Taking on several tasks in the first release of a generator can open up too many issues at once and muddle the decision making. You should focus your effort on solving one or two key problems.

2.3.2 Engineers will ignore the "do not edit" comments

One of the most common problems with a generated code base is that engineers will ignore the plentiful warnings in the comments of the file indicating that the code should not be edited.

I can't stress enough that your first reaction to someone breaking the "do not edit" rule should be sympathy. Engineers break the rule because they want to get something done and either they don't understand how to run the generator or the generator simply could not do what they needed. In both cases, you need to educate your team and perhaps alter the function of the generator to address their reasons for ignoring the comments. The important thing is not the infraction, but the fact that a team member was using the code and possibly using the generator—which is a great starting point for the deployment of the generator.

If engineers continue to violate the "do not edit" rule, you may need to go back to the drawing board with the generator, the deployment, or both. Engineers who are conscious of the value of the generator and who understand how the generator works should not alter the output by hand and expect that their changes will be maintained.

2.3.3 If the generator can't build it, the feature will take weeks to build

Suppose you've developed a generator for a user interface builds assembly code from a set of high-level UI definitions. It builds everything: the window drawing code, the message handling, the button drawing—everything, right down to the machine code.

What happens when you need to add a dialog box to your UI that cannot be built with this generator? In the worst-case scenario, you get out your assembly language manual and go for it.

This is an unrealistic and extreme example, but it proves the point that you always want your generator building code that sits on a powerful framework. An example is the Qt cross-platform UI toolkit. Figure 2.10 shows a generator for Qt code.

Should a generator replace the functionality of Qt? No. It should generate code for Qt from high-level UI definitions: the same high-level UI definitions that can be used to build the web interfaces that Qt can't build. There is also nothing wrong with having the generator write code that makes use of your own libraries, which sit on top of powerful frameworks.

As with any software engineering project, you will want to spend the time picking an appropriate and powerful architecture and development environment. Using code generation techniques in combination with the right development tools can significantly enhance the quality and reduce the development time of your application development.

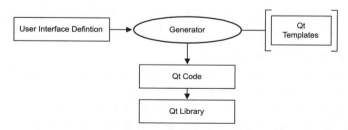

Figure 2.10 Generating code for the Qt framework

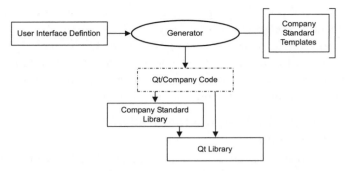

Figure 2.11   Generating code for a combination of Qt and a company-specific interface library

Figure 2.11 shows a generator that builds to both Qt and a company-specific interface library. Including code to manage the interface can make the generator run more smoothly, as well as make it much easier for an implementer to build the dialog boxes that cannot be created by the generator.

2.4   CODE GENERATION SKILLS

In this section, we discuss the specific technical skills you'll need to build generators. If you are unfamiliar with some of these skills, consider using them in practical code generation projects as an ideal opportunity to learn them.

2.4.1   Using text templates

Generating code programmatically means building complex structured text files en masse. To maintain your sanity and the simplicity of the generator, you should use a text-template tool such as HTML::Mason, JSP, ASP, or ERb. Using a text template means that you can keep the formatting of the code separate from the logic that determines what should be built. This separation between the code definition logic and the code formatting logic is an ideal abstraction, which we maintain in the generators presented in this book as case studies.

2.4.2   Writing regular expressions

Regular expressions are a tool for searching and replacing within a block of text. Reading in configuration files or scanning source files is greatly simplified by using regular expressions. Regular expressions allow you to specify a format for text, and then check to see whether the text matches in addition to extracting any information you require from the text.

If you have always thought of regular expressions as indecipherable line noise, now is the time to learn them. The regular expressions used in this book are fairly simple, and you should be able to learn from the examples in the text through context.

For an immersion course in regular expressions, I recommend the book *Mastering Regular Expressions*, by Jeffrey Friedl (O'Reilly, 2002). This excellent book gives you a solid grounding in the art of regular expression construction. Many people learn to use regular expressions as invocations of black magic; they use them without knowing precisely *why* they work. Regular expressions are an invaluable tool and worth your time to learn thoroughly. Once you have mastered them, the idea of writing string parsing code by hand will be forever dashed from your mind.

Appendix F shows examples of regular expressions implemented in Ruby, Perl, Python, Java, C#, and C.

2.4.3 Parsing XML

XML is an ideal format for configuration and abstract definition files. In addition, using schema or Document Type Definition (DTD) validation on the XML can save you from building elaborate error handling into the file-reading code.

There are two styles of XML parsers:

- *Streaming*—Streaming parsers (e.g., Simple API for XML-SAX) send the XML to handlers in the host code as the file is being read. The advantage is that the memory footprint is low and the performance is good, allowing for very large XML files to be read.

- *DOM*—DOM parsers read the entire XML stream, apply validation, and then return a set of in-memory objects to the host code. The memory footprint is much larger than a streaming parser, and the performance is significantly lower. The advantage of using a DOM parser is that the host code is much less complex than the corresponding host code for a streaming parser.

The case studies in this book use a DOM parser because the overall complexity of the code is much lower with DOM. Performance is usually not an issue because the code generator is run during development on fast machines.

2.4.4 File and directory handling

Code generators do a lot of file reading and writing as well as directory handling. If you have had experience only with the Win32 API or the standard C library for file and directory handling, you may be rolling your eyes at the concept of lots of directory access. Now is an ideal time to learn the joy of simple and portable file and directory handling available in Perl, Python, or Ruby.

The most common scripting languages have built-in, easy-to-use APIs for directory construction, directory traversal, and pathname munging, which work on any operating system without code alteration or special cases. The same is also true of file I/O, which is implemented in the core libraries of these languages.

2.4.5   Command-line handling

Code generators are usually command-line based. They are invoked either directly, as part of a check-in or build process, or from an IDE. The example code generators shown in this book are run off the command line.

On Macintosh OS X and other Unix derivatives (e.g., Linux or FreeBSD), the command line is accessible through terminal emulators. On Windows you may want investigate Cygwin, which is a Unix emulator that runs on top of Windows.

2.5   *CHOOSING A LANGUAGE FOR YOUR CODE GENERATOR*

One of the advantages of separating the code writing from the production code itself is that you don't have to use the same language for both tasks. In fact, it is often a good idea to use a different language for each task if only to distinguish the generator code from the code being generated.

Code generators are text processing-intensive applications. A generator reads a number of text files (such as configuration or template files), uses these files to create the output code, and stores the output code in production files.

So what makes a good language for building a generator?

- The ability to easily read, parse, and search text files is critical.
- Text templating is fundamental to code generation, which means support for easy-to-use and powerful text-template tools is important.
- Native handling for XML would be handy, though support through an external library is acceptable. Today a number of high-quality XML authoring and validation tools are available. For that reason alone, XML is a good choice for a configuration file format. The ability to read and manipulate XML data structures is therefore essential.
- Easy and portable file and directory maintenance and searching is necessary; it will be the job of the code generator to find and read input files and manage the output files for the generated code.

On the other hand, some language factors are not important for code generation:

- Language performance is not a high priority because the code generator itself is not in production. It is the generated code that must match the performance metrics of the project.
- Memory space efficiency is also of little concern because the generator is run off-line during development.

On the whole, you need a language that is efficient to develop and easy to maintain, and that supports the range of programming models—from simple scripts to advanced object-oriented designs.

2.5.1   Comparing code generator languages

Table 2.1 shows the pros and cons of using various computer languages for code generation. The differences in each of these languages make them good for some applications and not so good for others.

Table 2.1   Using computer languages for code generation

Language	Pros	Cons
C C++	• If the generator is shipped to customers, they will not be able to read or alter the source.	• The languages are suited to text parsing tasks. • Strong typing is not ideal for text processing applications. • The exceptional execution speed of C is not that important. • Directory I/O is not portable. • XML and regular expression tools are difficult to use.
Java	• If the generator is shipped to customers, they will not be able to read or alter the source. • The code is portable to a number of different operating systems. • XML tools are available. • Text-template tools are available.	• Java is not ideal for text parsing. • Strong typing is not ideal for text processing applications. • The implementation overhead is large for small generators.
Perl Ruby Python	• The code is portable to a number of different operating systems. • The languages scale from small to large generators. • Text parsing is easy. • You can use built-in regular expressions. • The XML APIs are easy to use. • Text-template tools are available.	• Other engineers will need to learn how to create and maintain code in these languages.

2.5.2   Using Ruby to write code generators

I have chosen Ruby as the programming language for the example code generators in this book for the following reasons:

- Ruby has built-in support for regular expressions. Regular expressions are critical for parsing, searching, and modifying text.
- Ruby has portable file and directory I/O constructs.
- Ruby supports several robust text-template tools, including ERb and ERuby.
- Ruby is easy to read and understand.
- Ruby programmers have access to two superb XML libraries in rexml and ruby-libxml.

- Ruby supports the full range of imperative programming models from one-line command-line invocations, to simple scripts, to functional decomposition, to full object-oriented designs.
- Ruby can pack a lot of functionality into a small amount of code. This keeps the code samples in the book shorter.

Ruby was designed and implemented by Yukihiro Matsumoto and released to the public in 1995. As he put it in his introduction to the book *Programming Ruby*, "I wanted a language more powerful than Perl, and more object-oriented than Python." What he developed was a language that is graceful, simple, consistent, and so fun and addictive to write in that you may find yourself wanting to use it in all of your projects.

Appendix A introduces Ruby and gives you a foundation for understanding all the examples in this book and extrapolating that information to whatever code-generation language you choose. You may even find that you feel comfortable enough with Ruby to make it your implementation language.

2.6   SUMMARY

Code generation comes in a few standard forms and you need to be familiar with each of them and how they work in order to select the best one for your project. Although the decision can be difficult, in general you will find that one method will always be clearly superior to the others based on your architecture and goals.

We have also addressed some of the cultural issues around generation so that you can better empathize with the engineering customers of your generator and address their concerns properly. A tool that goes unused or neglected by the people it was meant to serve provides a service to no one, so special care must be given to the successful deployment of the tool.

This chapter provided some insights into the kinds of skills you need to write generators. In the next chapter, we examine the tools you can use to build generators. In addition, we introduce some simple generators that you can use as templates for your own work, as well as generators that fit vertical needs such as user interfaces, test cases, web services, and database access.

C H A P T E R   3

Code generation tools

This chapter discusses the tools used in this book for developing code generators. Like any application, a code generator uses a set of generic tools to perform its function. In this chapter we examine the Ruby programming language itself, as well as a utility for reading XML, a text-template library, and a parsing toolkit for computer languages (C, C++, Java, and SQL). All of these tools will be used in the generators presented in this book. Regardless of whether you use these particular tools in practice, you should familiarize yourself with them so that you can understand the example generators we present in the book.

3.1 BUILDING GENERATORS WITH RUBY

All of the code generators described in this book are implemented in Ruby. Ruby is a general-purpose programming language similar to Perl or Python. One of the key advantages to Ruby—one it shares with Perl and Python—is the ability to scale the complexity of a program from simple scripts to elaborate object-oriented designs. The examples in this book demonstrate Ruby's full range—from small scripts to very large applications. An introduction to the Ruby programming language is provided in appendix A.

The main site for the Ruby language is www.ruby-lang.org. There you'll find a Ruby installation kit appropriate for your machine. Windows users should check out www.rubycentral.com for a convenient Windows installer.

After you have compiled and installed Ruby, you will need to install Rexml (a tool for reading XML files) and ERb (a text-template tool). We'll take a look at these two utilities next.

3.2   PARSING XML WITH REXML

Although Ruby does not include an XML parser as part of its standard libraries, you can select from among several alternatives for reading XML in Ruby—including lib-xml, Rexml, and XMLParser. We chose Rexml for this book because of its ease of use and portability. Rexml is written completely in Ruby, so as long as your Ruby installation works, you can use Rexml.

To download Rexml, go to the Germane Software site (www.germane-software.-com/software/rexml/) and download the latest release. At the time of publication, the latest release was version 2.5.2. Installation instructions are provided on the Germane Software site along with the source code. There you will also find an excellent tutorial.

3.2.1   Using Rexml

In this section we provide some examples of using the Rexml API for reading and writing XML files.

Reading XML text

This example shows how to read the interior text fragments within the XML node. To start with, we need an example XML file:

```
<names>
  <name><first>Charles</first><last>Bronson</last></name>
  <name><first>Chuck</first><last>Norris</last></name>
  <name><first>Stephen</first><last>Segal</last></name>
</names>
```

This XML defines a set of action movie actors' names. Each name node has child first and last nodes, which contain the first and last names of the actors as interior text. The Ruby code shown here will read this XML and print the names:

```
require 'rexml/document'

doc = REXML::Document.new( File.open( "names.xml" ) )    ◄──①  Creates the root
doc.root.each_element( "name" ) { |name_obj|                     document node

                                                          ②  Iterates through
  first = name_obj.elements[ "first" ].text                   each name
  last = name_obj.elements[ "last" ].text
                                                          ③  Gets the first
  print "#{first} #{last}\n"                                   and last names

}
```

① This code creates the Rexml document object by passing the Document constructor with an open File object.

② This code iterates through each of the `name` elements within the root element. Each `name` node is then passed into the block through the `name_obj` variable.

③ The element's hash table is used to find the `first` and `last` nodes; then, the text method is used to return the interior text of the node.

Reading XML attributes

Data can also be stored in the attributes of a tag. The next example shows the same data encoded as attributes:

```
<names>
  <name first="Charles" last="Bronson" />
  <name first="Chuck" last="Norris" />
  <name first="Stephen" last="Segal" />
</names>
```

Here, the first and last names are defined as attributes on the `name` node. The following code reads the names from the attributes:

```
require 'rexml/document'

doc = REXML::Document.new( File.open( "names.xml" ) )
doc.root.each_element( "name" ) { |name_obj|

  first = name_obj.attributes[ "first" ]
  last = name_obj.attributes[ "last" ]

  print "#{first} #{last}\n"

}
```

❶ Getting the first and last name attributes

❶ Using the `attributes` hash table returns the attribute with the specified name. This returns an `Attribute` object, which then implicitly calls the to-string method (`to_s`). This method converts the attribute value to text.

Writing updated XML

The next example builds on the previous one by adding a new attribute called `fullname` to each `name` element. The `fullname` element is the concatenation of the first and last names.

```
require 'rexml/document'

doc = REXML::Document.new( File.open( "names.xml" ) )
doc.root.each_element( "name" ) { |name_obj|

  first = name_obj.attributes[ "first" ]
  last = name_obj.attributes[ "last" ]

  fullname = REXML::Attribute.new( "fullname", "#{first} #{last}" )

  name_obj.add_attribute( fullname )

}

print doc.root
```

❶ Creating the new attribute

❷ Adding the attribute to the node

❸ Converting the nodes back to text

❶ This code creates a new `Attribute` object by providing the key value pair of `full-name` and then the concatenation of the `first` and `last` strings.

❷ The `add_attribute` method takes a single `Attribute` object and adds it to the attribute list for the element.

❸ The `print` method implicitly calls the `to_s` method on the `doc.root` object. The `to_s` method returns a text string with the full XML of the tree.

3.3 ERB: A GREAT TOOL FOR TEMPLATES

ERb is a text-template tool similar to JSP, ASP, PHP, or HTML::Mason. Template tools are invaluable in code generation. Without them, the code you generate is interspersed within the code that manages the output code, directory handling, configuration management, and any other tasks. That mixing results in confusing and difficult-to-maintain code. For example, when you are generating Java with Java, it is difficult to differentiate the output Java from the generator Java.

We chose to use ERb in this book because it is small, simple, reliable, and portable. Other template packages in Ruby require compilation; ERb does not, which means that, like Rexml, if you can run Ruby you can use ERb.

ERb is maintained in Japan, so finding the English documentation and getting to the download can be difficult. However, the ERb download is available on the web site for this book, www.codegeneration.net/erb, and we have provided some simple documentation here.

We discuss some simple alternatives to the ERb toolkit in appendix E.

3.3.1 Installing and using ERb

Once you download the install zip file, unpack it in any directory. Using the shell, run:

```
ruby install.rb
```

in the top directory. You may need root permissions to do this on a Unix system. A successful install will tell you that files have been copied to Ruby's site directory.

You can run ERb directly from the command line, but for our purposes this is unnecessary. We will be invoking the ERb library from our generators and handling the output ourselves.

This simple script reads an ERb template and executes it:

```
require 'erb/erb'

File.open( ARGV[0] ) { |fh|          ❶ Opens the input file

    erb = ERb.new( fh.read )         ❷ Creates a new template

    print erb.result( binding )      ←— Runs the template

}
```

❶ This code creates a new ERb object with the contents of the input file.

❷ This code runs the template and returns the output text. The `binding` method call in-side the `result` method call is actually a call to a method called `binding` that returns the variable bindings within the current context. In this case, it means that the template will have access to the `erb` and `fh` local variables. This is how you pass arguments to an ERb template—you create the variables within the current scope and pass the bindings within that scope to the template.

3.3.2 ERb templates

ERb has a simple template syntax. The simplest ERb template is just text with no replacement areas, like this:

```
Hello World
```

The result of running this template is:

```
Hello World
```

To do something more complex requires knowing the two key constructs of ERb. The first is the `<% ... %>` construct, which embeds Ruby code in the template. The code is executed, but the result is ignored for output purposes. For example:

```
<% name = "Jack" %>          ◁─┐ Sets the value
Hello World                     │ of the name
                                │ variable
```

The output does not change:

```
Hello World
```

Nothing new happens because the result of `name = "Jack"` is ignored. The value of `name` is set and that code is run, but because we haven't used the `<%= ... %>` construct to output the name, we would never know. Let's remedy that:

```
<% name = "Jack" %>          ◁─┐ Uses the value
Hello <%= name %>               │ of the name
                                │ variable
```

This evaluates to:

```
Hello Jack
```

Now you are getting somewhere. The `<%= ... %>` takes the result of the expression within the block and puts it into the output stream.

Any output to standard I/O within an ERb template is output into the ERb result stream. For example:

```
<% name = "Jack" %>
Hello <% print name %>        ◁── Using print instead of <%= %>
```

gives the same output as our earlier example, `"Hello Jack"`. Sometimes using the `print` method can make the template easier to write and understand. You should also notice that the `<% ... %>` and `<%= ... %>` constructs can span multiple lines, and those extra lines will not appear in the output. For example:

```
<%
name = "Jack"
%>
Hello <%= name %>
```

This will still result in `"Hello Jack"`, as above.

You should know how to use an iterator within an ERb template. It's an important pattern that we make extensive use of later in the book. Here is an example:

```
<%
names = []
names.push( { 'first' => "Jack", 'last' => "Herrington" } )    Creates and
names.push( { 'first' => "Lori", 'last' => "Herrington" } )    populates the
names.push( { 'first' => "Megan", 'last' => "Herrington" } )   names array
%>
<% names.each { |name| %>
Hello <%= name[ 'first' ] %> <%= name[ 'last' ] %>            Iterates through names
<% } %>                                                       and builds the output
```

This code will output:

```
Hello Jack Herrington
Hello Lori Herrington
Hello Megan Herrington
```

Notice how the `each` method call block wraps around some ERb template code. This makes it easy to build templates that create multiple output items.

Passing values to an ERb template

Templates don't stand alone; you will need to pass the template values so that it can work on them and produce an acceptable result. Passing values to an ERb template is easy. Let's take the `names` example above. Here is the example host application:

```
require 'erb/erb'

names=[]
names.push( { 'first' => "Jack", 'last' => "Herrington" } )    Creates and
names.push( { 'first' => "Lori", 'last' => "Herrington" } )    populates the
names.push( { 'first' => "Megan", 'last' => "Herrington" } )   list of names

File.open( ARGV[0] ) { |fh|          ◁— Opens the template

   erb = ERb.new( fh.read )          ◁— Creates a new ERb object with the template

   print erb.result( binding )       ◁— Runs the template and prints the result

}
```

The template looks like this:

```
<% names.each { |name| %>
Hello <%= name[ 'first' ] %> <%= name[ 'last' ] %>
<%}%>
```

**Iterates through
names and builds
the output**

Here's the resulting output:

```
Hello Jack Herrington
Hello Lori Herrington
Hello Megan Herrington
```

The template can see the `names` variable because of the call to `binding`, which gives the ERb template handler access to all of the variables within the local scope, including `names`.

3.3.3   Building ASP, JSP, etc. with ERb

One condition that can complicate using templates to build code is when your target is another template. For example, what would happen if you needed to output the `<%` or `%>` values to the ERb template result? The author of ERb thought of this issue and provided a solution using the `<%%` and `%%>` constructs. Here's an example:

```
<edit name="<%= field %>" value="<%% myBean.get<%=  field.capitalize %>()
%%>">
```

If `field` is equal to `"first"` then the output of this template will be

```
<edit name="first" value="<% myBean.getFirst() %>">
```

ready for deployment on your JSP server.

3.4   BUILDING THE LANGUAGE PARSER TOOLKIT

Code generation often involves reading programming language code files and looking for various language constructs, such as comments; class, function, or method definitions; or specially formatted code fragments. For simple jobs like reading specially formatted comments that could appear anywhere in the file, you can get by with regular expressions. For more complex tasks—such as reading function prototypes, matching up comments associated with particular methods or classes, or finding function invocations—you will have to parse the language directly in order to reliably gather the information.

For this reason a set of classes that can parse the important language features of C, C++, Java, SQL, and PostgreSQL is provided with the code for this book. You should be able to use these classes directly if they match your input language, or you could use them as a starting point to parse your input language.

You can build a language parser toolkit using a standard two-phase parsing approach. The first pass takes the input text and turns it into a set of tokens. Tokens are a way of organizing structured text into a set of blocks, which are more easily

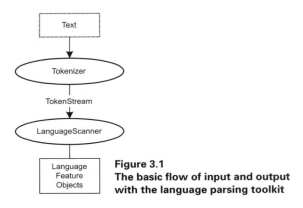

Figure 3.1
The basic flow of input and output with the language parsing toolkit

parsed by downstream code. The `Tokenizer` classes turn the text into tokens. The output of the `Tokenizer` is an object derived from an array called a `TokenStream`.

In the second phase, you analyze the tokens and look for specific language features. The classes that perform this analysis derive from the `LanguageScanner` class. This flow is shown in figure 3.1.

As you can see in figure 3.1, the text goes into the `Tokenizer`, which builds a `TokenStream`. The `TokenStream` is taken as input by the `LanguageScanner`, which analyzes the `TokenStream` and populates an internal store of language features.

The term language features includes elements such as function prototypes, class definitions, comments, and table definitions. The language features that the scanner looks for depends on the input language. For example, the `CLanguageScanner`, which analyzes C code, looks for function prototypes and their associated comments.

3.4.1   Inside the Tokenizers

All of the `Tokenizers` build just three types of tokens: `CodeTokens`, `White-spaceTokens`, and `CommentTokens`. Figure 3.2 shows an example string of C as it is broken out into tokens.

The segment of C in figure 3.2 is tokenized by the `CTokenizer`. Any text that is not inside a comment is considered a `CodeToken`. For special operands (e.g., +, -, * , and ;), a new token is always created. That's why you see b and ; as separate tokens.

Figure 3.2
A sample tokenization of a C expression

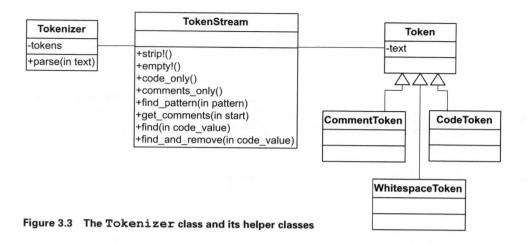

Figure 3.3   The Tokenizer class and its helper classes

Figure 3.3 shows the UML for the relationship between the Tokenizer, Token-Stream, and Tokens objects.

The Tokenizer contains an instance of the TokenStream class. Token-Stream stores an ordered array of Tokens. TokenStream is a derived class of Array, which adds methods that are specific to both creating and analyzing tokens.

I've included two Tokenizer classes with the toolkit: CTokenizer and SQL-Tokenizer. See figure 3.4.

Both of the Tokenizer classes derive from the Tokenizer base class. SQLTokenizer handles both standard SQL and PostgreSQL; CTokenizer handles C, C++, and Java.

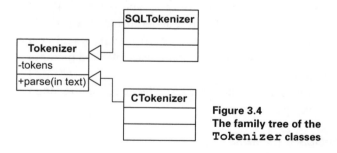

**Figure 3.4
The family tree of the
Tokenizer classes**

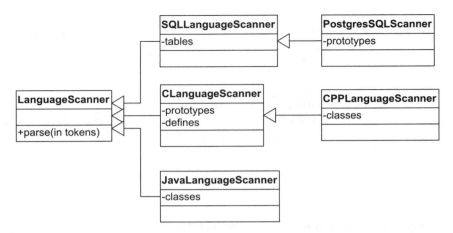

Figure 3.5   The family tree of the `LanguageScanner` **classes**

3.4.2   Inside the LanguageScanners

Layered on top of the `Tokenizers` is a set of language scanners. There is one language scanner for each language the toolkit supports. Figure 3.5 illustrates the relationship between these classes.

All of the classes inherit from the `LanguageScanner` base class, which is an interface providing the one common entry point, `parse()`, that takes a `TokenStream`. On the SQL side of the fence the basic `SQLLanguageScanner` class adds the parsing for tables, and `PostgreSQLScanner` adds support for parsing PostgreSQL-stored procedure prototypes.

The C language tree starts with `CLanguageScanner`, which reads C files and builds a list of function prototypes and `#define` preprocessor macro values. `CPPLanguageScanner` derives from the C scanner and parses C++. In order to handle C++ classes, it adds an array of class objects that define instance variables and methods.

Finally, as you'd expect, `JavaLanguageScanner` parses Java code. It parses the Java class and creates an internal store of instance variables and methods as well as their related JavaDoc comments.

Next, we'll examine each of these classes. The code for the language scanners is available on the book's web site.

The LanguageScanner class

The `LanguageScanner` class and its related classes provide the foundation for all of the specialized language scanners. It contains the basic constructs—prototypes, classes, and class variables—that are used by all of the other scanners. See figure 3.6.

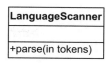

Figure 3.6
The LanguageScanner base class

The LanguageScanner class defines an interface with a single entry point that all of the derived scanners implement. Each language scanner stores the features specific to that language. For example, SQLLanguageScanner stores table information, while CLanguageScanner stores function prototypes and #define values.

The other classes that are related to the LanguageScanner class are shown in figure 3.7.

Along with the LanguageScanner interface, there is an infrastructure for storing details about both plain functions (through the Prototype object) and object-oriented classes (through the definition of the LanguageClass and ClassVariable classes).

In derived language scanners, one or more LanguageClass objects are used to store information about class definitions found in the token stream. Each LanguageClass object contains the class name, information about the class lineage as well as the variables in the class (defined by an array of ClassVariable objects), and any methods (as an array of Prototype objects.)

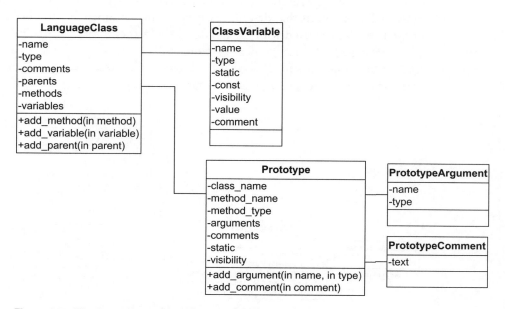

Figure 3.7 The LanguageScanner helper classes

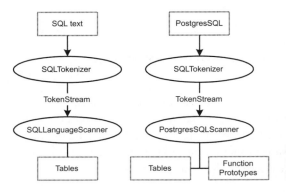

**Figure 3.8
Parsing SQL and PostgreSQL
using the language parsing toolkit**

The SQL scanners

The processing flow for ANSI SQL and PostgreSQL is shown in figure 3.8.

Each code flow starts with running the text through the `SQLTokenizer`, which creates a `TokenStream` from the text. This `TokenStream` is then passed to either `SQLLanguageScanner` (for ANSI SQL) or `PostgreSQLScanner` (for PostgreSQL). Figure 3.9 shows the UML for these SQL language-scanning classes.

`SQLLangaugeScanner` reads `TokenStreams` and then parses and stores information about any table definitions it found. The `Tables` array stores `SQLTable` objects for each table found. Each of the `SQLTable` objects in turn contains an array of `SQLField` objects that describe each field. Any comments found before the table or the fields is associated with the table or field in the `comment` attribute.

`PostgreSQLScanner` derives from `SQLLanguageScanner` and handles reading the prototypes for PostgreSQL-stored procedures. Listings 3.1 and 3.2 show example code for parsing SQL and PostgreSQL, respectively.

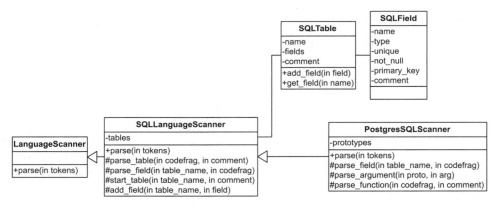

Figure 3.9   The SQL scanning classes

Listing 3.1 Example code for parsing SQL

```
require "SQLTokenizer"              Includes the Tokenizer definitions
require "SQLLanguageScanner"        Includes the Scanner definitions

File.open( ARGV[0] ) { |fh|
  in_text = fh.read()               Opens and reads the file
  tokenizer = SQLTokenizer.new( )
  tokenizer.parse( in_text )        Tokenizes the SQL
  languagescanner = SQLLanguageScanner.new()
  languagescanner.parse( tokenizer.tokens )   Scans the TokenStream
  languagescanner.tables.each{ |table|
     print "#{table.name}\n"        Prints out names of tables
  }
}
```

Listing 3.2 Example code for parsing PostgreSQL

```
require "SQLTokenizer"              Includes the Tokenizer definitions
require "SQLLanguageScanner"        Includes the Scanner definitions

File.open( ARGV[0] ) { |fh|
  in_text = fh.read()               Opens and reads the file
  tokenizer = SQLTokenizer.new( )
  tokenizer.parse( in_text )        Tokenizes the SQL
  languagescanner = PostgreSQLScanner.new()
  languagescanner.parse( tokenizer.tokens )   Scans the TokenStream
  languagescanner.prototypes.each{ |proto|
     print "#{proto.method_name}\n"  Prints out names of tables
  }

}
```

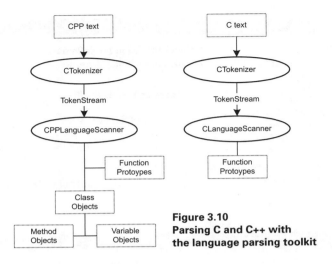

Figure 3.10
Parsing C and C++ with
the language parsing toolkit

The C and C++ scanners

The processing flow of C and C++ files is shown in figure 3.10.

Both C and C++ text is run through a `CTokenizer`, which returns a `Token-Stream`. This `TokenStream` is then fed to either the `CLanguage` or `CPP-LanguageScanner` scanner. These classes are shown in figure 3.11.

The `CLanguageScanner` looks for C function prototypes and preprocessor `#define` macros. It stores the prototypes in an array called `prototypes` and the macros in a hash table called `defines`, which is keyed on the `#define` symbol name.

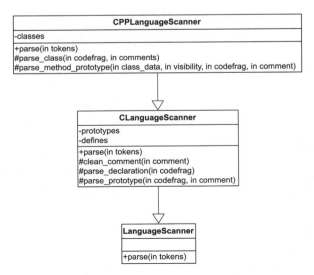

Figure 3.11   The C and C++ language scanner classes

The `CPPLanguageScanner` looks for classes in C++ code that have been tokenized using `CTokenizer`. The resulting classes array is populated with `Language-Class` objects that describe each class as well as its instance variables and methods. Because this derives from `CLanguageScanner`, any standard function prototypes will be read as well. Listing 3.3 contains example code for parsing C, and listing 3.4 shows example code for parsing C++.

Listing 3.3   Example code for parsing C

```
require "CTokenizer"                                    Includes the Tokenizer definitions
require "CLanguageScanner"                              Includes the Scanner definitions

File.open( ARGV[0] ) { |fh|
  in_text = fh.read()
  tokenizer = CTokenizer.new( )                         Tokenizes the C
  tokenizer.parse( in_text )
  languagescanner = CLanguageScanner.new()             Scans the TokenStream
  languagescanner.parse( tokenizer.tokens )
  languagescanner.prototypes.each{ |proto|             Prints out any function names
    print "#{proto.method_name}\n"
  }
}
```

Listing 3.4   Example code for parsing C++

```
require "CTokenizer"                                    Includes the Tokenizer definitions
require "CPPLanguageScanner"                            Includes the Scanner definitions

File.open( ARGV[0] ) { |fh|
  in_text = fh.read()
  tokenizer = CTokenizer.new( )                         Tokenizes the C++
  tokenizer.parse( in_text )
  languagescanner = CPPLanguageScanner.new()           Scans the TokenStream
  languagescanner.parse( tokenizer.tokens )
  languagescanner.classes.each{ |cpp_class|            Prints out any class names
    print "#{cpp_class.name}\n"
  }
}
```

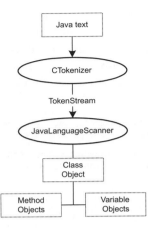

Figure 3.12
Parsing Java using the language parsing toolkit

The Java scanner

Figure 3.12 shows the processing flow for parsing a Java file.

The Java code is fed to the `CTokenizer`, which returns a `TokenStream`. The `TokenStream` is passed to the `JavaLanguageScanner`, which parses the tokens and stores information about the classes and JavaDoc comments. The `Java-LanguageScanner` class and its helper classes are shown in figure 3.13.

This is less complicated than it looks. As with `CPPLanguageScanner`, it is `JavaLanguageScanner`'s responsibility to read the class definitions in the `TokenStream` and store relevant information. The surrounding Java classes are derivations of the basic storage classes with JavaDoc elements added.

For example, the `JavaClass` class is derived from `LanguageClass` and adds an instance of the JavaDoc object. The JavaDoc object is added to allow handling of any JavaDoc comments associated with the class definition. The `JavaVariable` and `JavaPrototype` classes derive from `ClassVariable` and `Prototype`

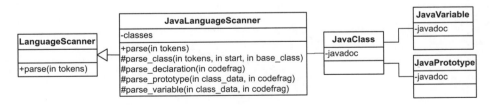

Figure 3.13   The Java language scanner and its related classes

classes, respectively, and add the JavaDoc handling object. Listing 3.5 shows example code for parsing Java.

Listing 3.5   Example code for parsing Java

```
require "CTokenizer"                              Includes the Tokenizer definitions
require "JavaLanguageScanner"                     Includes the Scanner definitions

File.open( ARGV[0] ) { |fh|
  in_text = fh.read()
  tokenizer = CTokenizer.new( )
  tokenizer.parse( in_text )                      Tokenizes the Java
  languagescanner = JavaLanguageScanner.new()
  languagescanner.parse( tokenizer.tokens )       Scans the TokenStream
  languagescanner.classes.each{ |jclass|
    print "#{jclass.name}\n"                       Prints out any class names
  }
}
```

NOTE   If your generation task is strictly Java based and the input to the generator is a set of class definitions, you may want to consider using the Doclet API (see chapter 6, section 6.4).

3.4.3   Language parsing tools

A number of excellent open source and off-the-shelf parsing tools are available; here's a selection:

- Recoder is a language parser and generator toolkit for Java: http://recoder.source-forge.net/.
- Spirit is a parser for domain-specific languages that is written in Java: http://spirit.sourceforge.net/.
- VisualParse from SandStone is a highly regarded parser-building product: www.sand-stone.com.
- The classic parsing tools, lex and yacc, are described in various books and on the Web. The lex and yacc page on the "Compiler Tools" web site is a good starting point: http://dinosaur.compilertools.net/.
- Generators that are written in Java that wish to scan Java code should use the Doclet API described in chapter 6, section 6.4.

3.5 SUMMARY

In this chapter, we explained the basic toolset used to build generators in this book, including the Ruby language, which is used to write the generators themselves. For partial and tier generators, reading XML is important, so we chose Rexml for XML parsing. All of the generators use text templates, and we chose to use ERb.

We also showed how to build a toolset to first parse your application code, creating tokens, and then demonstrated how to analyze those tokens to find important language features in the code. This is an essential step in building a generator that uses source code as input. We included examples of such language parsers for C, C++, Java, SQL, and PostgreSQL.

With those basics established, you're now ready to move on to chapter 4, where we'll build some simple generators.

Building simple generators

In this chapter, we show you how to build simple generators based on the models presented in chapter 2. They provide an introduction to the practical aspect of building generators as well as a starting point for building your own generators. This is an ideal starting point for someone new to code generators. It's also valuable for those experienced with code generators to see how this book approaches their construction.

Here are some points to keep in mind before delving into the examples:

- Some of these generators are so simple that they could be accomplished with existing Unix utilities. While those utilities are powerful, as examples they would provide little insight into building code generators, and as such would give you no foundation for understanding the larger code generators presented in the chapters that follow.

- The Ruby code we present in this chapter is deliberately simple. No functions or classes are specified, and we use only the most basic methods. You should not consider these examples as an indication of what can or cannot be coded in Ruby. Ruby supports the full range of programming models, from simple macros, to function decomposition, to object-oriented programming, to aspect-oriented programming.

4.1   THE CODE MUNGER GENERATOR TYPE

Code munging is the simplest of the code generation models and thus serves as the starting point for our introduction to developing code generators. The code munger takes executable code (e.g., C, Java, C++, SQL), parses the file, and produces some useful output. In this section, we explain what a code munger does and show you six different variants on this fundamental generator type.

4.1.1   Uses and example code

Simple as they are, code mungers solve quite a few difficult problems. For instance, you can use them to:

- Create documentation by reading special comments from a file and creating HTML as output. (An example of this is a JavaDoc.)
- Catalog strings that will require internationalization.
- Report on resource identifier usage.
- Analyze code and report compliance with company standards.
- Create indices of classes, methods, or functions.
- Find and catalog global variable declarations.

A code munger takes an input file, often source code, and searches it for patterns. Once it finds those patterns, it creates a set of one or more output files, as figure 4.1 shows.

Now let's take a look at some specific types of mungers.

Code munger 1—parsing C macros

Our first code munger reads C files looking for #define macros. A #define macro in C looks like this:

```
#define MY_SYMBOL "a value"
```

For example:

```
#define PI 3.4159
```

The munger should find any #define macros and create an output file that contains a line for each symbol, using this format:

```
[symbol name],[symbol value]
```

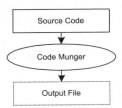

Figure 4.1
The input and output
flow of a code munger

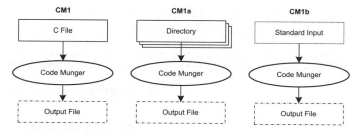

Figure 4.2   The three basic code munger input models, which handle a file, a directory, and standard input

We'll show four variants of the code. The first reads a single file; the second scans a directory and reads all of the eligible files; the third reads the file contents from standard input; and the fourth reads from a file but uses the language parser toolkit to read the `#define` values. Figure 4.2 shows the first three variants in block architecture form.

The advantages of each approach are:

- *Reading from a single file*—This type of code munger is ideal for integration within a Makefile or build process, since it works in the standard compiler style of one input or one or more output files. This type of I/O flow works with the external tool model as described in appendix D.

- *Reading from a directory*—This approach is valuable because the code munger can handle a growing repository of files without the need for code alterations.

- *Reading from standard input*—If the munger reads from standard input, then it can be embedded into IDEs. This type of I/O flow works with the filter model described in appendix D.

Here is our input file for the first variant, which reads from a single file:

```
#include <stdio.h>
#define HELLO "hello"
#define THERE "there"
int main( int argc, char *argv[] )
{
        printf( "%s %s\n", HELLO, THERE );
        return 0;
}
```

The two `#define` macros define `HELLO` and `THERE`. The output file should look like this:

```
HELLO,"hello"
THERE,"there"
```

The two symbols and their values are dumped into the file in comma-separated values (CSV) format. The Ruby generator to accomplish this is shown in listing 4.1.

```
unless ARGV[0]
  print "cm1 usage: cm1 file.c\n"        ❶ Checks the command-line argument
  exit
end
                                          ❷ Opens the output file
File.open( "out.txt", "w" ) { |out_fh|   ❸ Reads a line from the input file
  File.open( ARGV[0] ).each_line { |line|
    next unless ( line =~ /^#define\s+(.*?)\s+(.*?)$/ )    ❹ Looks for the
    out_fh.print "#{$1},#{$2}\n"                               #define macros
  }                                       ◁— Prints to the
}                                             output file
```

❶ This code checks to make sure that you have a value from the command line. If you don't, then it prints a friendly usage statement and exits the program.

❷ The first call to `File.open` opens a new file for output. The first parameter is the file-name and the second optional flag is the mode, in this case w (for *writing*). The default mode is r (for *reading*). If the file can be opened for writing, then the code block is executed and the file handle is passed to the block.

❸ The second call to `File.open` opens the input file that was specified on the command line. This time, however, we use the `each_line` iterator to walk through the file line by line.

❹ This regular expression serves two purposes. First, the expression checks to see if the line is a `#define` macro. If it isn't a `#define` macro, then the `next` operator is executed and the regular expression goes on to the next line. The second function gets the symbol and value text items from the `#define` macro if it finds one. The regular expression is broken out in figure 4.3. The expression looks for a full line because the ^ and $ markers are specified. The line should start with `#define` followed by some white space, followed directly by two segments delimited by white space.

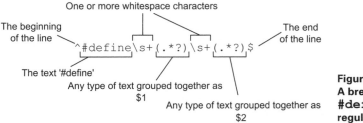

Figure 4.3
A breakout of the
#define macro
regular expression

CHAPTER 4 BUILDING SIMPLE GENERATORS

It is a shame that regular expressions are often regarded as line noise. They are extremely powerful once you get a knack for the syntax. An easy way to learn regular expressions is to use your favorite editor to test regular expression search patterns against the file you want to read. Although regular expression syntax is not consistent across all applications and languages, there is usually a great deal of similarity, and it should be easy to convert the regular expression you develop to the Ruby regular expression syntax.

The second code munger variant reads a directory, finds any C files, and scans them for macros. The code is shown in listing 4.2.

Listing 4.2 Code munger 1, second variant: parsing a directory

```
unless ARGV[0]                                       ❶ Checks the command-
  print "cm1a usage: cm1a dir\n"                       line arguments
  exit
end

File.open( "out.txt", "w" ) { |out_fh|
  Dir.open( ARGV[0] ).each { |file|                  ❷ Reads the directory
    next unless ( file =~ /[.]c$/ )                   ❸ Ignores anything
    print "Reading #{file}\n"                           other than C files
    File.open( file ).each_line { |line|
      next unless ( line =~ /^#define\s+(.*?)\s+(.*?)$/ )
      out_fh.print "#{$1},#{$2}\n"
    }
  }
}
```

❶ This code checks to make sure that you have a value from the command line. If you don't, then it prints a friendly usage statement and exits the program.

❷ The Ruby Dir class is a portable directory access class. The open method opens the directory for reading. The each iterator then walks through every file in the directory and sends the files into the code block one by one.

❸ This code uses a simple regular expression to disqualify any files that do not end with .c. This regular expression is broken out in figure 4.4. The period character in a regular expression represents any character, so when you actually want to specify a period you need to use the [.] syntax. The c string matches "c" and the $ means the end of the line. The expression reads *search for .c at the end of the string*. When applied to a file-name string, this means *match any filename that has a .c extension*.

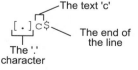

Figure 4.4
A breakout of the .c regular expression

The third variant (listing 4.3) uses the standard input for the contents of the C file and then creates the out.txt file in response.

Listing 4.3   Code munger 1, third variant: reading from standard input

```
File.open( "out.txt", "w" ) { |out_fh|
  $stdin.each_line { |line|                          ❶ Reads input
    next unless ( line =~ /^#define\s+(.*?)\s+(.*?)$/ )   from stdin
    out_fh.print "#{$1},#{$2}\n"
  }
}
```

❶ The global $stdin stands for standard input. This object can be used as if it were any file that was opened as read only.

The fourth variant (listing 4.4) reads from a file but uses the language parser toolkit to get the macro names.

**Listing 4.4   Code munger 1, fourth variant: reading from a file
using the language parser toolkit**

```
require "CTokenizer"                       Imports the tokenizer
require "CLanguageScanner"                 and scanner

unless ARGV[0]
  print "cm1c usage: cm1c file.c\n"
  exit
end

File.open( "out.txt", "w" ) { |out_fh|
  tokenizer = CTokenizer.new( )                        Builds the tokenizer
  tokenizer.parse( File.open( ARGV[0] ).read() )       and reads input
  languagescanner = CLanguageScanner.new()
  languagescanner.parse( tokenizer.tokens )            Scans for C language constructs
  languagescanner.defines.each{ |key,value|
    out_fh.print "#{key},#{value}\n"                   Outputs any
  }                                                     #define values
}
```

Code munger 2—parsing C comments

The second example code munger looks for special comments in a C file. You'll find this example useful if you want to create a special markup language that can be used in close proximity with the code. Here is our example input file:

```
// @important Something important
// @important Something very important

int main( int argc, char *argv[] )
{
```

```
        printf( "Hello World\n" );
        return 0;
}
```

The special comment format is:

```
// @important ...
```

Everything after the `//  @important` prefix is the content of the comment. You can choose whatever terms you like for your comment tags by altering the regular expression in the sample code.

This code munger's job is to find the comments and then store the contents of the comments in an output file. The output file should look like this:

```
Something important
Something very important
```

Listing 4.5 contains the Ruby code you use to implement this.

```
unless ARGV[0]                                          ❶ Checks the
  print "cm2 usage: cm2 file.c\n"                          command line
  exit
end

File.open( "out.txt", "w" ) { |out_fh|
  File.open( ARGV[0] ).each_line { |line|
    next unless ( line =~ /^\/\/\s+@important\s+(.*?)$/ )  ❷ Looks for
    out_fh.print "#{$1}\n"                                    comments
  }
}
```

❶ This code checks to make sure that you have a value from the command line. If you don't, then it prints a friendly usage statement and exits the program.

❷ The heart of this code is the regular expression, which is shown broken out in figure 4.5. The caret symbol (^) at the beginning of the expression symbolizes the beginning of the line. The next four characters—the ones that look like a steeplechase—are the two forward slashes of the comment. Because the forward slash is a reserved character, it needs to be escaped, which means putting a backslash before the character. This is how you end up with the steeplechase pattern: \/\/.

After that, you want to look for one or more whitespace characters and then the @important string. Following that is one or more whitespace characters. Then, use the parentheses to gather together all of the text until the end of the line, which is specified by the $ character.

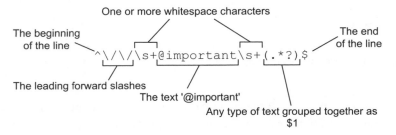

Figure 4.5   A breakout of the @important comment regular expression

Code munger 3: pretty printing C as HTML

One very common use of a code munger is the wholesale conversion of the input file into an entirely new format. Our next example does exactly this type of conversion: the input is a C file and the output is HTML. A typical use for this type of converter would be to generate code fragments for documentation or to create standalone pages that are the end point of some code documentation.

Here is our example C file that we would like to turn into HTML:

```
// A test file for CM2
//
#include <stdio.h>

// @important Something important
// @important Something very important

int main( int argc, char *argv[] )
{
        printf( "Hello World\n" );
        return 0;
}
```

We don't want anything too fancy in the HTML. The title should be the name of the file, and the code should be displayed in Courier. In the next version, you can consider doing some syntax coloring. Here is the type of HTML you should expect from the generator:

```
<html>
<head>
<title>test.c</title>
</head>
<body>
<font face="Courier">
// A test file for cm2<br>
//<br>
#include &lt;stdio.h&gt;<br>
<br>
// @important Something important<br>
// @important Something very important<br>
```

```
<br>
int main( int argc, char *argv[] )<br>
{<br>
   printf( "Hello World\n" );<br>
   return 0;<br>
}<br>
</font>
</body>
</html>
```

Figure 4.6 shows the result when viewed in a web browser.

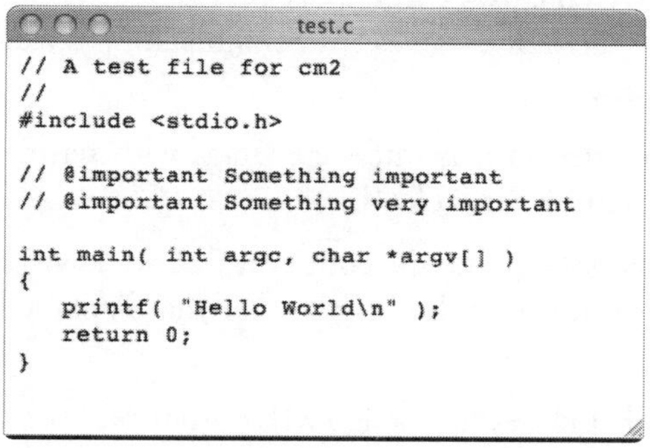

```
// A test file for cm2
//
#include <stdio.h>

// @important Something important
// @important Something very important

int main( int argc, char *argv[] )
{
    printf( "Hello World\n" );
    return 0;
}
```

Figure 4.6
The HTML generated for
test.c shown in a browser

The Ruby for our HTML-converting code munger is shown in listing 4.6.

Listing 4.6   Code munger 3: Converts a C file to HTML

```
unless ARGV[0]                                     ⟵  Checks the
  print "cm3 usage: cm3 files ...\n"                   command line
  exit
end

ARGV.each { |file|

  text = File.open( file ).read()

  text.gsub!( /\&/, "&amp;" )                       ❶  Replaces special
  text.gsub!( /\</, "&lt;" )                            characters with
  text.gsub!( /\>/, "&gt;" )                            HTML entities

  text.gsub!( / /, " " )                       ❷  Replaces
  text.gsub!( /\t/, "   " )             white space

  text.gsub!( /\n/m, "<br>\n" )                     ❸  Replaces end-of-
                                                       line characters
  html_file_name = "#{file}.html"
  print "Creating #{html_file_name}\n"
  File.open( html_file_name, "w" ) { |fh|
    fh.print "<html>\n<head>\n"                     ❹  Contains the
    fh.print "<title>#{file}</title>\n</head>\n"       HTML header
    fh.print "<body>\n<font face=\"Courier\">\n"
```

THE CODE MUNGER GENERATOR TYPE

```
    fh.print text          ◄─── Generates the HTML body
    fh.print "</font>\n</body>\n</html>\n"        ❺ Contains the HTML footer
  }
}
```

❶ The first set of regular expression substitutions scans the complete text and turns special characters into entity references. HTML uses <, > and & in place of <, >, and &.

❷ The second section of regular expressions turns spaces and tabs into nonbreaking spaces. We do this because HTML collapses white space on display. To preserve our formatting, we need to turn our spaces and tables into nonbreaking spaces, which are specified using the   entity.

❸ The last regular expression turns the returns into <br> tags with returns after them. These <br> tags are line break symbols in HTML.

❹ This is the HTML preamble that goes before the code text that we have converted into HTML. The important thing to notice is the insertion of the filename using Ruby's #{expression} syntax.

❺ This is the HTML post-amble that closes up the HTML output file.

Code munger 4: filtering XML

Another common use for a code munger is to filter the input file into a new output file. These types of code mungers are usually built as a one-off to do some type of processing on a file where the output is then used as the new master file. The original file and the generator are then discarded.

This code munger example takes some XML as input and adds some attributes to it, and then creates a new output file with the adjusted XML. Here is our example input file:

```
<classes>
        <class name="foo">
                <field>bar1</field>
                <field>bar2</field>
        </class>
</classes>
```

We want to add a type attribute to each field. To keep the example small, the type will always be integer. The output file should look like this:

```
<classes>
        <class name='foo'>
                <field type='integer'>bar1</field>
                <field type='integer'>bar2</field>
        </class>
</classes>
```

CHAPTER 4   BUILDING SIMPLE GENERATORS

One approach to transform between two XML schemas is to use Extensible Stylesheet Language Transformations (XSLT). Another is to make a dedicated code munger that acts as a filter. The code for the XML filter code munger appears in listing 4.7.

```
require "rexml/document"

unless ARGV[0]
  print "cm4 usage: cm4 files ...\n"
  exit
end
                                                    ❶ Reads the
                                                       original XML
doc = REXML::Document.new( File.open( ARGV[0] ).read ) ⭠

doc.root.each_element( "class/field" ) { |field|   ❷ Inspects each field
  field.attributes.add( REXML::Attribute.new( "type", "integer" ) ) ⭠
}
                                                    Adds the new    ❸
new_file_name = "#{ARGV[0]}.new"                     attribute
print "Creating #{new_file_name}\n"
File.open( new_file_name, "w" ).write( doc.to_s )  ❹ Creates the new file
```

❶ Using REXML::Document.new we construct a new XML document object from the contents of the input file. If this is successful, then all of the XML in the input file will be in memory.

❷ The each_element iterator finds all of the elements that match the given pattern and then passes them into the code block. You should note that the code uses a hierarchical specification for the node by passing in the string "class/field". This tells each_element that we want the field elements within the class elements.

❸ Using the add method we add a new attribute object to the field. This attribute object is created with a key and value pair where the key is type and the value is integer.

❹ Rexml makes building an XML file easy. You create the file using the standard Ruby File object, then use the to-string method (to_s) on the rexml root object to create the text of the altered XML.

Code munger 5: generating C static data from a CSV file

This munger uses the data stored in a CSV file to build a C implementation file that contains all of the data in an array of structures. You could use this file in building static lookup data for use during execution from the output of a database or spreadsheet.

Here's our example data file:

```
"Larry","Wall"
"Brian","Kerninghan"
"Dennis","Ritchie"
```

We would like to take the names of these legends of computer science and store them in C as an array of structures, as shown here:

```
struct {
  char *first;
  char *last;
} g_names[] =
{
  { "Larry","Wall" },
  { "Brian","Kerninghan" },
  { "Dennis","Ritchie" },
  { "","" }
};
```

This code munger is different from the previous code mungers because it uses an ERb template to generate the output code. The Ruby portion of the generator is shown in listing 4.8 and the template is shown in listing 4.9.

Listing 4.8   Listing 4.8 Code munger 5: Creates C constants from a CSV file

```
require "erb/erb"

Name = Struct.new( "Name", :first, :last )        ❶ Creates a new
                                                     Name structure
names = []
File.open( "data.txt" ).each_line { |line|        ⟵— Reads the data file
  name = Name.new()                               ⟵— Creates a new Name object
  ( name.first, name.last ) = line.split( "," ).map{ |val| val.chomp } ⟵
  names.push( name )         ⟵┐ Adds the Name              Gets the first ❷
}                              │ object to the list         and last names
erb = ERb.new( File.open( "data.template.c" ).read )
new_code = erb.result( binding )                  ❸ Runs the
                                                     ERb template
file_name = "data.c"
print "Creating #{file_name}\n"          Creates the
File.open( file_name, "w" ).write( new_code )   output file
```

❶ The `Struct` class facilitates the creation of classes that are just structures. In this case, we create a new class called `Name` with the member variables `first` and `last`. The Struct builder also creates get and set methods for each field. In this case, it means that you can use the `obj.last` or `obj.last = "smith"`.

❷ Here we split the line into its two components, the first and last names, which are delimited by a comma. The `map` method is used to iterate over the fields and to remove any trailing carriage returns by calling the `chomp` method on each item.

❸ This code builds and executes the ERb template for the C data file. The template is run when the `result` method is called. The local variables are passed in by using the `binding` method.

Listing 4.9   Template for code munger 5

```
struct {
  char *first;
  char *last;
} g_names[] =              ⟵ Iterates through each name
{ <% names.each { |name| %>        ⟵ Outputs the first and last name
  { <%= name.first %>,<%= name.last %> },
<% } %>
  { "", "" }
};
```

Code munger 6: building base classes

The last code munger in this chapter shows an easy way of building base classes with rudimentary functionality; you can then derive from those classes to create a completed product.

This may seem a little backward, but it will make sense by the end of the example. You start with the derived class. The base class is specified by the derived class, but the base class itself does not yet exist. The derived class has some comments that specify the design of the base class. The derived class is fed into the code munger, which creates the base class using these instructions. The derived class and base class are then compiled to create the output. This flow is shown in figure 4.7.

This example builds base classes that are primitive data structure objects. A data structure object contains only private instance variables and simple get and set

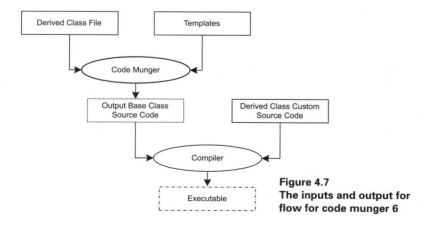

Figure 4.7
The inputs and output for flow for code munger 6

methods to alter the values. These types of classes are grunt work to build so they are ideal for a simple generator.

Let's start with the derived class:

```
// @field first
// @field middle
// @field last

public class Person extends PersonBase
{
  public String toString()
  {
    return _first + " " + _middle + " " + _last;
  }
}
```

Here we have created a new class called `Person`, which should inherit from the as-yet nonexistent base class `PersonBase`. `PersonBase` will be created by the generator. We would like the `Person` class to have three fields: first, middle, and last. To make that happen, we write the three comments at the top of the file; they start with `// @field`. These comments tell the generator that the base class should have three fields: first, middle, and last. You could add an extension to handle types.

The base class looks like this:

```
public class PersonBase {

  protected String _first;
  protected String _middle;
  protected String _last;

  public PersonBase()
  {
    _first = new String();
    _middle = new String();
    _last = new String();
  }

  public String getFirst() {
    return _first;
  }
  public void setFirst( String value ) {
    _first = value;
  }

  public String getMiddle() {
    return _middle;
  }
  public void setMiddle( String value ) {
    _middle = value;
  }

  public String getLast() {
    return _last;
```

```
  }
  public void setLast( String value ) {
    _last = value;
  }

}
```

This base class has the three instance variable declarations: the constructor, and the get and set methods for each instance. We removed the JavaDoc comments for brevity. You need to make sure that the output has JavaDoc when a generator such as this is used in production.

The Ruby code for the generator is shown in listing 4.10. It is similar to the generators we examined at the beginning of this chapter. The new feature is the use of an ERb template to build the output.

Listing 4.10   Code munger 6: Creates Java base classes for data storage

```
require "erb/erb"

unless ARGV[0]
  print "cm6 usage: cm6 file.java\n"
  exit
end

fh = File.open( ARGV[0] )                                    Reads the
text = fh.read()                                             input file
fh.close
                                                       ❶  Creates the
class_name = ARGV[0]                                       output file
class_name.gsub!( /[.]java$/, "" )

new_class_name = "#{class_name}Base"                        Creates the new
                                                              filename    ❷
fields = []
text.scan( /\/\/\s+@field\s+(.*?)\n/m ) { fields.push( $1 ) }   ◀┘

erb = ERb.new( File.open( "base.template.java" ).read )   ❸  Reads the
new_code = erb.result( binding )                              @field comments

print "Creating #{new_class_name}.java\n"                    Runs the ERb
File.open( "#{new_class_name}.java", "w" ).write( new_code )  template
```

❶ This regular expression replacement code finds the `.java` at the end of the filename and replaces it with a null string, effectively removing it. The regular expression is shown in more detail in figure 4.8.

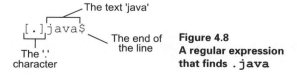

Figure 4.8
A regular expression
that finds .java

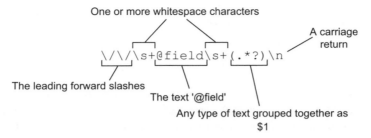

Figure 4.9   A regular expression for finding a field definition comment

❷ This regular expression finds the `// @field field-name` comments in the file. The field name is put into `$1`. Figure 4.9 is a diagram of the regular expression broken out into more detail. The steeplechase segment at the beginning (`\/\/`) corresponds to the two forward slashes at the start of the comment. After that, we look for some white space (`\s+`), the text `@field`, and some more white space (`\s+`). Then we group all of the text together before the return (`\n`).

❸ Here you create the ERb object with the contents of the template file. Run the template to get the output text. The call to `binding` gives the ERb template access to all of the variables and functions within the current scope.

Listing 4.11 shows the ERb template that is used by code munger 6.

Listing 4.11   Base.template.java

```
public class <%= new_class_name %> {          <──  Builds the
<% fields.each { |field| %>                         class name
  protected String _<%= field %>;<% } %>
                                              ❶  Creates each
  public <%= new_class_name %>()                  instance variable
  { <% fields.each { |field| %>
    _<%= field %> = new String();<% } %>      ❷  Creates the
  }                                               constructor
<% fields.each { |field| %>
  public String get<%= field.capitalize %>() {
   return _<%= field %>;                      ❸  Creates
  }                                              get and set
  public void set<%= field.capitalize %>( String value ) {  methods
   _<%= field %> = value;
  }
<% } %>
}
```

❶ Here the template uses the `each` iterator on the `fields` variable to build each field definition.

❷ Next, we use the `fields` array to create `new` invocations for each of the fields in the structure.

❸ The `fields` array builds the get and set methods. The `capitalize` method capitalizes the first character of the string.

4.1.2   Developing the generator

Developing a code munger is straightforward. The process flow in figure 4.10 shows the steps involved.

Let's look at these steps in more detail:

- *Build output test code*—First, determine what the output is supposed to look like. That will give you a target to shoot for and will make it easy to figure out what you need to extract from the input files.

- *Design the generator*—How should the code munger get its input? How should it parse the input? How should the output be built—using templates or just by printing the output? You should work out these issues before diving into the code.

- *Develop the input parser*—The first coding step is to write the input processor. This code will read the input file and extract the information from it that is required to build the output.

- *Develop templates from the test code*—Once the input is handled, the next step is to take the output test code that was originally developed and use it to either create templates or build the code that will create the output.

- *Develop the output code builder*—The last step is to write the glue that takes the data extracted by the input parser and feed it to the output formatter. Then, you must store the output in the appropriate output files.

This is not meant to be a blueprint for your development. Each code munger is slightly different, and you'll add and remove development phases accordingly.

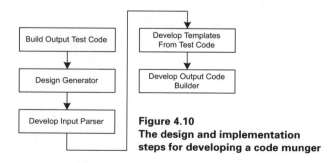

Figure 4.10
The design and implementation
steps for developing a code munger

4.2 THE INLINE-CODE EXPANSION GENERATOR MODEL

Inline-code expansion is an easy way to simplify source code. Sometimes your source code is so mired in infrastructure work that the actual purpose of the code gets lost in its implementation. Inline-code expansion simplifies your code by adding support for a specialized syntax, in which you specify the requirements for the code to be generated. This syntax is parsed by the generator, which then implements code based on the requirements.

A standard use of inline-code expansion is embedding SQL statements within code. SQL access requires a lot of infrastructure: you have to get the database connection handle, prepare the SQL, marshal the arguments, run the command, and parse and store the output. All of this infrastructure code obscures the fact that you are running a simple SELECT. The goal of inline expansion is to allow the engineer to concentrate on the SQL syntax and leave the infrastructure code to the generator.

Here is an example of some code marked up with an inline SQL statement, which is fed into the generator as input:

```
void main( int argc, char *argv[] )
{

    <sql-select: SELECT first, last FROM names>
    return;
}
```

The output of the generator is:

```
void main( int argc, char *argv[] )
{
    struct {
      char *first;
      char *last;
    } *sql_output_1;
    {
      db_connection *db = get_connection();
      sql_statement *sth = db->prepare( "SELECT first, last FROM names" );
      sth->execute();
      sql_output_1 = malloc( sizeof( *sql_output_1 ) * sth->count() );
      for( long index = 0; index < sth->count(); index++ )
      {
          // ... marshal data
      }
    }
    return;
}
```

This output is C pseudo-code and not for any particular SQL access system, but it demonstrates that the actual intent of the original SELECT statement is lost in a quagmire of code.

In this example, we have created a new language on top of C; let's call it SQL-C. The job of the generator is to convert SQL-C into production C for the compiler.

From the design and implementation perspective, the inline-code expander model is a formalized code munger. The input is source code from any computer language. That said, the source code is augmented with some type of markup that will be replaced during the generation cycle with actual production code. The output file has all of the original code, but the special markup has been replaced with production code. This output file is then used for compilation to build the actual product.

4.2.1 Uses and examples

Among the many possible uses for inline-code expansion are:

- Embedding SQL in implementation files
- Embedding performance-critical assembler sections
- Embedding mathematical equations, which are then implemented by the generator

The decision of when to use an inline-code expander versus object-oriented or functional library techniques can be critical. C++ has support for templating and inline expansion within the language. You should look to these tools before contemplating the building of a new language style based on inline-code expansion.

One important reason to avoid inline-code expansion is that the technique can make debugging difficult because you are debugging against the output of the generator and not the original source code. Therefore, the choice to use inline code expansion should be made with great regard for the both the positives and the negatives associated with using this technique. The technique has been used successfully in products such as Pro*C and SQLJ, which embed SQL in C and Java respectively, but there are issues with debugging the resulting code.

Figure 4.11 depicts the input and output flow for the inline-code expansion model.

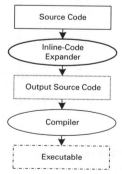

Figure 4.11
The input and output flow for an inline-code expansion generator

The code expander reads the input source code file, replaces any comments, and creates an output file with the resulting code. The output code is fed to the compiler and is used directly as part of the production application.

Let's take a look at an example. This inline-code expander will take strings marked in brackets and implement them with `printf`. The input filename is test.cx; the output filename is test.c. Here's our test input file:

```
int main( int argc, char *argv[] )
{
        <Hello World>
        return 0;
}
```

Our input file specifies that the "Hello World" string should be printed to standard output. The input file is fed to the generator, which outputs the following:

```
int main( int argc, char *argv[] )
{
        printf("Hello World");
        return 0;
}
```

As you can see, the "Hello World" string has been wrapped in a call to `printf` to send it to the standard output. While this example is not particularly useful on its own, it demonstrates the simplest form of the inline-code expansion technique.

The Ruby code that implements this generator is shown in listing 4.12.

Listing 4.12   Listing 4.12 Inline-code expander: Printf maker

```
unless ARGV[0]
  print "ilce1 usage: ilce1 file.cx\n"
  exit
end

fh = File.open( ARGV[0] )                                    Reads
text = fh.read()                                             the file
fh.close

text.gsub!( /<(.*?)>/ ) { "printf(\"#{$1}\");" }      ❶ Replaces <text> items

new_file_name = ARGV[0]
new_file_name.gsub!( /[.]cx$/, ".c" )                 ❷ Builds the new filename

print "Creating #{new_file_name}\n"                          Creates the
File.open( new_file_name, "w" ).write( text )               new file
```

❶ The regular expression substitution routine replaces every occurrence of `<text>` with `printf("text");`. The gsub! method finds all of the occurrences of the regular expression within the string. It then invokes the block on each occurrence and replaces

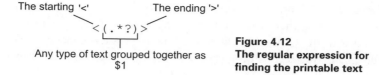

Figure 4.12
The regular expression for finding the printable text

the occurrence with the result of the block. The regular expression is shown in exploded form in figure 4.12.

The < and > characters in the regular expression need to match exactly. In between the two you can place any sequence of characters. In practice, you may want to tighten up the expression to avoid grabbing legitimate C code and regarding it as an expression.

❷ This regular expression substitution replaces the .cx and the end of the filename with .c. Figure 4.13 describes the regular expression. The [.] matches an actual period, the cx matches the string "cx", and the end of the string is marked by $. This expression will match any .cx at the end of a string or, in this case, a filename.

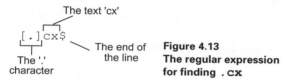

Figure 4.13
The regular expression for finding .cx

4.2.2 Developing the generator

Figure 4.14 shows a sample process for developing an inline-code expansion code generator. Let's examine these steps in greater detail:

- *Build the test code*—First, build the code you would like the generator to create. That way, you can compile it and see if it works for you.

- *Design the generator*—Next, design the input file format for the generator. You should also sketch out the flow of your generator.

- *Develop the input parser*—The first step in building the generator is to read the input file and extract any information from it that is not related to the code

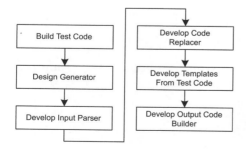

Figure 4.14
The design and implementation steps for developing an inline-code expansion generator

replacement sections. Our code does not do this because the example was too simple. However, there is an advantage to being able to specify global options embedded in the C file that will affect how the code is generated. These options would not be replaced during generation; they would only set flags that would change the style of code that is generated.

- *Develop the code replacer*—The next step is to build the code replacement regular expressions. These are the expressions that will find the special markup sections within the input file.

- *Develop the templates from the test code*—Once you have found the special markup, you can spend time building the templates that will build the output code. In our example code, we didn't use a template because our generator was too simple. For more complex generators, you can use a template-based approach. To create the templates, use the test code that you developed at the beginning of this process as a basis.

- *Develop the output code builder*—The last step is to merge the code replacer and the output code builder. Once this is completed, you will have the finalized output code in memory, and all you need to do is build the output file.

4.3   *THE MIXED-CODE GENERATOR MODEL*

The mixed-code generator is a more practical implementation of the inline-code expansion model. The generator reads the input file, makes some modifications to the file, and then saves it back into the input file after backing up the original.

The potential uses are similar. Using special markup, the generator builds implementation code to match the requirements specified in the markup.

The key difference between the two models is the I/O flow. In the mixed-code generation model, the input file is the output file. Mixed-code generation thus avoids the debugging problems inherent with inline-code generation.

To demonstrate the difference between the two models, we'll show the same example from the inline-code expansion introduction implemented as mixed-code generation, starting with the input:

```
void main( int argc, char *argv[] )
{
    // sql-select: SELECT first, last FROM names
    // sql-select-end
    return;
}
```

Note that the <sql-select: ...> syntax has been replaced with specially formatted comments.

The output of the generator is:

```
void main( int argc, char *argv[] )
{
```

```
// sql-select: SELECT first, last FROM names
struct {
  char *first;
  char *last;
} *sql_output_1;
{
  db_connection *db = get_connection();
  sql_statement *sth = db->prepare( "SELECT first, last FROM names" );
  sth->execute();
  sql_output_1 = malloc( sizeof( *sql_output_1 ) * sth->count() );
  for( long index = 0; index < sth->count(); index++ )
  {
    // ... marshal data
  }
}
// sql-select-end
return;
}
```

Notice how the comments are maintained but that now the interior is populated with code. The code that implements the requirements is specified in the comments. The next time the generator is run, the interior will be removed and updated with newly generated code.

Mixed-code generation has advantages over inline-code expansion:

- The use of comments avoids any syntax corruption with the surrounding code.
- By using comments in the original file, you can take advantage of special features of any IDE, such as syntax coloring or code hints.
- You can use a debugger because the input file is the same as the output file.
- The output code is located right next to the specification, so there is a clear visual correspondence between what you want and how it is implemented.

4.3.1   Uses and examples

The potential uses for mixed-code generation are similar to those for inline-code expansion. However, because of the proximity of the markup code to the generated code you may think of using it for other types of utility coding, such as:

- Building rudimentary get/set methods
- Building marshalling code for user interfaces or dialog boxes
- Building redundant infrastructure code, such as C++ copy constructors or `operator=` methods.

As we mentioned earlier, the major difference between inline-code generation and mixed-code generation is the flow between the input and the output. Figure 4.15 shows the flow for mixed-code generation. As you can see, the generation cycle uses the source code as both the input and the output. This is the same code that is sent to the compiler and used as production code.

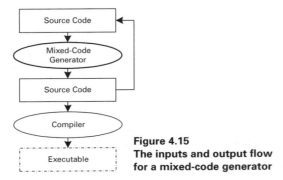

Figure 4.15
The inputs and output flow
for a mixed-code generator

It is the responsibility of the generator to retain a backup of the original code before replacing it with the newly generated code. When you use this model, make sure that you manage the backups and have a reliable source code control system.

Our first example of the mixed-code generation type will build print statements. Here is the input file for our example:

```
int main( int argc, char *argv[] )
{
// print Hello World
// print-end
        return 0;
}
```

We've changed the <...> syntax into comments. There are two reasons for this change. First, the code is compilable both before and after generation. Second, the comments are maintained between generation cycles so that the generator knows which parts of the code to maintain. The output of the generator, which is in the same file as the input, is shown here:

```
int main( int argc, char *argv[] )
{
// print Hello World
printf("Hello World");
// print-end
        return 0;
}
```

The original comments are retained and the implementation code has been put in-between the start and end comments.

Do you need start and end comments? Yes. You need a predictable ending marker for the regular expression. Otherwise, you would not know which code belonged to the generator and therefore could be replaced. You could end up replacing the contents of the file from the starting marker to the end of the file.

Listing 4.13 contains the code that implements our simple mixed-code generator.

Listing 4.13   Mixed-code generator 1: building printfs

```
require "ftools"

unless ARGV[0]
  print "mc1 usage: mc1 file.c\n"
  exit
end

fh = File.open( ARGV[0] )                    Reads the                              Searches for
text = fh.read()                             input file                               start and
fh.close                                                                          end markers  ❶

text.gsub!( /(\/\/\s*print\s+)(.*?)\n(.*?)(\/\/\s*print-end\n)/m ) {  ↵
  code = "printf(\"#{$2}\");\n"                    ❷ Creates the code
  $1 + $2 + "\n" + code + $4                       ❸ Returns the replacement code
}

File.copy( ARGV[0], "#{ARGV[0]}.bak" )        ←— Backs up the original file

File.open( ARGV[0], "w").write( text )        ←— Writes the new file
```

❶ This regular expression finds the `//` `print` … and `//` `print-end` markers and all of the content between the two. The `//` `print` text goes into `$1`; the print specification goes into `$2`. The generated code in the middle, if it is there, goes into `$3`, and the `//` `print-end` goes into `$4`.

The regular expression is shown in exploded form in figure 4.16.

❷ This creates a `printf` call from the string that was specified in the comment.

❸ This puts the expression back together by adding the `code` text to the `$1`, `$2`, and `$4` groups that we preserved from the regular expression.

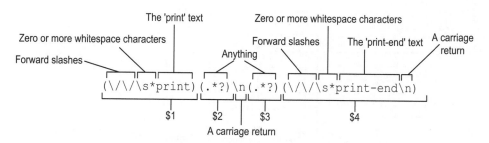

Figure 4.16   The regular expression that finds the special markup comments

4.3.2 Developing the generator

Figure 4.17 shows a simple development process for building a mixed-code generator.

As you can see, this is very similar to the process for developing an inline-code expander:

- *Build the test code*—First, build the code you want to see come out of the generator. That means writing some special markup comments and also identifying the code to be generated.

- *Design the generator*—Sketch out the code flow for the generator.

- *Develop the input parser*—If you want to include any options that you can specify in the input file, this is the time to implement the parsing for that. You need to develop the code that reads the input file and scans for any options that will be used to modify the behavior of the generator. Our earlier example doesn't have any options, but you could imagine that there might be an option for specifying a custom procedure instead of `printf`.

- *Develop the code replacer*—Next, build the regular expression that will read the replacement sections. This expression should find the starting and ending blocks, as well as the arguments and the code in the interior. The example code shows a typical regular expression for this purpose.

- *Develop the templates from the test code*—Now that you have identified replacement regions, you need to develop the code that will populate them with the generated code. The example code is so simple that all you need is to do is some string formatting to build the `printf` statement. If the requirements of your generator are more complex, you may want to use some of the ERb templating techniques shown in chapter 3, "Code generation tools."

- *Develop the output code builder*—The final step is to merge the code replacer with the output code builder to create the final output code. Then you need to back up the original file and replace it with the newly generated code.

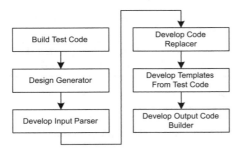

Figure 4.17
The design and implementation steps for developing a mixed-code generator

4.4 THE PARTIAL-CLASS GENERATOR MODEL

The partial-class generation model is the first of the code generators to build code from an abstract model. The previous generators used executable code (e.g., C, Java, C++, SQL) as input. This is the first generator to use an abstract definition of the code to be created as input. Instead of filtering or replacing code fragments, the partial-class generation model takes a description of the code to be created and builds a full set of implementation code.

The difference between this model and tier generation is that the output of a partial-class generator should be used in conjunction with some derived classes that will augment and override the output. Both the base class and the derived class are required to create the fully functioning production form. Tier generation requires no such derived classes because it takes responsibility for building and maintaining all of the code for the tier.

Partial-class generation is a good starting point for tier generation. The advantage of building only part of a class is that you have the ability to override the logic in the generated classes if your business logic has custom requirements that are not covered by the generator. Then, as you add more functionality to the generator, you can migrate the custom code from the user-derived classes back into the generated classes.

4.4.1 Uses and examples

Here are some common uses for partial-class generation:

- Building data access classes that you can override to add business logic
- Developing basic data marshalling for user interfaces
- Creating RPC layers that can be overridden to alter behavior

Figure 4.18 shows the I/O flow using a definition file as the source of the base class structure information.

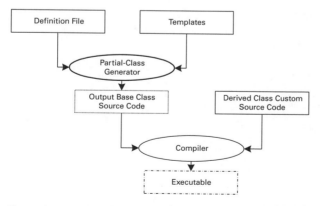

Figure 4.18   A partial-class generator using a definition file for input.
Note that the output of the generator relates to the handwritten code.

In a partial-class generation model, your application code should never create instances of the base classes directly—you should always instantiate the derived classes. This will allow the partial-class generator to transition to a full-tier generator by generating the derived classes directly and removing the original base classes from the project.

Let's look an example. This partial-class generator is closely related to code munger 6. Both generators are building classes for structured storage based on a defined set of the required fields. The output of the generator is a set of classes based on the contents of a simple text definition file, shown here:

```
Person:first,middle,last
```

This small test file specifies one class, Person, which has fields named first, middle, and last. We could have specified more classes by adding extra lines, but just having one class keeps the example simple.

The output class, Person, is shown here:

```
public class PersonBase {

  protected String _first;
  protected String _middle;
  protected String _last;

  public PersonBase()
  {
    _first = new String();
    _middle = new String();
    _last = new String();
  }

  public String getFirst() { return _first; }
  public void setFirst( String value ) { _first = value; }

  public String getMiddle() { return _middle; }
  public void setMiddle( String value ) { _middle = value; }

  public String getLast() { return _last; }
  public void setLast( String value ) { _last = value; }

}
```

Listing 4.14 shows the code for the generator.

```
require "erb/erb"

File.open( "fields.txt" ).each_line { |line|  <—  Reads each line of the input file
  ( class_name, field_text ) = line.split( ":" )  ❶ Reads the class name and fields
  fields = field_text.strip.split( "," )          ❷ Splits the fields into an array
  erb = ERb.new( File.open( "field_class.template.java" ).read )
  new_code = erb.result( binding )                 Runs the ERb template ❸
  print "Creating #{class_name}Base.java\n"        Creates the
  File.open( "#{class_name}Base.java", "w" ).write( new_code )  new file
}
```

❶ The `split` method splits a string into an array on the specified delineator. In this case, we use the `:` character as a delineator. The two elements of the string are then put into the `class_name` and `field_text` variables.

❷ After you have the `field_text`, you want to break it up into an array of `fields`. Use the `split` method again to break up the string, using the comma character as a delineator.

❸ Here you create an ERb object with the contents of the text template. Then, invoke the template using the `result` method. Pass in the variables from the current scope using the `binding` method.

The t1.rb generator uses one template, field_class.template.java:

```
public class <%= class_name %>Base {          <—  Adds the class name
<% fields.each { |field| %>
  protected String _<%= field %>;<% } %>       ❶ Creates the instance variables

  public <%= class_name %>Base()
  { <% fields.each { |field| %>
    _<%= field %> = new String();<% } %>        ❷ Creates the constructor
  }
<% fields.each { |field| %>                     ❸ Creates the get and set methods
  public String get<%= field.capitalize %>() { return _<%= field %>; }
  public void set<%= field.capitalize %>( String value ) { _<%= field %> =
value; }
<% } %>
}
```

❶ Here you iterate through each field and create a `String` instance variable for the field.

❷ In the constructor, this code replaces the class name and then creates calls to `new` for each field.

❸ Finally, this code iterates through each field to create get and set routines with the right field name.

4.4.2 Developing the generator

The example process flow shown in figure 4.19 could be used to develop a partial-class generator.

Let's examine these steps in detail:

- *Build the base class test code*—First, design and build the base class you want the generator to create.

- *Build the derived class test code*—Next, build the derived class that will use the base class as a test case. You should also build the definition file that specifies the base class. The generator will take this file as input.

- *Design the generator*—After building the input, output, and definition files, you need to spend some time creating a simple design for the generator.

- *Develop the input parser*—Your first implementation step is to develop the parser that will read the definition file and store any elements that are required by the generator.

- *Develop the templates from the test code*—The next step is to take your original base class code and to turn it into an ERb template for use by the generator.

- *Develop the output code builder*—The final step is to merge the input parser with the template invocation code and to write the code that will create the output files.

4.5 THE TIER GENERATOR MODEL

A tier generator builds all of the code for one tier or section of an application. The most common example is the constructor of a database access layer tier of a web or client/server application. In this section, we show several forms of a very basic tier generator. You can use the code here as the basis for your tier generator.

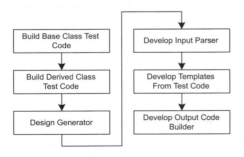

Figure 4.19
A set of design and implementation steps for building a partial-class generator

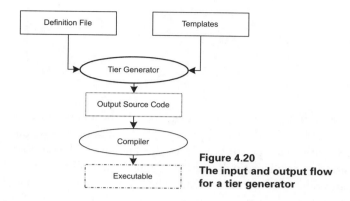

Figure 4.20
The input and output flow for a tier generator

4.5.1   Uses and examples

Besides building database access layers, there are a number of possible uses for a tier generator. These include creating:

- The RPC layer of an application that exports a web services interface
- The stub code in a variety of different languages for your RPC layer
- The dialog boxes for a desktop application.
- The stored procedure layer for managing access to your database schema
- Data export, import, or conversion layers

The input to a tier generator is a definition file from which it gathers all of the information required to build the complete code for the tier. The basic I/O flow is shown in figure 4.20.

The generator takes a definition file, which contains enough information to build all of the classes and functions of the tier. It then uses this information in conjunction with a reservoir of templates to build the output source code. This output code is production ready and waiting for integration into the application.

Our first example of tier generator builds structure classes from XML. It is very closely related to the partial-class generator example. The only difference is the name of the classes that it generates and the format of the definition file. At the implementation level, the two types of generators are very similar—it's in the *roles* of the two types of generators that there is a larger divergence.

The role of the tier generator is to take responsibility for all of the code in the tier. The partial-class generator model opts instead to take partial responsibility for the tier and then lets the engineer create the rest of the derived classes that will complete the functionality for the tier.

This structure generator uses XML to specify the classes and their fields, as opposed to the simple text file in the partial-class generator version. The XML version of the same file used in the original generator is shown here:

```
<classes>
        <class name="Person">
                <field>first</field>
                <field>middle</field>
                <field>last</field>
        </class>
</classes>
```

Note that although this XML file is much bigger, it has the ability to expand to handle extra information more easily than a simple text file. For example, you could add types to each field by specifying a type attribute on the field tag. To do the same on the text file would require creating an increasingly complex syntax. XML also has the advantage of having editing and validation tools that come in handy as your XML files grows larger.

Listing 4.15 contains the code that implements the XML version of the structure class tier generator.

Listing 4.15   The tier generator: building structure classes from XML

```
require 'rexml/document'
require "erb/erb"

doc = REXML::Document.new( File.open( "fields.xml" ) )        ◁— Reads the XML file
doc.root.each_element( "class" ) { |class_obj|               ❶ Iterates through each class
  class_name = class_obj.attributes()[ "name" ]             ❷ Gets the class name
  fields = []
  class_obj.each_element( "field" ) { |field|
    fields.push( field.text.strip )
  }                                                          ❸ Gets the field names
  erb = ERb.new( File.open( "field_class.template.java" ).read )
  new_code = erb.result( binding )                          Runs the  ❹
  print "Creating #{class_name}.java\n"                     ERb template        Writes the
  File.open( "#{class_name}.java", "w" ).write( new_code )                      output file
}
```

❶ The each_element iterator finds all of the elements matching the specified name and passes it into the code block. Here you use the each_element iterator to get all of the class elements in the XML file.

❷ Next, use the attributes method to get an array of the attributes on the class element and dereference the array to get the name attribute.

❸ This code uses the same each_element iterator to get the fields from the class element. Inside the code block, you push the field name into the array of fields. Use the text method to get the text of the element and the strip method to remove any leading or trailing white space.

❹ This code creates the ERb template object from the text template. It then runs the template using the `result` method and passes the variables in the current scope into the template with the `binding` method.

Listing 4.16 shows the template used by the tier generator to build the data structure classes.

Listing 4.16   field_class.template.java

```
public class <%= class_name %> {
<% fields.each { |field| %>
  protected String _<%= field %>;<% } %>

  public <%= class_name %>()
  { <% fields.each { |field| %>
    _<%= field %> = new String();<% } %>
  }
<% fields.each { |field| %>
  public String get<%= field.capitalize %>() { return _<%= field %>; }
  public void set<%= field.capitalize %>( String value ) { _<%= field %> =
value; }
<% } %>
}
```

4.5.2   Developing the generator

Developing a tier generator is much like building any of the other generators in this chapter. We show the steps in figure 4.21, but you should follow your own path; these steps are merely a starting point.

Let's examine these steps in detail:

- *Build the test code*—One of the great things about building a code generator is that you start at the end. The first step is to prototype what you would like to generate by building the output code by hand. In most cases you already have the code you want to generate in hand because it's already part of the application.

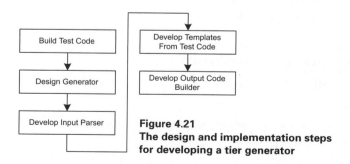

Figure 4.21
The design and implementation steps for developing a tier generator

- *Design the generator*—Once you have the output, you need to determine how you are going to build a generator that will create the test code as output. The most important job is to specify the data requirements. What is the smallest possible collection of knowledge that you need to build the output class? Once you have the data requirements, you will want to design the input definition file format.

- *Develop the input parser*—The first implementation step is to build the definition file parser. In the case of XML, this means writing the Rexml access code to read in the XML and to store it in some internal structures that are easy for the templates to handle.

- *Develop the templates from the test code*—Once the input is coming into the generator, you must create the templates that will build the output files. The easiest way to do this is to take the test code you started as the starting point for the template.

- *Develop the output code builder*—The final step is to write the glue code that runs the templates on the input specification from the definition file and builds the output files. At the end of the development, you should be able to run the generator on your definition file and have the output match the test code that you created in the beginning of the process.

4.6 GENERATING FOR VARIOUS LANGUAGES

Each language creates unique issues for code generation. Each has a unique coding style; in addition to this implicit style, most companies have coding guidelines that enforce additional style requirements. Your generated code should follow this style, just as if you had written the code by hand. This is one of the most important reasons to use templates when building code. Templates allow you the freedom to add white space and position generated code as if you were writing it yourself.

A common complaint about generated code is that the code is not visually appealing. Ugly code conveys a lack of care to the reader and disrespect for the output language and the production code. You should strive to make your templates and their resulting code as clean as if you had written every line yourself. In this section, we explore each of the popular languages and offer advice on using generation techniques and avoiding the common pitfalls.

4.6.1 C

For C, you'll need to keep these considerations in mind:

- Only externally visible functions and constants should be visible in generated header files.

- Internal functions and constants generated within the implementation files should be marked as static.

- Choose and use an inline documentation standard (e.g., Doxygen).

- If you have a development environment that allows for code collapsing while editing, be sure to develop the code in a way that matches the code-collapsing standard.

- Set your compiler to the highest warning level and generate code that compiles without warnings.

- Consider bundling all of the generated code into a single library and then importing that as a component into the application.

4.6.2   C++

In addition to the guidelines for C generation, you should take into account these factors when generating C++:

- Consider using C++ namespaces to contain the generated code in a logical grouping.

- Consider using a pattern where you expose an abstract base class with only public members. This base class is exported in the header. Then, use this abstract class as the basis for an implementation class, which is implemented only in the .cpp file. A factory method can be exported that creates a new instance of the derived class. This will ensure that recompiles will not be necessary when private methods or variables are changed by the generator.

4.6.3   C#

C# appears to have been designed for generation. You should use the inherent language features to your advantage:

- Use the `#region` pragma to allow for code collapsing in the editor.

- Consider packaging all of the generated code as an assembly to reduce compile times and to create logical boundaries between system components.

- Make use of the XML markup capabilities to allow for easy documentation generation.

4.6.4   Java

Here are some suggestions when generating Java:

- For generator input, use the JavaDoc standard when appropriate and the Doclet API for access to your JavaDoc comments.

- For generator output, be sure to include JavaDoc markup in your templates to ensure that you can use the JavaDoc documentation generation system.

- Consider generating interfaces for each of your output classes. Then, generate concrete classes for these interfaces. This will reduce compile and link times as well as loosen the coupling between classes.

4.6.5 Perl

Here are some suggestions when generating Perl:

- You should always include use strict in the code you generate and run perl with the −w option.
- Generate POD documentation along with the code.
- Be sure to use package containment and explicit exports to ensure that your functions don't bleed into the main namespace.

4.6.6 SQL

Keep these suggestions in mind when generating SQL:

- You should spend the time to make sure that the output SQL is marked up with the portions of the SQL code that diverge from the SQL standard to use vendor-specific options.
- You should separate the schema, any stored procedures, and any test data into separate files.
- When generating SQL within another language (e.g., Java executing SQL using strings and JDBC), be sure to use the argument replacement syntax within the driver. In Java this means using the PreparedStatement class and the question mark replacement syntax.

4.7 SUMMARY

This chapter provided you with a set of starting points that you can use to build your own generators. From this point on, we will be taking these generators and building on them to show how they can be used to solve a number of common software engineering problems. In the next chapter, we'll begin building generators for specific types of uses, starting with generators for user interface elements such as web forms.

P A R T II

Code generation solutions

The first part of this book concentrated on theory and technique; the second part applies these techniques to real-world problems. Each chapter provides a number of generator architectures and a case study that includes complete source code.

All of the chapters have a similar format. The chapter first presents the problem, and then describes several high-level generator architectures for addressing a variety of platforms and technologies. We then include a case study that shows an end-to-end example of using generation to solve the problem at hand.

Each case study uses a different type of generation to solve the problem. By mixing the generator designs, it is our intention not only to offer an overview of what generators can be used for but also to explain how each type works.

Reading all of the chapters in this part will give you a solid grounding in both the application and construction of generators.

I suggest that you avoid reading just the one chapter that is relevant to your current project because you may find that you do not agree with how we apply the generator architecture to solve the problem. Reading all of the chapters will allow you to pick the generator architecture that best suits your application.

CHAPTER 5

Generating user interfaces

In this chapter, we'll cover the design and implementation of a generator that builds user interface (UI) elements and code, such as web forms and desktop application dialog boxes. Some engineers stay away from user interface generation because they think that the result will be boring, dry or unusable, or that there are just too many edge cases. We give some practical advice for how to avoid these issues so that you can get the benefit of consistency when generating your user interface.

The prime advantage of generating a user interface is that you can create an abstracted form of the user interface, which is generated into executable user interface code. This abstracted form—which details when and where user interaction is required—can be generated into any number of target forms, from web pages to dialog boxes for Windows or Macintosh applications.

This chapter provides a practical example of the type of generator used in the case study from chapter 1, "Introducing code generation." We include sample designs for generators that build UI code based on other architectures.

While this approach is commonplace in commercial products (most notably Microsoft), many readers may be wary because that has been their only exposure to UI code generation.

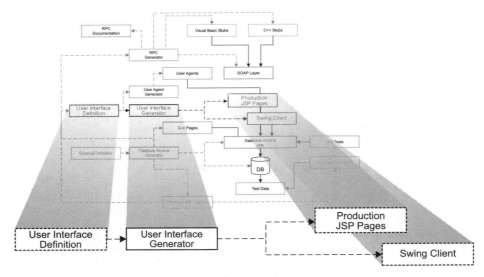

Figure 5.1   The user interface generator from the chapter 1 case study

5.1   *THE BIG PICTURE*

In the case study presented in chapter 1, the user interface generator builds the JSP and Swing pages for the application. Figure 5.1 shows how the user interface generator fits into the whole of the generation system.

The user interface generator gets its input from a UI definition file and an API definition (which is built by the database access generator; see chapter 10).

Before we go any further, here are some terms we'll use in this chapter:

- *User interface*—Either web pages and forms, or dialog boxes for desktop and client/server applications.

- *Form definitions*—The files used by the generator to define what fields and values should be presented to the user.

- *Templates*—Files used by the generator in the process of building the target files. These templates could be fragments of HTML or resource definition files, in the case of a Windows or Mac application, as well as fragments of production code to be used on the server or in the application itself.

- *Usability*—A measure of an application's ease of use.

5.1.1   Why generate the user interface?

The major advantage of generating a user interface is that you can create a layer of *abstraction* between the business rules for the interface and their implementation. User interface code can be particularly messy, with lots of system calls that create a sea of minutiae within which lies some semblance of your business rules and the usability standards of your application.

The three-tier architecture clearly defines three components: the *interface, business logic,* and *storage.* That may sound great on paper, but things are not always so clean in implementation for several reasons:

- To have a reasonable user interface with client-side validation, you will need to have some of the business logic copied to the user interface tier.

- Some fields require cross-field validation. You must account for this in both the business logic and the interface layer. An easy solution is to submit a record to the business logic layer, and if there is a conflict, the form is re-sent by the server with error information. Usability would be improved if the form were validated before submission. Because this means hand-coding the cross-validation rules in two places (the user interface and the business logic layer), it is not often done. Code generation makes this enhanced usability possible by building both layers simultaneously.

- Removing hyperlinks from the pages of a web application that link to pages that the user cannot access for security reasons makes for an easy-to-use application, but it also means that some of the security information will have to migrate its way to the user interface.

Let's take our accounting application as an example. The business rules of the application say that any `Person` object within the system that has selected external vendor must specify the ID of that vendor. Certainly rules like this one are codified in the business layer, but at the interface layer such a rule has to be hand-coded. This hand-coding creates possible synchronization problems because the front-end field validations can get out of sync with their back-end business rule counterparts.

Another common solution is to send the possibly errant record to the business logic layer for validation. This is a clean implementation, but the usability suffers because the user may be presented with a cryptic message and returned to the form.

Using code generation, you can specify the security and validation parameters for each object in one definition and have the generators use that definition when creating the data access, business logic, and user interface layers. Changing a security or validation parameter in the definition file modifies every tier of the application so that the new rule is consistent throughout.

In summary, here are some of the key benefits of user interface generation:

- *Consistency*—Generating forms en masse creates forms that are consistent and that present uniform usability standards to the user.

- *Flexibility*—Using a tool to build your interfaces means that you can respond to requirement changes quickly. Security changes underscore this flexibility; if you change and enhance your security API you can alter the templates to match, regenerate, and have an interface that conforms to the new security standards.

- *Portability*—As good as some of today's user interface toolkits (e.g., Qt or Tk) are, they still bind the business logic of the forms to the implementation details. Having a high-level representation of the business requirements of the forms in your application allows you to retarget the generator to any number of different interface technologies. For example, from one form definition you should be able to generate both web and client/server interfaces.

5.1.2 Integration with existing tools and other generators

Many high-quality tools are available for building web pages and dialog boxes for desktop applications. Are we suggesting that you scrap those tools? Of course not.

Say you're using Microsoft's Visual Studio to build desktop applications. Visual Studio's dialog editor creates text-based dialog resource files that a generator can read. The generator can then check the controls specified by the business logic layer against the controls on the dialog box.

To increase your overall productivity, we recommend you continue using existing tools while building generators that work in conjunction with those tools.

While the UI is the first thing the customer encounters, it is the end of the line when it comes to implementation. This makes sense because you must implement the interfaces the UI talks to before implementing the UI itself. The case study in chapter 1 showed a user interface generator working in conjunction with the back-end generator. This is a powerful architecture because it reduces redundant data entry and ensures the user interface layer has information about the back end so that it is able to provide a high-quality user experience. Interface generators can gain by pairing with the back-end generator if there is one.

5.2 DESIGNING A GOOD INTERFACE

The first question about a generated user interface is often, "Won't it look like dreck?" Frankly, it's possible. Bad templates and poor design will make for a bad interface. Generation will not make your UI better; all it will do is create the interface more quickly and more consistently than if you used hand-coding.

A user interface can be thought of in two pieces. The first is the look of the interface. Generated code can look as good as a hand-coded interface as long as you use well-written templates. The other piece of the UI equation is the usability of the interface. It takes great care to build usable interfaces with code generation.

Figure 5.2 shows an example record from a project management system and the associated simple interface. This is the type of interface that simple generators or wizards will give you. The dialog box maps one to one with the fields in the record. At most, the generator will alter the types of controls based on the types of the fields in the record.

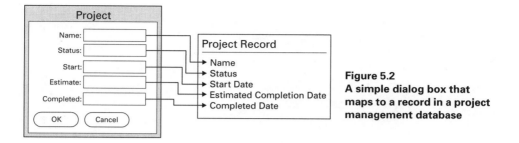

Figure 5.2
A simple dialog box that maps to a record in a project management database

This simplistic interface is not an ideal interface for the end user. An ideal interface matches users' workflow and makes it easy for them to interact with the system in a way that reduces input error. An example three-dialog box system is shown in figure 5.3.

These three dialog boxes map more closely to the workflow of the project manager. The first dialog box presents all of the fields required when a user starts a project. The second maintains the estimated completion time of the project. The user employs the third dialog box once the project is finished. Each dialog box shows only a portion of the complete record.

This example illustrates the difference between an interface built directly from the data definition and one built from an understanding of the user requirements and the need to create a usable system. Looking back to the case study in chapter 1, the user interface generator merged the data representation delivered by the database generator with an interface definition to create the final interface. It's within this interface definition that the usability requirements play a key role. The interface definition details

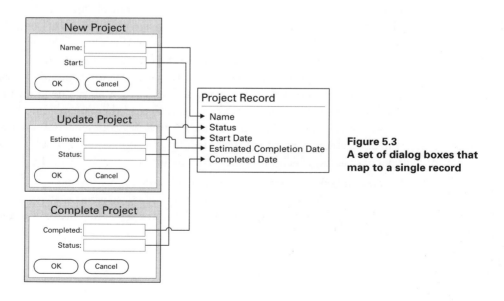

Figure 5.3
A set of dialog boxes that map to a single record

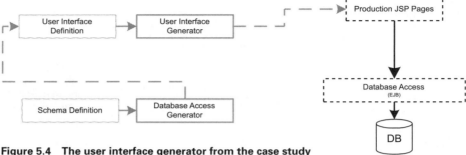

Figure 5.4   The user interface generator from the case study

what fields are put where and when. The relationship between the database generator and the user interface generator (from the case study) is illustrated in figure 5.4.

As engineers and architects, we spend a lot of time with our customers going through their workflow and capturing the data requirements as we design the schema. It's a mistake to capture just the data requirements and discard the workflow information. The workflow information allows the engineers and usability and interface experts to design and construct an interface that is usable by the customer. Usability is the key to the successful deployment of an application. You can be sure that applications that are difficult to use drive users away.

Here are some additional techniques to avoid building bad interfaces:

- *Include your graphic designer in the process early on*—The designer can use any web development tool to build one or two basic forms that present a variety of controls. Once you have these forms, you can decompose them into modular templates for the body of the page, the menus, the control types, and so forth. The role of the generator is then to compose new pages from the form definition using the modular templates. I can't emphasize enough the value of this workflow. Web development shops in recent years have used graphic designers to build complete forms for their applications. This is nonsensical. Talented graphic designers are great at coming up with web layout and style, as well as providing insight on novel ways to present data to the customer. To turn these people into form builders is a waste of talent. In addition, today's web development tools are not geared to making changes across the structure of pages en masse. The resulting pages will lack consistency, which hurts the flexibility and the testability of the application.

- *Use multiple layout types*—Not all pages and dialog boxes should be organized in the same way. Developing a number of different meta-layouts that you can use on a form-by-form basis can mean better usability and a pleasing break from monotony.

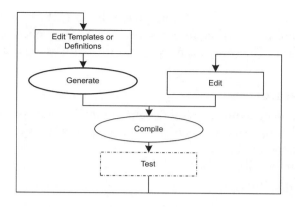

Figure 5.5
The edit, compile, and test workflow along with the generation steps

5.3   WORKFLOW COMPARISON

Figure 5.5 shows the standard UI generation workflow. You begin by editing either the templates or the definition files and then running the generator. The next step is to deploy the generated output with the rest of the application code and test it. You can fix any flaws that are found during testing on the next iteration of the cycle.

5.4   A CASE STUDY: GENERATING JSP

In this section, we introduce a new case study for UI generation. You'll build a generator that creates JSPs from an abstracted definition file.

5.4.1   Why generate JSPs?

JSPs are an ideal target for generation because of the lack of modularity in the JSP 1.0 specification. An ideal generator for JSP would abstract control types—such as selects, edit fields, check boxes, and radio buttons—so that the form definition need only specify a control type and the generator would create the appropriate HTML and structural JSP to build the form properly.

Your goal

Your purpose is to create a fairly basic generator that can build database forms and tables. Generally in database applications you are either creating or editing a database entity using a form or displaying the result of a query in a table as a report. The generator should support both of these use cases and be flexible enough to handle additional types of pages.

You want to specify as few requirements as possible for the creation of a page. These initial elements include:

- Data source—In this case the entity bean
- Layout—Either an entry form or a data table
- Fields—The fields that display within the form or table

In case you aren't familiar with the Java 2 Enterprise Edition (J2EE) architecture, JavaServer Pages (JSPs) use methods on an entity bean to perform queries, get field data, set values, and so forth. The entity bean represents the business logic layer to the user interface.

5.4.2 The role of the generator

Before embarking on the architecture, physical design, and implementation, let's spend some time examining what the generator is responsible for and outputs for which the generator does not take responsibility.

The generator takes responsibility for:

- All of the code for the JSP pages.

The generator does not take responsibility for:

- Any business logic underneath the user interface layer.
- User interfaces based on other technologies, such as Swing.
- Programmatic interfaces, such as SOAP or XML-RPC.

It's important to establish from the beginning what you can expect from this generator. You must draw the lines of responsibility in the design of your generator as well as in the deployment of any generator that you use off the shelf.

5.4.3 The high-level architecture

The block architecture for the JSP generator appears in figure 5.6. The generator takes a single definition file as input. For each input definition file, this generator builds one output file. To build the output file, the generator uses a set of nested templates. At the top level are a number of page templates, which invoke interior templates depending on the type of JSP you want to generate.

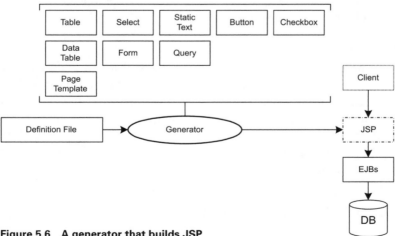

Figure 5.6   A generator that builds JSP

Figure 5.6 shows a data table, a form, and a query. These are just different types of pages. Each of these templates in turn uses another set of nested components to build the data table, form, or query given the contents of the definition file.

Form validation can be done by invoking another set of templates that act as input controls for various types of dates (integers, monetary values, dates, etc.). To keep this example as simple as possible, we left out the validation code.

Some JSP frameworks (e.g., Struts) require multiple output files. To support this, you will need to modify the generator I/O code.

5.4.4 A table definition file

Your interface to the generator is the *definition file*. The format of the definition file is the language you use to express the requirements for the JSP file that will be generated. You want to make it as simple and readable as possible.

The case study generator uses XML as the definition file format. Here is an example definition for a table page:

```
<file name="table1.jsp" title="Edit Name">
  <container name="table_page" bean="NameBean">
    <column title="First" name="first" field="first" />
    <column title="Middle" name="middle" field="middle" />
    <column title="Last" name="last" field="last" />
  </container>
</file>
```

The `file` tag contains the name and title of the output file. Within the `file` tag can be any set of nested containers and `field` tags. Anything that is not a `container` tag is considered a `field` tag. `field` tags have corresponding templates. For example, a `column field` tag is going to invoke the `column` template.

Our example definition file creates a *table page*. This page builds JSP that runs a query and displays a table showing the result. The table contains rows and columns; the number of rows depends on the result of the query at runtime. The columns are specified within the definition file inside the `table_page` XML element.

Each `column` represents a single field in a result set. The column specifies the title that will be displayed in the table header, as well as the field you want to use as the source of the data.

It is up to the `table_page` template to access the bean (which is why the name of the bean is specified), to run the query, and to build the logic that iterates over the results. It's the role of the `column` template to generate the JSP code required to render each cell.

5.4.5   A form definition file

The following file definition builds an input form:

```
<file name="form1.jsp" title="Edit Name">
  <container name="edit_form" bean="NameBean">
    <edit name="first" field="first" />
    <edit name="middle" field="middle" />
    <edit name="last" field="last" />
  </container>
</file>
```

The `file` tag specifies the output file and the title of the page. Within the `file` tag is an `edit_form` container. The container is meant to host a set of form fields. In this example, it contains three edit items, each of which specify a different field of the `NameBean` object.

It is the role of `edit_form` to create and manage a `NameBean` instance. You design the individual field templates to build the JSP that in turn generates HTML edit fields populated with the correct data.

5.4.6   Processing flow

JSP generator

The processing flow of the generator begins with these steps:

- Read the definition XML file and keep it in the DOM format.
- Create the output file.
- For each top-level container, you follow these steps:
  - Add the XML attribute information to the context.
  - Run the `container` template and store the result text.
  - Pop the XML attribute information off of the top of the context stack.
  - Add the text to the output file.
  - Close up the output file.
- Each container follows these processing steps:
  - Output any preamble.
  - Iterate through interior fields and follow these steps:
    - Add the XML attribute for the interior node to the context.
    - Run the template for the interior node and store the result text.
    - Pop the XML interior node attribute information from the context.
    - Output the interior node text.
    - Output the post-amble.

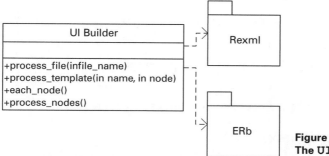

Figure 5.7
The `UIBuilder` class

5.4.7   Designing the generator

Now that you have the requirements, the high-level architecture, and the input files, it's time to think about the design of the generator itself. Figure 5.7 shows the UML for the `UIBuilder` generator class.

Rexml is used to parse the input definition files, and ERb is used to run the templates with the data from the definition files.

This generator is simply a recursive template invoker. You pass the name of the definition file to the `process_file` command, which reads the definition file, invokes the `container` templates, and stores the output in the specified output file.

The `container` template is given a reference to its XML node as well as its children, so it can in turn ask the `UIBuilder` to invoke sub-templates.

This nested template invocation is a very powerful paradigm. It's worth spending some time to understand. The relationship between the `UIBuilder` and the templates is symbiotic, as shown in figure 5.8.

The `UIBuilder` uses ERb to invoke templates. These templates can then in turn use `UIBuilder` as a resource to invoke more templates. The results from these sub-templates is then integrated into the result of the host template.

The generator reads the definition file, and then uses the `UIBuilder` class to invoke the first template, which then invokes all of the appropriate templates for the nested fields. The result of the first template result is stored as the output of the generation cycle for the given definition file.

In this design, the generator is simply a generic framework. The real intelligence of the system is contained within the templates.

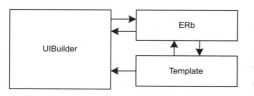

Figure 5.8
The relationship between the `UIBuilder` class and the templates within the generator

The UIBuilder class

The `UIBuilder` class is at the center of the JSP generator design. It is responsible for:

- Reading the definition file
- Managing the `file` tag by creating the output file
- Invoking the top level of `container` tags
- Handling any nested template invocations that are required by the templates

The UIBuilder context

Templates in the `UIBuilder` framework are like functions in a programming language. They take arguments and return values. Templates get their arguments through a context variable, and their return value is the text of the template.

For example, take this node:

```
<edit name="middle" field="middle" />
```

The `edit` template is shown here:

```
<edit name="<%= context[ 'field' ] %>" value="<%% myBean.get<%= context['field'].capitalize %>() %%>">
```

The edit template needs the `name` and `field` attributes from the XML. The template obtains these through the `context` variable. The `context` for any template consists of the attributes of the XML tag that invokes the template. In this case, the `context` has both `name` and `field`, both of which are defined as `middle` by the XML.

Nested context

The case study JSP generator implements a *nested context*. The nested context sent to the template is the sum of all of the parent XML nodes, with the most recent values taking precedence.

Figure 5.9 shows examples of the context at each level of the XML tree in our form definition file.

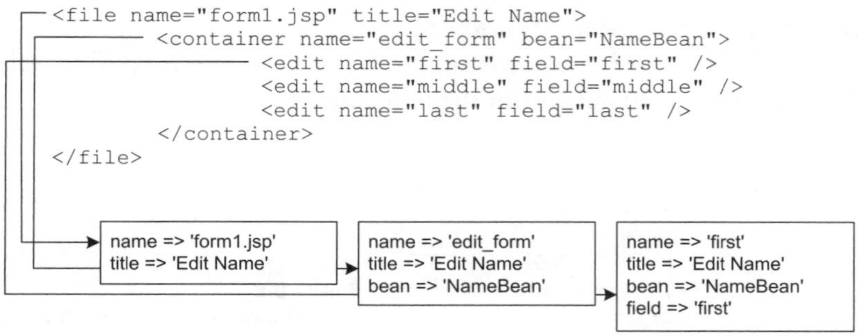

```
<file name="form1.jsp" title="Edit Name">
    <container name="edit_form" bean="NameBean">
        <edit name="first" field="first" />
        <edit name="middle" field="middle" />
        <edit name="last" field="last" />
    </container>
</file>
```

```
name => 'form1.jsp'        name => 'edit_form'        name => 'first'
title => 'Edit Name'       title => 'Edit Name'       title => 'Edit Name'
                           bean => 'NameBean'         bean => 'NameBean'
                                                      field => 'first'
```

Figure 5.9 Examples of nested context at the various levels of the XML as it builds JSP pages

At the top level only `name` and `title` are defined. As we get to the container, we add the `bean` value, and the value of `name` changes to `edit_form` because `container` is the nearest tag that defines the value. Then we go into the `edit` tags, where we add the `field` value, and redefine the `name` value to `first`, then `middle`, and finally `last`.

The advantage of a nested context is that, should the `edit` form, for example, need to know the bean name, it gets the bean value because it inherits that value automatically from its parent.

Listing 5.1 contains the code for the JSP generator.

Listing 5.1 Listuibuilder.rb

```ruby
require 'rexml/document'
require 'erb/erb'

class UIBuilder

  def initialize
    @out_file = nil                              ❶ Sets up the output variables
    @output_file_name = nil
    @output_full_name = nil
    @output_directory = "output"                 ❷ Sets up some filename
    @templates_directory = "templates"             locations
    @context_stack = []                          ❸ Initializes the context array
    @node_stack = []                             ❹ Initializes the node stack
  end

  def process_file( file_name )                  ❺ Creates the main public entry point
    begin
      doc = REXML::Document.new( File.open( file_name ) )    ⊲┐ Reads the
    rescue                                                    │ XML file
      raise "Could not open or parse #{file_name}"
    end

    @output_file_name = doc.root.attributes[ 'name' ]  ⊲┐ Gets the output
    unless( @output_file_name )                          │ filename
      print "#{file_name}: No name attached to the file element.\n"
      exit -1
    end                                                Builds the out-
                                                       put file path ┐
    @output_full_name = "#{@output_directory}/#{@output_file_name}"  ⊲┘

    begin                                              Creates the ┐
      @out_file = File.open( @output_full_name, "w")  ⊲ output file ┘
    rescue
      raise "Could not create #{@output_full_name}"
    end

    push_context( doc.root )    ⊲── Starts the context stack

    nodes = doc.root.elements
    nodes.each() { |node|                    Finds top-level
      if ( node.name() == "container" )      containers and
                                             runs them
```

```
        @out_file.write( process_container( node ) )       ⤴ Finds top-level
      end                                                     containers and
    }                              ┌── Pushes the node onto    runs them
    pop_context()          ◁──────┤   the context and gets
    @out_file.close()             └── the context stack
    print "#{file_name}\n"
  end

private

  def process_container( container )
    process_template( container.attributes[ 'name' ], container )
  end
                                         ┌── Pushes the node onto
  def process_template( name, node )     │   the context and gets
    context = push_context( node )  ◁────┤   the context stack
    template_full_name = "#{@templates_directory}/#{name}"
    begin
      fh = File.new( template_full_name )      ┌── Gets the
      erb_script = fh.read                     │   template
      fh.close()
    rescue
      raise "Could not read template #{name}"
    end
    begin
      erb = ERb.new( erb_script )              ┌── Runs the
      erb_result = erb.result( binding )       │   template
    rescue => err
      raise err #, "There was a problem interpreting template #{name}"
    end
    pop_context()          ◁──┐ Pops our node
    erb_result                │ from the context
  end

  def each_node()                ❻ Iterates the interior node
    current_node = get_current_node()
    result = ""
    nodes = current_node.elements
    nodes.each() { |node|
      text = ""
      if ( node.name == "container" )
        text = process_container( node )
      else
        text = process_template( node.name, node )
      end
      result += ERbStrIO.as_stdout { yield( node, text ) }
    }
    result
  end

  def process_nodes()            ❼ Prints the interior node
    result = ""
    each_node() { |node, text|
```

```
      result += text
    }
    result
  end

  def build_context()
    context = {}
    @context_stack.each { |values|
      values.each { |key,value|
        context[ key ] = value;
      }
    }
    context
  end

  def get_current_node()
    @node_stack.last
  end

  def push_context( node )                    ❽ Adds a level to
    @node_stack.push( node )                     the context
    values = {}
    node.attributes.each() { |key,value|
      values[ key ] = value;
    }
    @context_stack.push( values )
    build_context()
  end

  def pop_context()                           ❾ Removes a level
    @node_stack.pop                              from the context
    @context_stack.pop()
  end
end
if ( ARGV[0] )
  proc = UIBuilder.new()          ⟵ Creates the UIBuilder object
  begin
    proc.process_file( ARGV[0] )       ⟵ Runs the definition file
  rescue => problem
    print "#{problem}\n"              | Handles errors
    exit -1                          | gracefully
  end
  exit 0
else
  print "No input file specified\n"
  exit -1
end
```

❶ The out_file variable is the output file handle. output_file_name is the name
of the output file, and output_full_name is the full pathname of the output file.

❷ These two instance variables store the location of the output directory and the templates directory. If you derive from this class, you can specify new locations for these values.

❸ This code initializes the context stack. The context stack is an array of hash tables. As context hashes are added, they are pushed onto the stack and then popped off as the XML tag processing is completed.

❹ `node_stack` holds an array of references to the all of the nodes before the current node.

❺ `process_file` is the main entry point for this class. `file_name` contains the name of the definition file. It is the job of `process_file` to read in the definition file, run the templates, and store the output.

❻ `each_node` is one of the methods that a container can use to deal with interior nodes. `each_node` runs each interior node and passes the text back to the template. The template can then wrap this text in some more HTML before going on to the next interior node.

❼ `process_nodes` processes each node in the container and returns the text of all the nodes concatenated together.

❽ `push_context` is called whenever you invoke a new field or container. It adds the attributes of the new XML node as a new layer in the context. When you've finished with the XML node, the layer is popped off by calling `pop_context`.

❾ `pop_context` pops one layer off the context stack.

Of course, the `UIBuilder class` is worthless without the set of templates that build the output code. The first template section of the code covers the templates used to build a query table.

First, we need to go back to the definition file that sets the requirements for our query table:

```
<file name="table1.jsp" title="Edit Name">
  <container name="table_page" bean="NameBean">
    <column title="First" name="first" field="first" />
    <column title="Middle" name="middle" field="middle" />
    <column title="Last" name="last" field="last" />
  </container>
</file>
```

This XML doesn't have any comments in it, but there is no reason it couldn't. You should treat definition files just like source code. They should include comments that describe the purpose, the author, the revision history, and so forth. XML allows for this using the `<!-- -->` comment standard.

The definition file shows us that we'll use two templates: `table_page` and `column`. The `table_page` is referenced by the `container` tag, and the `column` template is referenced by the `column` tag. Remember that the design of this generator specifies that anything that isn't explicitly a "container" (excluding the `file` tag at the top) is a template reference, wherein the name of the tag is actually the name of the template. So the `column` tag becomes a reference to the `column` template. Listing 5.2 contains the code for the `table_page` template.

Listing 5.2   table_page

```
<jsp:useBean id="myBean" class="<%= context[ 'bean' ] %>" scope=request></
jsp:useBean>                        ❶ References
<html>                                 the EJB beans
<head>
<title><%= context[ 'title' ] %></title>
</head>
<body>

<table>
<tr>
<% print each_node() { |node,text| %>
<th><%= node.attributes[ 'title' ] %></th>       ❷ Builds the
<% } %>                                             interior nodes
</tr>
% ResultSet result = myBean.query();
% while( result.next ) {
<tr>
<%= process_nodes() %>
</tr>
% }
</table>

</body>
</html>
```

❶ The template uses the local context to specify the bean, in addition to setting the title of the page.

❷ The `each_node` iterator is used to build the header for the table. Then you use `process_nodes()` to fill in the interior of the Java table iterator, which builds all of the `<tr>` and `<td>` nodes of the table.

The next template used in this example is the `column` template, shown here:

```
<td><%%= result.get<%= context['field'].capitalize %>() %%></td>
```

This is a simple template that creates a single JSP `<td>` tag builder.

The `capitalize` method on `Strings` in Ruby uppercases the first character in the string and lowercases the rest of the string. If your field has camel case characters (e.g., `myValue`), be warned that `capitalize` may not give you the result you expect. If you have this problem, you should write your own routine to handle your case-sensitivity variants.

The <%%= is the ERb method for specifying <%= in the output. The %%> sequence creates %> in the output.

Now, here's the output of the generator for the definition file:

```
<jsp:useBean id="myBean" class="NameBean" scope=request></jsp:useBean>
<html>
<head>
<title>Edit Name</title>
</head>
<body>

<table>
<tr>

<th>First</th>

<th>Middle</th>

<th>Last</th>

</tr>
% ResultSet result = myBean.query();
% while( result.next ) {
<tr>
<td><%= result.getFirst() %></td>
<td><%= result.getMiddle() %></td>
<td><%= result.getLast() %></td>

</tr>
% }
</table>

</body>
</html>
```

In the production code, you will likely need to add URL argument handling to the templates so that the resulting JSP can send query parameters to the bean. Depending on your application architecture, you could hard-code these parameters into different types of page_templates, or you could migrate the URL parameters into the definition file and then have the page_template respond to those by generating the URL-handling JSP.

Another goal of the generator is to build HTML forms. An example HTML form definition is shown in listing 5.3. The edit_form template (listing 5.4) creates a page of form controls.

Listing 5.3   Form template code

```
<file name="form1.jsp" title="Edit Name">
  <container name="edit_form" bean="NameBean">
    <edit name="first" field="first" />
    <edit name="middle" field="middle" />
    <edit name="last" field="last" />
  </container>
</file>
```

Listing 5.4   edit_form

```
<jsp:useBean id="myBean" class="<%= context[ 'bean' ] %>" scope=request></
jsp:useBean>              ❶ References
<html>                      the EJB bean
<head>
<title><%= context[ 'title' ] %></title>
</head>
<body>
<form action="<%= @output_file_name %>" method="post">      ❷ Inserts interior
<%= process_nodes() %>                                          form elements
</form>
</body>
</html>
```

❶ The template uses the context to get the bean and to set the title for the HTML page.

❷ The template also uses the `@output_file_name` class member of the host `UIBuilder` object. It can do this because the binding of the `UIBuilder` object is sent to the ERb template. This binding includes the `context` hash, but it also includes anything in the current scope of execution, such as member variables. If this design does not suit you, one alternative would be to use specially named values in the context for elements like the output filename.

Now, here's the code for the `edit` template:

```
<edit name="<%= context[ 'field' ] %>" value="<%% myBean.get<%= con-
text['field'].capitalize %>() %%>">
```

This simple template uses the context to build the HTML for the edit control and to build the JSP that sets the value of the field at runtime.

The output of the JSP generator for this form definition should look like this:

```
<jsp:useBean id="myBean" class="NameBean" scope=request></jsp:useBean>
<html>
<head>
<title>Edit Name</title>
</head>
<body>
<form action="form1.jsp" method="post">
<edit name="first" value="<% myBean.getFirst() %>">
<edit name="middle" value="<% myBean.getMiddle() %>">
<edit name="last" value="<% myBean.getLast() %>">

</form>
</body>
</html>
```

We deliberately simplified this example; in a production environment you will need to include field validation, page-level security, and URL-handling code.

For this generator, let's use the system test utility (described in appendix B) with the following definition file:

```
<ut kgdir="kg">
 <test cmd="ruby uigen.rb definitions/form1.def" out="output/form1.jsp" />
 <test cmd="ruby uigen.rb definitions/form2.def" out="output/form2.jsp" />
 <test cmd="ruby uigen.rb definitions/table1.def" out="output/table1.jsp" /
>
</ut>
```

The first time you run the JSP generator, you want to create a set of known good output. The known good output is a copy of the output that you certify as perfect. To create the known good output, run the following:

```
% ruby ../ut1/ut1.rb -m -f ut.def
ruby uigen.rb definitions/form1.def
definitions/form1.def
Known good kg/form1.jsp stored

ruby uigen.rb definitions/form2.def
definitions/form2.def
Known good kg/form2.jsp stored

ruby uigen.rb definitions/table1.def
definitions/table1.def
Known good kg/table1.jsp stored
```

Of course, you should inspect the known good output files to make sure they are really "good." Then you can make whatever modifications you like to the generator and rerun the tests:

```
% ruby ../ut1/ut1.rb -f ut.def
ruby uigen.rb definitions/form1.def
definitions/form1.def

ruby uigen.rb definitions/form2.def
definitions/form2.def

ruby uigen.rb definitions/table1.def
definitions/table1.def

No test failures
```

At this point you can be reasonably sure that, as long as your tests covered a reasonable gamut of functionality, your system is still performing well after alterations.

5.5   TECHNIQUE: GENERATING SWING DIALOG BOXES

Swing is a cross-platform UI class library built entirely in Java. The Swing class library is intended for desktop application development and supports all of the modern interaction models, such as documents, modal and modeless dialog boxes, menus, and toolbars. Not only is Swing portable between all of the common operating systems, it also emulates the look and feel of those platforms. An application written in Swing looks as if it were written for its operating system directly. In this section, we'll discuss a generator that builds a Swing-based UI.

5.5.1   Generator requirements

Swing implements dialog boxes as code; there is no resource file from which the Swing library reads a dialog definition and creates controls. Building a dialog box involves building a set of control objects, containers, and callbacks in Java code. As with most interface toolkits, the business rules that drive the interface get lost in all of the construction and maintenance minutiae. An ideal generator architecture allows you to keep the business logic of the interface separate from its Swing implementation.

The details in a Swing dialog box can be divided into two groups. The first group includes the relevant details for the business side:

- A data source for getting and setting the data
- Fields
- Basic types of the fields (e.g., `String`, `Integer`)
- The layout of the fields
- Which fields are editable
- Which validations should be applied to each field
- Which cross-field validations are required

The next set of items provide the implementation details:

- Swing objects that represent each field
- The dialog class
- The constructor that builds the class and lays out the fields
- Event responders that listen for button presses
- Code that implements the field and cross-field validations

In a hand-coded dialog box, the items in both lists are mixed together in the implementation. The generator handles the implementation details and thus allows you to concentrate on the business details.

We have to be realistic, however. A generator will not be able to handle all of the edge cases in the user interface. Login pages are an example of edge case pages that are

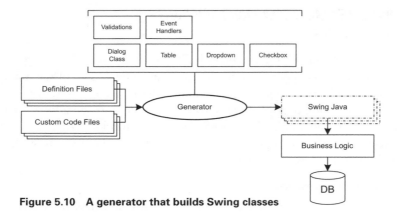

Figure 5.10   A generator that builds Swing classes

often custom built. This is because the logic for supporting the page, validating the login information and privileges, and initiating the session is singular to the login page alone. So generating this one-off page is inefficient. For that reason, we need to be able to add custom code to the process so that we can override or extend the output of the generator to handle edge cases.

Note that with the exception of the Java types in the business details and any custom edge case code, the business details are platform neutral. This lets you maintain the portability of the business logic for the interface. If you decide to change platforms, you can move the dialog boxes by mapping the Java types and porting the edge case code. Even if the generated output isn't a complete solution, you will still be further along than if you had tried to port the Swing code directly.

5.5.2   Architectural recommendation

In this example, the business requirements tell you that you need to take the business details and custom code as input and create the Java Swing code to manage the dialog boxes. The block architecture for a Swing dialog generator, based on the tier generator model, is shown in figure 5.10.

The generator reads the business details from an XML definition file. When custom code is required, the definition files reference an external file that contains the required Java code. The generator takes both of these inputs and merges them, using a reservoir of templates, into Java implementation files.

The templates are fairly simple. First you have a framework template that builds the basics of the dialog class. Then, there are control templates for building each of the types of controls for each of the fields specified and for doing the validation of those controls when processing the OK click.

5.5.3 Processing flow

The processing flow of the generator is as follows:

- Reads and validates the definition XML files and stores the information in local structures.

- Checks for any custom code references. Reads in the code files and stores them in the local structures.

- Iterates the following steps over every dialog box defined in the XML file:

  ○ Initializes caches of code for the variable declarations and the methods.

  ○ Iterates over each field and performs the following steps:

    ▸ Builds and caches the field definitions.

    ▸ Builds the event handlers and adds to the methods cache.

    ▸ Adds any custom per-field to the methods cache.

- Handles any per-dialog custom code by adding the code to the methods cache.

- Uses the Java Dialog Class template to create the implementation for the class. This template should contain the class, the constructor, and the standard event handlers. The variables and methods text from the field processing steps should be merged into the output.

- Stores the output of this template in the .java file with the correct name.

5.6 TECHNIQUE: GENERATING MFC DIALOG BOXES

The Microsoft Foundation Classes (MFC) are a set of C++ classes that provide a wrapper around the Win32 API. To build a dialog box in MFC, you use the Resource Editor provided with the Microsoft Visual C++ IDE. You then build the C++ class to handle the dialog events using the Dialog Wizard. The Dialog Wizard creates classes, maps controls to classes, and handles some rudimentary validations. This wizard follows the mixed-code generation model by managing the C++ code within special comments. You are free to override the default behavior by adding custom C++ outside the comments.

5.6.1 Generator requirements

So why write another generator if Microsoft already has developed one? There are some drawbacks to the Dialog Wizard approach:

- The business details of the dialog box are mixed in with the code that maintains the state of the controls.

- The validations are fairly rudimentary, and there is no way to generate cross-field validations.

- You have no method of telling the Dialog Wizard how to read and write data to your API. For example, if your code is factored into a Model-View-Controller model, you can't adjust the Dialog Wizard to fit that model.

Because the Dialog Wizard is usually very valuable, the generator should provide compelling value in these areas.

To separate the business details from the implementation details, first decide which business details are important to capture:

- The data source to get and set the data
- The fields and their mapping to the dialog resource
- Validations for each field
- Cross-validations between fields
- Custom requirements on a per-dialog or per-field basis

With this information, the generator should be able to handle these details:

- Building the MFC infrastructure to create the control objects and mapping them to the windows controls
- Building the data get and set code that initializes the controls properly and handles the OK button press
- Implementing the field and cross-field validations
- Implementing or importing the code for custom requirements

Clearly the case for building this generator is not as compelling as the Swing generator because of the excellent up-front work that Microsoft has done with the Resource Editor and the Dialog Wizard. However, there are some scenarios where you should make the investment in this generator:

- You are already generating a web interface for an application and you want a client/server interface. This generator could use your existing web interface definitions to create the client/server dialog boxes.
- You are building an application with a large number of dialog boxes.
- The Dialog Wizard is not helping you because of your application data model or other specific requirements.
- You are not satisfied with the data exchange and data validation (DDX/DDV) model provided by the MFC and you cannot easily overcome those limitations within the MFC framework or by using C++ inheritance or templates.

5.6.2   Recommended tier generator architecture

The tier generator model shown in figure 5.11 creates MFC dialog classes directly from a set of business detail files written in XML.

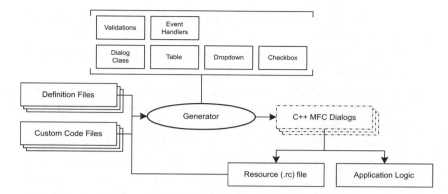

Figure 5.11   A generator that builds the C++ for MFC dialog boxes

Using the business detail and custom code input files, the generator takes a set of templates and creates the MFC dialog classes. The generator also validates the resource mappings in the business detail files against the resource (.rc) file.

5.6.3   Processing flow

MFC generator

The processing engine of the generator follows these steps:

- Reads and validates the definition XML files and stores the information in local structures.
- Checks for any custom code references. Reads in the code files and stores them in the local structures.
- Reads in the resource file and stores the dialog boxes and their control IDs and types.
- Checks the local structures against the dialog boxes and controls that were read from the resource file.
- Merges the control type information in the .rc file with the definition file so you know which code templates to use to handle the control.
- Iterates the following steps over every dialog box defined in the XML file:
  - Initializes code caches that will be used for the CPP and HPP files.
  - Iterates over each field and follows these steps:
    - Builds and caches the field definitions for the HPP file and the constructor code for the CPP file.
    - Builds the event handlers for the CPP file and adds the prototypes to the HPP method list.

- Adds any custom per-field code to the CPP file and adds the prototypes to the HPP method list.
- Handles any per-dialog custom code by adding the code onto the HPP and CPP code caches.
- Uses the Dialog Class CPP template to create the implementation for the class. This template should contain the class, the constructor, destructor, and message map. The code text from the field processing steps should be merged in. Stores the output of this template in the CPP file with the correct name.
  - Uses the Dialog Class HPP template to create the header for the class. This template should have the infrastructure methods (e.g., constructor and destructor). The template should then merge in the code created during the field processing. Stores the output of this template in the HPP file with the correct name.

5.6.4 Recommended mixed-code generation architecture

An alternative to tier generation for MFC classes is to use a mixed-code generation model on top of the mixed-code generation model already used by the Class Wizard. If your requirements are simple enough to fit into this model, then you will still be able to use the Class Wizard, which is not an option in the tier generator described previously. Figure 5.12 shows the mixed-code generation model.

In this generator, you look for your own custom comments and augment them with custom code. As with the mixed-code generator shown in chapter 4, the generator takes its input from the comments to generate the code for implementing the comment, and then replaces the existing comment with the original comment plus the new code.

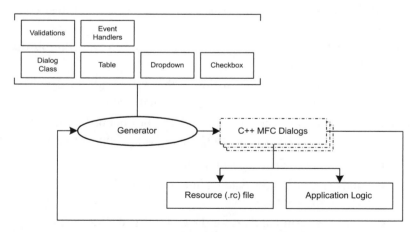

Figure 5.12   A generator that builds MFC dialog boxes using the C++ dialog boxes in a manner similar to the Class Wizard

If your implementation only requires modification to the CPP or HPP file, you should consider integrating the generator into the Microsoft Studio Visual C++ MSVC IDE so that you can access it from the menu and have the generator work with standard I/O.

5.6.5 Processing flow

MFC generator mixed-code generator architecture

Here is a very basic process flow for this mixed-code generation model. You will have to adapt it to suit your requirements:

- Reads in both the CPP and HPP files
- Scans the files for your special comments
- Performs these steps for each comment:
  - Parses any information required for generation from the comment
  - Generates the code based on the information in the comment using a template
  - Replaces the comment with the original comment text and the generated code
  - Creates backups of the CPP and HPP files
  - Replaces the CPP and HPP files with the next text

5.7 DESIGN TIPS

Here are some tips on how to design your solution up front so that you can generate large portions of the UI at implementation time.

- Try to break down your interface into three or four large types of interaction models. Database application HTML pages, for example, usually break up into table, form and query pages.

- Recognize that in most systems there will be more than a few exception cases that cannot be generated. The login page of a web application is a good example. In some cases, this means providing for custom code; in others, it means that the page will need to be handwritten.

- For HTML pages, design your pages as a set of nested components and containers so that you can build consistency and quality through reuse.

- Again on HTML pages, work with designers and product management staff to keep the page flows simple and consistent. This will make the pages easy to generate and to use.

- For dialog boxes, try to establish two or three basic layouts for tabs and controls.

- Also when building dialog boxes, you may want to use the nested template architecture that was implemented in the case study in section 5.4 to create the popular sand struts style of layout.

5.8   TOOLS FOR GENERATING UIS

Here is a list of web sites where you can find tools available for purchase off the shelf to generate user interfaces:

- CodeCharge (www.codecharge.com/studio/) has an integrated development environment that can generate a single interface definition to multiple target environments (JSP, ASP, etc.).
- Visual Studio (http://msdn.microsoft.com/vstudio/) has interface tools and a Class Wizard that will write some of the Win32 dialog management code for you.
- X-Designer (www.ist.co.uk/xd/index.html) can generate code for a number of different platforms from a single definition.
- Proc-Blaster from Lockwood Software (www.lockwoodtech.com/index_pb.htm) uses template-based code generation, as we discussed in section 5.4.

5.9   SUMMARY

Don't fall prey to the idea that code generation will make your pages bland. Code generation can build user interfaces that are of high quality, consistent, and elegant. Hand-tweaking tags and JSP code on hundreds of pages is wasted engineering time.

The user interface is easily one of the highest impact areas to use code generation. Find a small portion of your project and use it to try one of the solutions in this chapter. You'll see immediate productivity and quality improvements, and you'll quickly be sold on this powerful technique.

In the next chapter, we'll look at ways of using code generation techniques to create documentation for several types of applications.

Generating documentation

It seems that every new language promises "self-documenting code"—code so clear that an engineer will be able to divine its purpose just by reading it. No commonly used language has ever succeeded at meeting the self-documenting challenge, but a few advances have made it easier for us to create well-documented code. Tools such as POD (for Perl), JavaDoc (for Java), and Doxygen (for C++) allow you to put specialized comments in your file along with your code. You can then employ a special tool to *parse* the code, extracting the comments and the code structure, and automatically generate documentation.

Even though you are using comments, the design is not to provide low-level, line-by-line documentation. These tools support capturing the design intent close to the code that implements that design. In this way, you keep your knowledge about the design maintained with the code. The code, the technical documentation, and the API aspect of the design documentation are all maintained as one unit and checked in and out of source code control as one unit.

You can use code generators to interpret inline documentation and turn it into external documentation in HTML, PDF, and other forms. If you understand how documentation generators work, you can build your own generators and extend the usefulness of your existing inline documentation.

This chapter introduces a new generator that supports structured comments in SQL files. After adding structured comments to the SQL code, you can run the generator on the code and the generator will output a set of HTML files that document the schema. We'll use a JavaDoc format for the structured SQL comments.

6.1 THE IMPORTANCE OF STRUCTURED COMMENTS

The fragment of Java code shown in listing 6.1 is augmented with JavaDoc comments. (We explain JavaDocs in more detail in section 6.4.) The JavaDoc comments explain the purpose of the class and describe all the member variables and methods. The Java-Doc tool takes these structured comments and creates HTML documentation for the class.

Listing 6.1 Example of Java using JavaDoc structured documentation standard

```
/**
 * This class stores a name and value pair.          ❶ Name and value pair
 */                                                     class documentation
public class NameValuePair {
    /**
     * The name                    ❷ Instance variable
     */                              documentation
    public String _name;

    /**
     * The value
     */
    public Object _value;

    /**
     * This constructor takes a name and value pair to build
     * the object.
     * @param name The name.                Constructor      ❸
     * @param value The value.            documentation
     */
    public NameValuePair( String name, Object value )
    {
      // Setting the values      ❹ Interior non-JavaDoc
      _name = name;               documentation
      _value = value;
    }
}
```

❶ Notice the proximity of the JavaDoc comment to the code element that it documents. This proximity is the largest single value of this type of inline documentation. Documentation that is close at hand has a high probability of being maintained. If the documentation is in another file, or another system, it will likely fall out of sync with the original code. By using JavaDoc, you check out the code and documentation, as well as check it in, all in one logical unit.

❷ The second major advantage of inline documentation is simplicity. To write a JavaDoc comment properly, all you need to do is add an asterisk to the beginning of the line, then type the comment as you normally would.

❸ If your method has arguments, you use the `@param` syntax to document each parameter. In the case of the constructor, you must document the incoming parameters. You do this by using the `@param` syntax, which takes the first word as the argument name and the rest of the string as the comment for the parameter.

❹ JavaDoc is held separately from regular comments by using the `/** ... */` syntax. In this way, it does not conflict with any standard comments spread throughout the file. In this code, the comment identifying what goes in the constructor is ignored because the `//` comment syntax is not used for JavaDocs.

Your documentation will stand a better chance of being both complete and up-to-date if it is easy to maintain. And your well-documented code will in turn produce a well-maintained application. Inline documentation tools, such as JavaDoc, put the documentation right next to the code it documents. This simple format is easy to read and means the documentation is more likely to be maintained throughout the life of the software.

6.2 THE BIG PICTURE

The case study generators in chapter 1, "Introducing code generation," used a JavaDoc to build documentation for all of the generated output code and libraries. This documentation is valuable not only for engineers who need to use the APIs internally to build the application, but also for users of the external SOAP interface. If the SOAP interface generator creates the Java client code, the JavaDoc embedded in that client code can be used as documentation for the external interface. This means that, along with the Java classes themselves, you can provide your customer with robust documentation in HTML format that describes all of the classes, their member variables, and their methods.

6.3 A CASE STUDY: AUGMENTED SQL CODE

Perl, C, C++, and Java all have inline documentation standards. SQL does not have an inline documentation standard despite its widespread use of complex tables and elaborate stored procedures—which would benefit greatly from quality documentation. For this reason, we've chosen to make the case study for this chapter a documentation generator for SQL that uses a JavaDoc-style syntax.

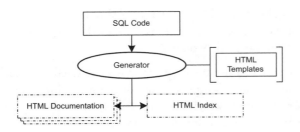

Figure 6.1
The input and output flow for the SQL documentation generator

6.3.1 Roles of the generator

The SQL documentation generator in this case study has one big responsibility: It builds the technical documentation for the SQL in your application, including all of the tables and stored procedures. The generator does not take responsibility for:

- Designing the documentation.
- Creating the end-user documentation.
- Cataloging or documenting the SQL queries or operations in the application layer.

By drawing these clear lines of responsibility, you can confidently lay out the feature set and the architecture for the generator.

6.3.2 Laying out the generator architecture

Let's build the generator using the code munger model (see chapter 2, "Code generation basics," section 2.1.1). We chose the code munger model because the input is executable code and the output is an external form other than code. The generator will take SQL as input and scan it for JavaDoc-style comments. Then, using templates, the generator will build a page for each table and an index page that contains references to all the pages. Figure 6.1 shows the I/O flow for the SQL documentation generator.

Keep in mind that all of the tables must be included in a single generation run. That way, you can ensure proper linkages between table pages in the documentation. The next step is to design the JavaDoc-style syntax. SQL does not support the /** ... */ comment syntax, so we developed a syntax for the comments based on the ANSI standard—the comment syntax. Here is some example SQL marked up with the Java-Doc syntax:

```
-- Book contains information about each book, the title,
-- the author, the publisher, etc.
--
-- @field bookID The primary key id
-- @field title The title of the book
-- @field ISBN The ISBN number of the book
-- @field authorID The author (as a foreign key relation)
-- @field publisherID The publisher (as a foreign key relation)
-- @field status The active or inactive state of the record
-- @field numCompies The number of copies in the library
```

1 General documentation for the table

2 Documentation for each field

```
-- @relates_to Author
-- @relates_to Publisher
create table Book (
   bookID integer not null primary key
   ,title varchar(80) not null
   ,ISBN varchar(80) not null unique
   ,authorID integer not null
   ,publisherID integer not null
   ,status integer not null
   ,numCopies integer not null
);
```

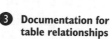

❸ Documentation for table relationships

❶ Comments outside of the @key syntax are related to the body of the table itself. Here, the text starting with Book contains… is taken as a description of the Book table itself.

❷ The @field syntax is directly followed by the field name. The words that follow it are considered documentation for the specified field. In this case, the bookID field is documented with the following text: The primary key id.

❸ The @relates_to key is used to specify relations between tables. The Book table is related to the Author and Publisher tables, so there are two @relates_to items, the first for Author and the second for Publisher. The HTML output should include links to the Author and Publisher documentation from the Book page because of these @relates_to keys.

6.3.3 Processing flow

SQL documentation generator

As it goes about its job of creating HTML documentation for your SQL code, the generator follows a series of steps:

- Reads the input SQL file.
- Tokenizes the SQL input.
- Parses the tokens to read the comments and the structure of the tables.
- Initializes a list of all pages.
- Follows these steps for each table:
  - Creates a page using the HTML template that contains the name of the table, a description of the purpose of the table, the fields of the table with their types and any description, and links to any pages for the tables to which this table relates.
  - Stores the name of this page in the list of all pages.
- Creates the HTML with the list of all the table description pages.

6.3.4   Building the code for the SQL generator

The case study generator is written in Ruby and uses the `Tokenizer` toolkit from chapter 3 ("Code generation tools") to read and parse the SQL file. The code then stores the table definitions and comments in memory and uses this material to generate the HTML pages. The generator creates the HTML pages with the help of templates from ERb. Listing 6.2 shows the code for the documentation generator.

Listing 6.2   docgen.rb

```
require "SQLTokenizer"                    ❶ Brings in the SQL Tokenizer
require "SQLLanguageScanner"

require "JavaDoc"                          ❷ Includes support for JavaDoc

require "erb/erb"                          ❸ Brings in the ERb template system

def run_template( template_name, bind )
  erb = ERb.new( File.new( "templates/#{template_name}" ).read )
  erb.result( bind )                                          Simple template ❹
end                                                                  processor

def convert_comment( comment )
  cleaned = ""
  comment.each_line { |line|
    line.sub!( /\s*\-\-\s*/, "" )
    line.strip!
    cleaned += "#{line}\n" if ( line.length > 0 )
  }

  converted = "/**\n"
  cleaned.each_line { |line| converted += " * #{line}" }
  converted += " */\n"
  converted
end

class ExtendedJavaDoc < JavaDoc          ❺ JavaDoc subclass for
                                            SQL documentation
  def initialize()
    super()
    @tableDescription = ""
    @fieldDescriptions = {}
    @relatesTo = []
  end

  attr_reader :tableDescription  # The table description string
  attr_reader :fieldDescriptions  # The hash of descriptions for each field
  attr_reader :relatesTo  # The array of tables this table relates to

  def add_to_tag( key, text )

    text.strip!
    if ( key == "@desc" )
      @tableDescription += text
    elsif ( key == "@field" )
      text =~ /(.*?)\s/
```

```
                field = $1
                text.sub!( /^#{field}\s*/, "" )
                @fieldDescriptions[ field.downcase.strip ] = text
        elsif ( key == "@relates_to" )
                @relatesTo.push( text )
        end
    end
end

def read_sql_file( file_name )

    print "Parsing #{file_name}...\n"
    fh = File.open( file_name              Reads the SQL
    in_text = fh.read()                    input file
    fh.close()

    tokenizer = SQLTokenizer.new( )        Tokenizes
    tokenizer.parse( in_text )             the SQL

    languagescanner = SQLLanguageScanner.new()
    languagescanner.parse( tokenizer.tokens )      Parses the SQL
                                                    token stream
    tables = languagescanner.tables

    tables.each { |table|          ❻ Iterates through each table
        print "Building #{table.name}.html\n"

        jd = ExtendedJavaDoc.new()
        jd.parse( convert_comment( table.comment ) )
                                                    ❼ Gets the
                                                       JavaDoc
        table.fields.each { |field|
            field.comment = jd.fieldDescriptions[ field.name.to_s.downcase.strip ]
        }
                                            Iterates over ❽
                                            each field
        table_comment = jd.tableDescription
        relates_to = jd.relatesTo

        fh = File.new ("output/#{table.name}.html", "w" )
        fh.print run_template( "table_page.html.template", binding )
        fh.close()                                  Creates the out- ❿
    }                                               put HTML file

    print "Building tables.html\n"                  Builds the
    fh = File.new ("output/tables.html", "w" )      main index
    fh.print run_template( "tables.html.template", binding )   of tables
    fh.close()

    print "Building index.html\n"                   Builds the
    fh = File.new ("output/index.html", "w" )       container
    fh.print run_template( "index.html.template", binding )   frame
    fh.close()
end

if ARGV[0]
    read_sql_file( ARGV[ 0 ] )
else                                    Sends the argument
    print "Must specify an input SQL file\n"   to the SQL documen-
end                                     tation builder
```

❶ This code imports the `Tokenizer` and parser that reads the SQL. These are from the language parsing toolkit described in chapter 3.

❷ The `JavaDoc` class is also from the language parsing toolkit. It reads JavaDoc comments and creates a hash of key value pairs that stores the data in the comment. Later in this chapter you'll create an `ExtendedJavaDoc` class that derives from the `JavaDoc` class to handle your requirements.

❸ ERb is the text-template handler.

❹ `run_template` is a wrapper for the ERb template mechanism that takes the filename of a template and the binding object that contains the local variables for template.

❺ The `ExtendedJavaDoc` class derives from the `JavaDoc` class and handles the `@field` and `@relates_to` keys. The `@field` descriptions are stored in the `fieldDescriptions` hash table; the `@relates_to` table names are stored in an array called `relatesTo`.

❻ This code iterates over every table. Within this loop the code reads the JavaDoc comments attached to the table, then uses a template to create the HTML page for the table.

❼ This code creates our `ExtendedJavaDoc` object for this table and passes along to it the comments that are attributed to the table.

❽ This code attaches a comment to every field by using the comment for the field in the `ExtendedJavaDoc` object.

❾ These two local variables—`table_comment` and `relates_to`—are passed to the ERb template by using the `binding` method call on `run_template`.

❿ This code runs the ERb template that generates the HTML page, which in turn describes the table.

Next you need a template that uses basic ERb substitution to build the header at the top of the page. This header describes the fundamentals of the table, including the name, and the comment. The template then iterates over each field to create the HTML table that describes the fields of the database table. The ERb template for the generator is shown in Listing 6.3.

Listing 6.3   table_page.html.template

```
<html><head>
<title><%= table.name %></title>          <—  Uses the table name as the title
</head>
<body>
<table width=100%>
<tr>
<td width=10% nowrap valign=top><b>Table Name:</td><td><%= table.name %></
td></tr>          <—  Shows the table name and comment
```

```
<td width=10% nowrap valign=top><b>Description:</td><td><%= table_comment
%></td></tr>
<td width=10% nowrap valign=top><b>Fields:</td><td>
<table cellspacing=1 cellpadding=0 bgcolor=#bbbbbb width=100%>
<tr>
<td width=20% nowrap valign=top><b>Name</b></td>
<td width=20% nowrap valign=top><b>Type</b></td>
<td width=20% nowrap valign=top><b>Constraints</b></td>
<td width=40% valign=top><b>Comments</b></td>
</tr>
<% table.fields.each { |field|
constraints = []
constraints.push( "Non-null" ) if ( field.not_null )
constraints.push( "Unique" ) if ( field.unique )
constraints.push( "Primary key" ) if ( field.primary_key )
%><tr>
<td bgcolor=white valign=top><%= field.name %></td>
<td bgcolor=white valign=top><%= field.type %></td>
<td bgcolor=white valign=top><%= constraints.join( ", " ) %></td>
<td bgcolor=white valign=top><%= field.comment %></td>
</tr><% } %>
</table>
</td></tr>
<% if ( relates_to.length > 0 )
rel_text = relates_to.map { |table| "<a href=\"#{table}.html\">#{table}"
}.join( ", " )
%><td width=10% nowrap valign=top><b>Relates To:</td>
<td valign=top><%= rel_text %></td>
</tr><% end %></table>
</body>
</
html>
```

Shows the beginning of the field table — points to `<td width=10% nowrap valign=top><b>Fields:</td><td>`

❶ Outputs each field

Shows the end of the field table — points to `</table>`

❷ Outputs the related table links

❶ This code loops through each field and outputs the cells that contain the names, the types, the constraints, and the comments.

❷ This code prints a list of related tables. The map creates the <a> tags and the join adds the comments between the completed <a> tags.

The tables.html file displays the left-hand menu in a framed layout (shown in figure 6.2). The menu contains the names of all the tables. When the user clicks on one of the table names, the right-hand frame shows the page specific to that table. The template for the tables.html file is shown here:

```
<html>
<body>
<% tables.each { |table| %>
<a href="<%= table.name %>.html" target="main"><%= table.name %></a><br>
<% } %>
</body>
</html>
```

Creates links to all of the Table pages

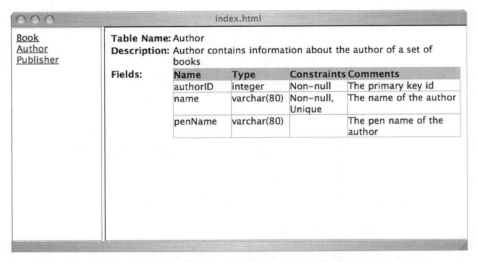

Figure 6.2 The generator builds this documentation for the Author table

Next you must write the template for the `index.html` file. No substitution is required in this template. The resulting HTML is a frameset that places the menu on the left-hand side and the table information in the right-hand panel. Here's the code:

```
<frameset cols="20%,*">
<frame src="tables.html">
<frame name="main" src="tables.html">
</frameset>
```

Figure 6.2 shows the output of the generator for the Book table. The HTML shows the name of the table, your description of it and all its fields, and the tables to which it relates.

6.3.5 Performing system tests

You are now ready to conduct system tests for your generator. You do this by using the system test framework described in appendix B. It's a simple process. The first time the test system runs, the generator stores the output as a set of known goods. After that, you run the generator and compare the outputs against the known goods. If there is a discrepancy, then you know that your definition of a good result has changed, your SQL has changed, or the generator is not creating the proper output. Once you identify the problem, you can re-create the known goods and start the process over again.

Here is the configuration file for the simple system test framework:

```
<ut kgdir="kg">
  <test cmd="ruby -I../lp docgen.rb examples/tables.sql">
        <out>output/Author.html</out>
        <out>output/Book.html</out>
        <out>output/Publisher.html</out>
        <out>output/index.html</out>
        <out>output/tables.html</out>
  </test>
</ut>
```

CHAPTER 6   GENERATING DOCUMENTATION

6.4 UNDERSTANDING THE JAVADOC AND THE DOCLET API

Long ago Sun realized the importance of embedded documentation in Java, and to address that, it created the JavaDoc standard. The JavaDoc engine is designed to have a replaceable back end. It reads and interprets the Java and creates a hierarchy of objects that are sent to the Doclet. This hierarchy contains not only the JavaDoc comments, but all of the information about the public, protected, and private member variables, methods, and classes.

The standard Doclet uses this information to create HTML documentation. You can write your own back end for JavaDoc using the Doclet API. Instead of you passing the hierarchy of objects to the HTML writing code, the objects are sent to your Doclet code, where you can use them however you like. A number of code generators have been built upon the Doclet API. Here are some of the more popular Doclets:

- XDoclet (http://xdoclet.sourceforge.net) is a code generation engine based on the Doclet standard. It is often used to build infrastructure beans around existing entity beans based on the JavaDoc markup found in the entity beans.
- CastorDoclet (http://castordoclet.sourceforge.net) is a database-mapping Doclet for Castor JDO.
- JELDoclet (http://jeldoclet.sourceforge.net/) converts the JavaDoc markup and the class structure information to XML.
- JUnitDoclet (www.junitdoclet.org/) is a unit-test creation tool based on the Doclet API.
- DocBookDoclet (freshmeat.net/projects/dbdoclet) generates DocBook documentation from JavaDoc.

If your generator requires input from a group of Java classes plus additional optional commenting information, you should consider using the Doclet structure. As an alternative, you can have the Doclet create an XML representation of the classes and comments, which you can then feed to the generator. This way, the generator is dependent neither on Java or the Doclet API.

You can find more information on the Doclet API, including technical documentation and tutorials, on Sun's Java site at http://java.sun.com. Additional information can be found at http://doclet.com/.

6.5 FINDING A TOOL TO DO IT FOR YOU

If you don't want to build your own documentation generator, you can download one of several free existing tools. Each popular language has at least one. We've listed a sampling of what's available here. Some of these generators have replaceable front or back ends, allowing them to read multiple languages and to output not only documentation but anything you require.

- Doxygen (www.doxygen.org) is an industry standard for inline documentation of C++.
- JavaDoc (http://java.sun.com/j2se/javadoc/) has been with Java since the beginning. It is used not only to generate HTML documentation but is integrated into IDE tools and provides API documentation on the fly within pop-ups.
- Synopsis (http://synopsis.sourceforge.net/) is an inline code documentation tool with support for multiple languages through a plug-and-play parser mechanism.
- ScanDoc (www.sylvantech.com/~talin/projects/scandoc/scandoc.html) is a Java-Doc syntax inline code documentation tool written in Perl and targeted at C++.
- PHPDoc (www.phpdoc.de/demo.html) is a JavaDoc comment style inline documentation tool for documenting PHP classes and pages.
- RDoc (http://rdoc.sourceforge.net/) and RDtool (www2.pos.to/~tosh/ruby/rdtool/en/index.html) are embedded source code documentation tools for Ruby.

6.6   SUMMARY

The case study generator shown in this chapter provides a glimpse into the value of tools that parse your code and comments to generate critical outputs such as documentation. With the tools provided in this book, you can build generators to parse C, C++, Java, and SQL, and from there use ERb to build whatever output you choose.

By using inline documentation, you add value to your code base because you include vital API documentation directly in the code. By building generators that further leverage the structure of the code base and its associated documentation, you extend your investment in creating the code.

In the next chapter, we show you how to build generators that perform unit tests of your applications.

CHAPTER 7

Generating unit tests

There is nothing like the feeling of editing your code with confidence. And that kind of confidence can only come from knowing you have tests that check every aspect of the code for defects. Unit tests are invaluable for performing this role and ensuring overall code quality. They run against an API, which tests both valid and invalid use cases. A robust unit test will invoke the system with a variety of methods and data, and then report back as to the success or failure of the system.

The downside of unit tests is that it takes a lot of work to create and maintain them. The upside is that you can apply generation to solve that problem.

In this chapter, we present a number of generators that make it easy to create and maintain unit tests that ensure code quality. Because each unit test application has different requirements, you will need to customize the generators in this chapter to use them effectively in your environment.

7.1 THE BIG PICTURE

The case study from chapter 1 used several generated unit tests. The first of these tested the database access interface through the EJB layer. The database unit test system uses test data from the database to build a test data loader. This data loader uses the EJB layer to set the database and to determine whether the data was properly written. Figure 7.1 shows the unit test from chapter 1.

The second set of unit tests we showed was a set of web robots that comes in the front door of the application through the web interface. Figure 7.2 shows how the user agents are generated and how they relate to the production pages.

The web robots use the same data as the database unit test but load that data in through the front end of the application. This tests the JSP pages, the database access layer, and the database schema. Using the web robots gives you an end-to-end test of your entire technology stack.

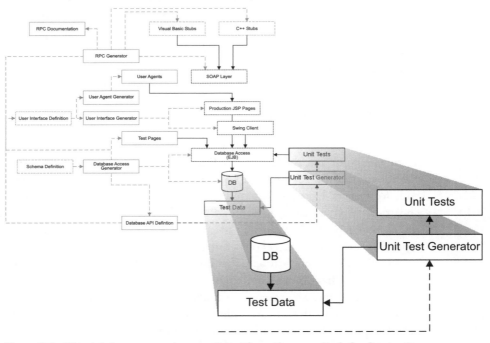

Figure 7.1   The database access layer unit test from the case study in chapter 1

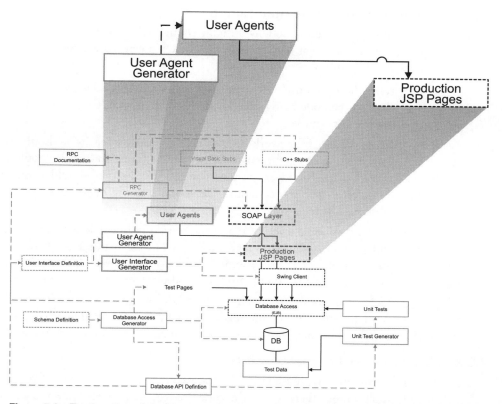

Figure 7.2 Testing the original case study system by loading data through the user interface

This chapter presents a case study that tests APIs in a manner similar to the database loader from the case study. In addition, we provide an architecture for the web robot unit test that was used in the study.

But before we start building our case study, it's useful to think about some of the common concerns that you might come up against when implementing unit tests with code generation.

7.2 PREPARING FOR COMMON CONCERNS

Who can argue with code quality? Because unit tests create higher quality, more reliable code, it's tough to argue against them, but the specter of time and money can cast a shadow on the value of code meant for testing instead of production. Here are some of the more common concerns about unit testing.

7.2.1 Unit tests won't be maintained

Maintaining production code is difficult enough without having to maintain the supporting unit tests. That may be true, but there are ways to ensure that your company's investment in unit tests is maintained:

- Keep the tests simple to create and maintain. One strategy is to keep your tests close to the code being tested. Another is to use code generation to make building the tests simple.

- Make the test framework visible and easy to run. Ideally it should also leverage your existing development tools, or the test framework tools should be installed as part of the build environment install. No barriers should exist between the intention to test the code and the actual running of the tests and receiving an understandable report.

- Support multiple levels of reporting. You should be able to test the overall system and get back a high-level report telling you what works and where you might run into problems. The user should be able to drill down on issues or rerun tests in specific areas to get more information about where issues are located.

- Make unit testing part of the culture. Ensure that time is allocated for unit test development. Run the unit tests automatically every night with email notification of failures so that everyone knows when and where unit tests are failing.

7.2.2 It's too hard to make unit tests

This is sometimes rephrased as "Unit tests won't work on my code." If you can write the code, tools are out there to test the code. It's true that some types of code are easier to test than others. You need to analyze how to spend your QA money and balance the importance of the code being tested against the difficulty and expense of testing it.

For all of the code domains (e.g., database access, interface, RPC) presented in this book, effective unit test tools are available both in the public domain or for purchase. If you are willing to spend the money and the time, tools are available that make building tests for your application easier. APIs can be tested through white box unit tests, web interfaces can be tested through robots, and client/server applications can be tested through front-end testing tools, such as those from Segue (www.segue.com).

7.2.3 Unit tests will limit our flexibility

It seems counterintuitive, but unit tests actually *increase* your flexibility by allowing you to accept more risks in refactoring code. If you have thorough unit tests for your module, then you can refactor the code any way you please; so long as the unit tests pass, you can be reasonably sure that the module is still running properly.

Working with unit tests is an immensely gratifying experience. If you have not worked with a solid unit test framework before, you are missing out on valuable peace of mind. It will be the end of sleepless nights spent worrying about application stability or reliability.

7.2.4 The interface isn't ready yet

When fully embraced, unit testing inverts the development process. You start by developing the unit tests, and then implement the interfaces to match the unit test cases. These tests should cover both normal and error conditions. Once the tests pass, you can feel confident that the interface is implemented completely.

When you invert the development process to create the unit tests before doing anything else, the question of whether the interfaces are sufficient for tests becomes a non-issue.

7.2.5 Unit tests are not worth the time

To understand the value of unit tests, you have to try using them at least once. I can guarantee that after you have experienced the confidence that comes with writing code with a unit test running as a bug-catching safety net, you'll never have to be convinced again.

7.2.6 Adding unit tests to a legacy system is painful

Let's face it: Doing almost anything with legacy code is painful. And that pain is multilayered. First, you have to try to understand the code. Then comes figuring out what changes need to be made. Finally, there is the fear that new changes will break the code.

This last part is where unit tests pay off. If you had unit tests in the first place, you wouldn't be worrying about the ramifications of code changes.

When you are modifying core components of a legacy system, it is worth the time to integrate unit tests before making the changes. If you have thorough unit tests and they pass after the modifications, you can be reasonably satisfied that the system is stable.

7.2.7 Unit tests can only prove the existence of errors

In 1968 Edsger Dijkstra wrote that "Testing can demonstrate the existence of errors, but never their absence." The idea is that you should be able to mathematically prove the validity of an algorithm and thus prove every possible test case. This is both fascinating and true. If you have algorithmic tests, you may not need unit tests. However, if your system does not have algorithmic tests you should consider using unit tests as a starting point to ensure code quality.

Our case study on unit test generation uses a generator that builds unit tests by parsing the test data directly from a C implementation file.

7.3 A CASE STUDY: AUGMENTED C CODE

The case study generator allows an engineer to add test cases to C code using specifically formatted comments. What follows is some C code with test data embedded into the comments. The placement of the test data is critical. The test data should be directly in *front* of the function to which the data will be sent. In this way, you keep the test data close to the function and obviate the need to specify to which function the test data applies.

```
// <test result="3"><a>1</a><b>2</b></test>          The test data
// <test result="6"><a>2</a><b>4</b></test>
int add( int a, int b ) { return a + b; }        ◁—— The function to test

int main( int argc, char *argv[] )
{
        run_tests();          ◁—— The test invocation
        printf( "%d\n", add( 1, 2 ) );
        return 0;
}
```

The output of the generator goes back into the input file. The following code fragment is the output of the generator using the input file:

```
// <test result="3"><a>1</a><b>2</b></test>
// <test result="6"><a>2</a><b>4</b></test>
int add( int a, int b ) { return a + b; }

int main( int argc, char *argv[] )
{
        run_tests();
        printf( "%d\n", add( 1, 2 ) );
        return 0;
}

// <test_start>          ◁—— The test marker comment
static int run_tests()          ◁—— The new unit test function
{
        if ( add( 1, 2 ) != 3 )          ◁—— A test invocation
        {
                printf( stderr, "Unit test add_1 failed!\n" );    The generated
                return 0;                                         failure handler
        }

        if ( add( 2, 4 ) != 6 )
        {
                printf( stderr, "Unit test add_2 failed!\n" );
                return 0;
        }

        return 1;
}

// </test_start>
```

In this code, we create a new function called `run_tests`, which is local to this module. This `run_tests` function calls `add` twice with the test data specified in the comments. If the `add` function does not respond properly, the system prints an error message and returns zero for failure. If all of the tests run properly, then `run_tests` returns 1 for success.

7.3.1 Roles of the generator

Before you architect a generator for the unit tests, you need to clearly define the role of the generator in your overall system. First, define which requirements are covered by the generator and which are not. Let's start with what *is* covered:

- Translation of technical unit test requirements into running unit tests (by technical requirements, we mean the input data for each test as well as the valid output for each set of input data).
- The framework within which the unit tests will be run.
- The assessment of the success or failure of the unit tests.

The generator does not take responsibility for:

- Designing the tests.
- Generating test data sets to test an arbitrary interface.
- Testing interfaces where the functions need to be called in a specific order.
- Testing object-oriented interfaces.

The limitation of the order dependency in the interface and the testing of object-oriented interfaces are addressed by other unit test generator designs presented in the sequential test case generator described later in section 7.4.

7.3.2 Laying out the generator architecture

The generator for the augmented C unit test system is based on the mixed-code generation model (see chapters 2 and 4 for more on mixed-code generation). It takes the C code as input, adds the test implementations using the test templates, and writes the new code back into the original file (after making a backup). Figure 7.3 is a block diagram of the generator.

In the next section, we'll look at a step-by-step view of how this generator operates as it executes.

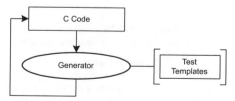

Figure 7.3   This generator takes C code, which embeds tests, implements the tests, and injects them back into the C.

7.3.3　Processing flow

The C unit test generator follows these processing steps:

- Reads the C file.
- Tokenizes the C.
- Parses the C tokens.
- Prepares an array to act as a list of tests.
- Inspects each function and follow these steps:
  - Looks at test data in the comments.
  - Adds the test data to the list of tests.
  - Uses a template to create the test function with all of the tests.
  - Adds the function into the original file text.
- Makes a backup of the original file.
- Writes the output into the original file.

7.3.4　Building the code for the unit test generator

We're ready to start writing the code for our generator. Our generator uses the `CTokenizer` and `CLanguageScanner` from the language parsing toolkit discussed in chapter 3. Once the C comments and function prototypes are parsed and stored in memory, the generator uses the ERb text-template system to build the new test function. Once the construction of the function is complete, the generator injects the function back into the original file using a regular expression. The source code for the C unit test generator is shown in Listing 7.1.

Listing 7.1　testgen.rb

```
require "ftools"

require "CTokenizer"
require "CLanguageScanner"

require "rexml/document"          <—— Imports the XML reader
require "erb/erb"                 <—— Imports the text-template handler

class PrototypeWithTests < Prototype       ❶ Prototype
  def initialize()                             subclass for
    super()                                    the test data
    @tests = []
  end
  attr_reader :tests   # The array of tests
  def add_tests( tests )
    tests.each { |test| @tests.push( test ); }
  end
end
```

```ruby
class TestData
  def initialize()
    @name = ""
    @result = ""
    @arguments = {}
  end

  attr_accessor :name       # The name of the test
  attr_accessor :result     # The expected result
  attr_reader :arguments    # The test data (a hash)

  def add_argument( name, value )
    @arguments[ name ] = value
  end
end

def parse_data( text )
  begin
    data = TestData.new()
    doc = REXML::Document.new( text )
    data.result = doc.root.attributes[ 'result' ]
    data.name = doc.root.attributes[ 'name' ]
    doc.root.elements.each { |elem|
      data.add_argument( elem.name, elem.text.strip )
    }
    data
  rescue
    nil
  end
end

def find_tests( comments )
  tests = []
  comments.each { |comment|
    found = comment.to_s.scan( /(<test.*?<\/test>)/ )
    if ( found )
      found.each { |items|
        data = parse_data( items[0] )
        tests.push( data ) if ( data )
      }
    end
  }
  tests
end

def generate_tests( file_name )
  fh = File.open( file_name )
  c_text = fh.read()
  fh.close()

  tokenizer = CTokenizer.new( )
  tokenizer.parse( c_text )
```

② Test data class

③ Parses the test data
from function comments

④ Finds the test data in
function comments

⑤ Shows the main
generator entry point

Reads the
C file

Tokenizes the C

```ruby
languagescanner = CLanguageScanner.new()                    ⟵ Creates the LanguageScanner
languagescanner.prototypeClass = PrototypeWithTests   ❻ Function proto-
languagescanner.parse( tokenizer.tokens )              ⟵      type subclass

count = 0                                                          Scans the
languagescanner.prototypes.each { |proto|                         tokens
  tests = find_tests( proto.comments )
  proto.add_tests( tests )                              ❼ Iterates over
                                                          each prototype
  index = 1
  proto.tests.each { |item|
    name = "#{proto.method_name}_#{index}"
    item.name = name unless ( item.name )              ❽ Iterates over
    index += 1                                            each test
    count += 1
  }                                                    ❾ Sets up a proto-
}                                                        types variable
                                                         for the template
prototypes = languagescanner.prototypes            ⟵
erb = ERb.new( File.new( "templates/c.template" ).read )   | Runs the template
template_result = erb.result( binding )

template_result="//<test_start>\n#{template_result}\n//</test_start>"  ❿

  File.copy file_name, "#{file_name}.bak"    ⟵  Backs up      Wraps the template
                                                the file      result in a comment
  if ( c_text =~ /\/\/ <test_start>.*?\/\/ <\/test_start>/m )
    c_text.sub!( /\/\/ <test_start>.*?\/\/ <\/test_start>/m,
template_result )
  else                                                       Puts new code into ⓫
    c_text += template_result                                the original file
  end

  File.open( file_name, "w" ).write( c_text )      ⟵  Creates the new file
  print "#{file_name}: #{count} tests found\n"     ⟵  Tells the user what we did
end

if ARGV[0]
  generate_tests( ARGV[ 0 ] )   ⟵  Sends a command-line argument to the test generator
else
  print "Must specify an input C file\n"
end
```

❶ PrototypeWithTests derives from the Prototype class defined in the language parser toolkit. The class adds an array of tests, which are TestData objects. Adding the tests to this class allows you to keep the test data in the same object as the function name and argument information.

❷ The TestData class wraps the name of the test, the expected result value, and the arguments for the function. There is one TestData object for each test, and it is attached to the PrototypeWithTests object to which the test is applied.

❸ `parse_data` uses the Rexml package to read the XML that defines a single set of test data. It takes the XML test as input and returns a `TestData` object.

❹ `find_tests` scans a comment string for all of the XML blocks of test data. The tests are returned as an array of strings, with each string containing one `<test>...</test>` block.

❺ `generate_tests` takes as input the name of the C file and processes the file, looking for tests and rebuilding the file with the test cases integrated. This function is the main entry point of the generator.

❻ By setting the `prototypeClass` member variable of the `LanguageScanner`, you are telling the `LanguageScanner` to use your class instead of `Prototype` when building new prototype objects. Your prototype objects have the tests member, which stores the array of tests associated with the prototype.

❼ After you have scanned the C file, you need to take each prototype and scan the comments for tests. Start by iterating over all the prototypes in the scanner by using the `each` method on the array of prototypes.

❽ If tests don't have names, you create pseudo-random test names using the name of the function and an ordinal value.

❾ Setting `prototypes` in the local scope to the `prototypes` array within the `LanguageScanner` means the template can get to the variable using just `prototypes`. The template can get to your local variables because you use the `binding` method to give the template access to your locals.

❿ This creates the string that contains all the test comment markers and the result of the template.

⓫ This code either finds the comments that bracket the test code and replaces them with the updated code, or if the comments cannot be found, the comments and the tests are appended to the end of the file.

Next we turn our attention to the template that both builds the tests and the function that holds the tests. The main body of the template is the `run_tests` C function. The template iterates over the prototypes and, within each prototype, it iterates over all the test data associated with that prototype. It's within this inner loop that we create the `if` statement that invokes the function with the test data and checks the result.

```
static int run_tests()
{
<%
prototypes.each { |proto|          <---  Iterates through each prototype
  name = proto.method_name
  proto.tests.each { |test|        <---  Iterates through each test
    values = []
```

```
      proto.arguments.each { |arg|
        values.push( test.arguments[ arg.name.to_s ] )    Orders the arguments
      }                                                     properly
      args = values.join( ", " )
      result = test.result
      test_name = test.name
%>
  if ( <%= name %>( <%= args %> ) != <%= result %> )
  {
    printf( stderr, "Unit test <%= test_name %> failed!" );
    return 0;
  }
<%
  }
}
%>
  return 1;
}
```

7.3.5 Finding tools for test cases

Unit testing is becoming increasingly popular, thanks to the advent of the XP programming style and its reliance on unit testing. As such, few unit test generators are available. At the time of this writing, the only one we could find was the JUnitDoclet open source generator for Java's JUnit testing framework (see www.junitdoclet.org/features.html).

In the next section, we'll look at a version of this generator that pays attention to sequence.

7.4 TECHNIQUE: THE ORDERED TEST GENERATOR

The case study generator illustrates a test system which works well against an API that does not require sequential ordering for the tests. But what about testing an API which requires that the functions or methods be called in a particular sequence—where values from one call are passed on to subsequent calls? Sequence-based test systems can also be built using a code generator.

One approach is to use a test data file with an ordered set of data, in which special mark-up can be used to show where data should be stored in variables and passed on to subsequent routines. Here is an example of a test data set for a sequential test generator:

```
:ret1,add,1,2
5,add,:ret1,2
```

The file format is a comma-separated file format. The first field is the return value. If the return value is a number (e.g., 5), then the function should return that value. If the return value is specified using a :name, then the return value should be stored in a variable with the specified name.

The second field is the function name. In both cases in the example, the function name is add. The remaining fields are the arguments to the function.

Here is the code generated for the input file:

```
// Test 1
int ret1=add(1,2);

// Test 2
if ( add( ret1, 2 ) != 5 ) { return 0; }
```

To implement the first line of the file, we have run the add function with the arguments 1 and 2. The output of the function is stored in the ret1 variable. The second line also calls add, but this time it passes in ret1 and the value 2. We then check the output against the value 5 to make sure we are adding properly.

This is a simplistic example, but it demonstrates the basic technique for building a sequential test data set and lets you see what the resulting code will look like.

7.4.1 Roles of the generator

The roles of the ordered unit test generator are the same as the roles of the unit test case study generator, as described in section 7.3.1.

7.4.2 Laying out the generator architecture

To build the test code that fits within the test framework, you'll use a tier generator model. We chose the tier model because you are building fully self-reliant code from an abstract model—the test data set. You take the ordered test data set as input. Then, using a set of invocation templates, you build the test code, which sits inside a test framework (e.g., JUnit, CPPUnit, Ruby/Unit). Figure 7.4 shows the block I/O architecture.

In the next section, we will walk through the steps of this ordered generator as it executes.

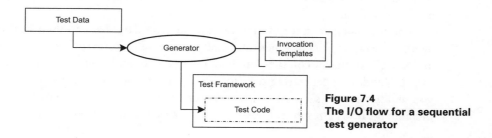

Figure 7.4
The I/O flow for a sequential test generator

7.4.3   Processing flow

Here is the process flow for the ordered generator:

- Reads the test data input file and stores it locally.
- Creates a buffer that will hold the test code.
- Iterates through each test in order and follows these steps:
  - Inspects the return value to see if you are going to check against the return value or store the return value. If you are storing the return value, it runs the template to create the variable and selects the proper template to handle the invocation. It stores the variable creation code, if you created it, in the test code buffer.
  - Runs the invocation handler that builds the call to the function with the right arguments and either stores or inspects the output.
  - Stores the result of the template in the test code buffer.
- Uses a template that provides a framework for the test code and adds the test code to the framework.
- Stores the final product in the output file.

At the end of the process, you will have test code that allows for sequential API access.

7.5   *TECHNIQUE: THE TEST DATA GENERATOR*

Testing a function or class well means running a lot of tests on it with a variety of data. Ideally you would use data that stresses the target code in a number of directions. The data would test the positive function of the API by sending in valid data. In addition, it would test negative conditions by sending in bad data or by calling the API out of sequence. The mechanism should also test the API under load by sending in large amounts of data.

The test data generator randomly generates test data that can then be used to test against the target class or function. Ideally, you would create the random output once and store it so that it could be predictably used over and over again against the same target. Randomly generating data for each test is troublesome for two reasons. First, you will not get the same coverage of test cases each time. Second, you will get unpredictable errors as a result of differing test data each time the test is run.

7.5.1   Roles of the generator

In order to define the physical architecture of the test data generator, you have to start by defining the role of the generator and declaring with certainty what the generator is responsible for—and what it is *not* responsible for. It has one main responsibility: creating test data sets for the application.

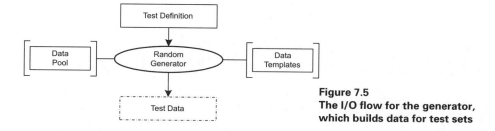

Figure 7.5
The I/O flow for the generator,
which builds data for test sets

And here are the tasks this generator is not responsible for:

- Building the test data loader.
- Building I/O functions or libraries to read the test data.
- Validating test data.

With these guidelines in mind, you can now design the architecture of the generator.

7.5.2 Laying out the generator architecture

You can define the test data generator as a tier generator because it uses an abstract model of the test data and the test definition, along with some data and data templates to create the finished test data.

The generator takes as input a test definition file. This file contains information about how much test data should be created, how many test data types there are, and what each test data type looks like.

To create the data, the generator uses a set of data pools, from which it randomly selects data elements. The generator then merges the input data with data templates, which are used to format the data for output.

The data pools can be sets of names or addresses, or just different types of strings or numeric values—any set of data from which you could derive some interesting tests. The block I/O flow for the test data generator is shown in Figure 7.5.

The next section shows how this generator works.

7.5.3 Processing flow

Test data generator

Here are the process steps for the test generator:

- Reads the test definition and stores it locally
- For each test data type:
  - Builds enough data for the amount of tests specified by selecting data randomly from the data pools for each of the fields
- Sends the data to the data templates for output formatting
- Stores the output in the test data file

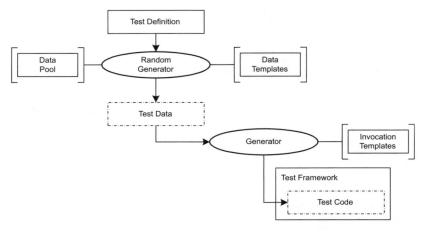

Figure 7.6   How the test data generator feeds the sequential test generator

7.5.4   Using the test data generator and the sequential test generator together

Figure 7.6 shows how the test data generator can be used in conjunction with the sequential test generator. The test data generator builds test data sets, which are then fed to the sequential test generator to create test code within the test framework.

You could argue that the generators should be merged, but by separating the data generation system from the test implementation system you extend the value of both systems. The test data generator can be used to build data for other systems, such as database loaders, while the sequential test generator can be used to find particular edge cases in either random data sets or test sets that are hand-coded.

7.6   TECHNIQUE: THE TEST ROBOT GENERATOR

When it comes to user interfaces, web applications are easier to test than desktop applications. To test a desktop application through the user interface, you need a framework that can shield your test code from the system-level keyboard and mouse event generation used to implement the test. To test a web application through the user interface, all you need is an HTTP access library.

Applications that walk through a web user interface are called *robots*. An example robot for an online auction system may follow these steps:

- Fetches the main page and checks for the login form.
- Sends the login information via a POST.
- Gets and stores the session cookie.
- Requests the main page and parses the HTML to find the available items.
- Iterates through each item and fetches its page. It checks each page for the proper data values against the database.

Each of these is a complete system test that makes use of the entire technology stack, from the database access layer through the persistence layer and the user interface. If a robot says your system is responding properly, then you are likely in good shape.

Robots have other uses as well:

- Stress-testing an application by sending lots of requests in a short period of time
- Random "monkey-testing" an application by fetching pages out of order
- Argument-testing an application by sending invalid or missing arguments from the POST or GET

When building robots you should insulate your test code from the HTTP transit code required to get the page, post requests, or parse responses. The generator in section 7.5.1 builds interface wrappers that can be used by robots to post data to the web application or to fetch pages and parse their data.

7.6.1 Roles of the generator

Test systems become a source of infinite features once engineers understand that they no longer need to tediously hand-test their code. To keep that from happening, it's ideal to lay down a set of responsibilities for the test system and its generator. The test robot generator has one main responsibility: building automated tests for the pages built to the predictable standards of the web user interface for the target application. Here we've listed those tasks the generator does not take responsibility for:

- Documenting the tests.
- Testing interfaces that extensively use client-side functionality, such as JavaScript or Flash; the automated testing agents cannot access or test that code because the test agent is not a complete web browser.

With these guidelines in hand, you can continue on to designing the architecture of the generator.

7.6.2 Laying out the generator architecture

The web generator in Figure 7.7 builds interface wrappers for your robots. The wrapper hides the web transit logic from the robot, leaving the robot free to simply specify which pages are to be called, with what arguments, and in what order. Multiple robots, serving different purposes, can use these wrappers. The robots may load data, stress test, or bridge between the application and other technologies, such as instant messaging.

Using page definitions, the generator builds wrappers that handle posting arguments and then parsing the returned HTML from the server. The page definition file must have this data about each page:

- The page URL
- The names and types GET or POST arguments
- The structure of the data returned on the page

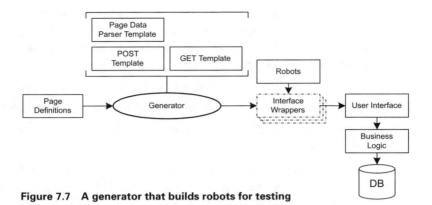

Figure 7.7 A generator that builds robots for testing

You can make it easy for the robots to find what they need by adding comments to the pages they will read. You can also bracket the important data on the page in DIV or SPAN tags, which are invisible to the user but are easily found using regular expressions. By targeting the page parser on specific DIV or SPAN tags within the page, you ensure that the robot will not break if the page structure changes for aesthetic reasons.

Let's go back to the online auction system we discussed earlier. The first thing the robot does after logging in is to see what is on sale. Here is some example HTML for the "What is on sale?" page:

```
<html><head><title>What is on sale</title><head>
<body>
Here is what is on sale today (<div id="today">1/23/03</div>):<br><br>
<table>
<tr><td>Name</td><td>Price</td></tr>
<tr>
<td><a href="item.cgi?id=2601"><div id="name_2601">Java In A Nutshell</
div></a></td>
<td><div id="price_2601">$26.95</div></td></tr>
<tr>
<tr>
<td><a href="item.cgi?id=2602"><div id="name_2602">Perl In A Nutshell</
div></a></td>
<td><div id="price_2602">$35.00</div></td></tr>
<tr>
<td>
```

If we use a regular expression that reads the DIV tags and gets the ID and contents, we get the following ordered pairs of information:

```
today      1/23/02
name_2601   Java In A Nutshell
cost_2601   $26.95
name_2602   Perl In A Nutshell
cost_2602   $35.00
```

This is the data that is important to the robot. The rest of the page is aesthetic information, which is important but not for this type of testing. The `DIV` tags insulate our robot from any changes to the aesthetic look of the page. The graphic designers can make any changes they like, so long as the `DIV` tags remain.

Next we'll look at how the robot goes about its work.

7.6.3   Processing flow

Test robot generator

The web robot page wrapper generator follows these steps:

- Reads in the page definitions and stores them locally.
- Goes through each page and follows these steps:
  - For a form page, builds a POST or GET wrapper to fill in the form variables.
  - For a report page, builds a page-parsing wrapper that reads and returns the contents of the `SPAN` or `DIV` tags.

Once this process is completed, you will have a set of wrappers that your robot can use to walk the site and that provides a level of abstraction between your robot logic and the layout of your site.

7.6.4   Generators for robots

Our wrapper generator merely built the interface wrappers for web pages that allows robots to walk our application with ease. Another type of generator can generate the robots themselves, using a dictionary of user actions. Here are two open source generators that build web robots:

- Sight is a toolkit for generating robots (http://jsight.sourceforge.net/index_SF.htm).
- Roboweb is a toolkit for building web robots (http://sourceforge.net/projects/roboweb/).

7.7   FINDING A TOOL TO DO IT FOR YOU

Unit tests fit within *test harnesses*. These harnesses provide reporting capabilities, test data generation capabilities, as well as other utilities useful in building unit tests. The following list shows some off-the-shelf testing tools for unit tests:

- Segue (www.segue.com) provides a set of programmable testing tools that can test Windows desktop and web application software.
- JUnit (www.junit.org/) is a unit test framework for Java.
- CppUnit (http://cppunit.sourceforge.net/) is a unit test framework for C++.
- HttpUnit (http://httpunit.sourceforge.net/) tests web applications through the user interface using HTTP.
- LWP::UserAgent (www.perldoc.com/perl5.6.1/lib/LWP/UserAgent.html) is a Perl library for writing HTTP robots.

- CsUnit (www.csunit.org) is a unit test framework for Microsoft's .NET technology stack.
- PHPUnit (http://wiki.berlios.de/index.php?PhpUnit) is a framework for testing PHP applications.
- PyUnit (http://pyunit.sourceforge.net/pyunit.html) is a unit testing framework for Python.
- DataFactory (www.quest.com/datafactory/) from Quest Software connects directly to a database to populate it with test data.

7.8   DESIGN TIPS

Here are some suggestions for designing your code so that you can build testing tools using generators:

- For interface code, consistency is king. Preferably all of your pages will be generated to make sure that GET and POST arguments are named consistently and processed the same way across the interface.
- For APIs, make sure your accessors and instance variables all use the same naming conventions. Also, your return types should be standardized across the interface.
- Use JavaDoc or special comments that the test case builder can use to configure itself to handle special API cases such as Singletons.

7.9   SUMMARY

The code base of any application is a valuable asset to the individual or company who owns or maintains the application. To maintain the code base long-term, software engineers have started to refactor code continuously. The term *refactoring* refers to the discipline of reworking the architecture of the application to match the current needs. As applications progress, you often find that the design decisions made in the beginning of the project are no longer valid, which means you have to refactor the code so that it will elegantly solve the current problem.

Unit tests are central to refactoring. If you have unit tests that test your component using test data and responses that match the current requirements, you can change the implementation of the component at will. As long as the output of the component still passes the unit tests, you can be reasonably sure the code is correct.

The key is having the unit tests in the first place. Having unit tests means that you can refactor. Refactoring means that you can keep the code base fresh with constant maintenance.

Using code generation for unit tests makes it easy to maintain and extend your unit tests. In this way, you avoid the common pitfall of not maintaining the unit tests or even failing to create them in the first place.

In the next chapter, we'll tackle a generator that embeds SQL into another language.

CHAPTER 8

Embedding SQL with generators

Code that implements SQL queries can often lose intent of the original SQL statements in the minutiae of the infrastructure requirements, such as managing the connection, creating input buffers, or handling error conditions. To solve this problem, vendors have created hybrid languages that embed SQL into an existing popular language. Pro*C is an implementation of this technique. SQL is written directly into the C code. During the compilation process, the Pro*C is turned into standard C by expanding the SQL code into pure C code that sets up the database connection and does the data marshalling and error checking.

We use the phrase *embedding* SQL to describe this process of building a domain-specific language by extending a language syntax with a syntax where SQL commands can be placed directly into the source without the infrastructure required to run the SQL. You then build a generator (or compiler) that translates this new domain-specific language into production code for deployment by implementing the code required to run the SQL.

In this chapter, we present a case study generator that specifies a new language called PerlSQL—Perl with embedded SQL. The PerlSQL is run through a generator that builds the production Perl with the embedded SQL converted into executable database interface (DBI) code.

8.1   PERLSQL

Code simplification is the primary advantage of embedding SQL into a language. SQL access requires creating infrastructure code that hides the intent of the author. The two code samples that follow show the before and after pictures of a PerlSQL sample. This first fragment of PerlSQL runs a **SELECT** against the database:

```
use PerlSQL::PerlSQL;
use Data::Dumper;
use DB;

my $dbh = DB::get();
my $id = 10;

my $data = eval {
  my $ps_sth0 = $dbh->prepare( "SELECT * FROM user_data WHERE id=:repvar1" );
  $ps_sth0->bind_param( "repvar1", $id );
  $ps_sth0->execute();
  my $ps_out = ();                                              The infra-
  while( my $ps_row_ref = $ps_sth0->fetchrow_hashref() ) {     structure
    push @$ps_out, $ps_row_ref;                                code around
  }                                                            the SQL
  $ps_row_ref;
}

print Dumper( $data );
```

As you can see, the SQL query is obscured by the infrastructure code required to implement the query. Here is the same code implemented as PerlSQL to simplify the use of the SQL:

```
use PerlSQL::PerlSQL;
use Data::Dumper;
use DB;

my $dbh = DB::get();
my $id = 10;

my $data = <select>                                The SELECT
SELECT * FROM user_data WHERE id=<<$id>>          statement that
</select>                                         we want to run

print Dumper( $data
);
```

The **<select>** syntax reduces the visual clutter and emphasizes the point of the code. It's obvious that the intent of the code is to run the **SELECT** statement with the **$id** value provided and to put the output into the **$data** variable.

The **select** tag tells PerlSQL to build the infrastructure to run the **SELECT** at that point in the code. The **<<$id>>** syntax lets the generator know that the local **$id** variable is to be used in the execute statement. With the exception of the **<select>...</select>** tag, this is valid Perl.

In the next section, we discuss the issues that you're likely to hear from your team about implementing this type of generator.

8.2   PREPARING FOR COMMON CONCERNS

There are some well-founded concerns involved with building a new language such as PerlSQL. We address these concerns in the sections that follow.

8.2.1   We are creating a new language

That is true: along with creating a language, you are taking responsibility for maintaining the language long-term and educating engineers in its use.

You should base the decision to implement something like PerlSQL on an assessment of your return on investment (ROI). Here are some advantages and disadvantages to the technique, which will aid in your ROI assessment:

Advantages:

- Reduced code complexity
- Embedded elements that stand out within the code
- Embedded elements that provide an obvious indication of purpose

Disadvantages:

- The ability to debug the code directly is lost.
- New engineers will need training on the syntax.
- The engineering team is responsible for the long-term maintenance of the language.

Consider these factors carefully when deciding whether to build this type of domain-specific language.

8.2.2   Debugging will be a pain

Because the PerlSQL code must be translated into Perl that resides in another file, debugging against the PerlSQL code will be difficult. Changes made to the production Perl code will have to be ported back into the PerlSQL code once the fix has been found.

As an alternative to the inline-code expander model, you could build PerlSQL using a mixed-code generation scheme. That would allow you to debug the code directly. You should consider this option when developing your generator.

8.2.3   With Perl you could do this within the language

Perl is an extremely flexible and powerful language. You could implement PerlSQL as a syntax extension, just as Damian Conway did with the `Lingua::Romana::Perligata` module, which allows you to write Perl in Latin.

This book focuses on the theory and implementation of generators. This chapter is intended to provide an example that you can use to understand the construction of inline-code expansion generators.

8.3 WORKFLOW COMPARISON

The standard workflow when you are writing code is edit, compile, and test. You edit your source code, compile it, test the compiled application; find any problems; and then repeat the process. The edit-compile-test workflow (shown in chapter 3, figure 3.8) changes significantly with PerlSQL. Figure 8.1 is an illustration of the altered workflow.

The most common workflow with PerlSQL is to edit the PerlSQL code, run the generator that creates Perl code, test the Perl code, and then alter the PerlSQL and repeat.

In the case where direct debugging against the production code is required, you will be debugging against the Perl output. Therefore, you will have to port any modifications into the PerlSQL code. At that point, you regenerate the Perl from the PerlSQL and follow the common workflow.

In the next section, we introduce a case study using PerlSQL.

8.4 A CASE STUDY: PERLSQL

The following case study builds the PerlSQL language using a template-based inline-code expansion generator. This means that the generator reads the PerlSQL and creates corresponding Perl to implement the PerlSQL code by expanding sections in the PerlSQL to create production Perl.

The PerlSQL generator is described in the sections that follow.

8.4.1 Roles of the generator

To design the generator, you need to specify the role of the generator within the complete architecture of the system. This role should spell out the functionality for which the generator takes responsibility and those elements for which the generator does not take responsibility. The generator has one main responsibility: translation of all the PerlSQL into Perl, with the proper infrastructure for executing the query or database operation.

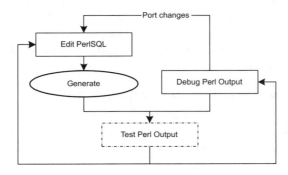

Figure 8.1
The edit, compile, and test cycle when using PerlSQL

The generator does not take responsibility for:

- Documenting the SQL code.
- Handling parameter validation for those parameters sent to the database. This would imply a level of understanding about the database structure that is implicit in the design of the generator.
- Verifying the syntax of the SQL. The generator would have to know a lot more about the database, the schema, and the stored procedures.

Now that you understand the high-level role of the generator, you can address its architecture and high-level design.

8.4.2 Laying out the generator architecture

The generator uses the PerlSQL as the base of the output Perl code. Then, using a set of regular expressions, the generator parses out the PerlSQL tags and replaces their contents with Perl implementations built using a pool of templates.

Figure 8.2 shows the block architecture of the PerlSQL inline-code expansion generator.

In the next section, we'll step through the process flow for the PerlSQL generator.

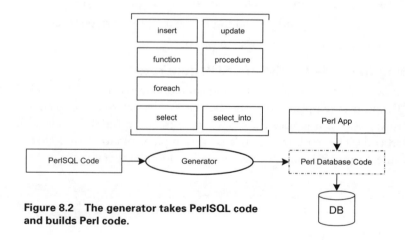

Figure 8.2   The generator takes PerlSQL code and builds Perl code.

8.4.3 Processing flow

Here are the high-level process steps that the generator makes:

- Reads the PerlSQL file.
- Uses the contents as the basis for the output text.
- Scans the text for any option tags. These option tags are used to manipulate the code that is generated. For example, one option changes the name of the database handle.
- Scans the text for tags that both open and close (e.g., `<select>...</select>`) and follows these steps:
  - Parses the SQL into its components: the SQL string, the `bind` variables, and the arguments for the execute command.
  - Executes the proper template with the decomposed SQL.
  - Replaces the tags with the output of the template in the code.
- Scans the text for standalone tags (e.g., `<select>`) and follows these steps:
  - Parses the SQL into its components.
  - Executes the proper template with the decomposed SQL.
  - Replaces the tag with the output of the template into the code.
  - Stores the altered text in the output file.

8.4.4 Building the code for the PerlSQL generator

You're now ready to write the underlying code of our generator. This code reads in the PerlSQL and uses templates to create the Perl for the database access code. It then uses regular expressions to replace the SQL segments in the PerlSQL code with the generated Perl code. The result is a completed Perl implementation that is then stored in the output file. Listing 8.1 contains the main code for the generator.

Listing 8.1 psqlgen.rb

```
require "FlexibleSQL"

require "erb/erb"
require "ftools"

$database_handle = "$dbh"        # The database handle Perl variable name
$next_sth        = 0             # The statement handle index
$sth_prefix      = "$ps_sth"     # The statement handle Perl variable prefix
$template_path   = "templates/"  # The directory for the templates
$output_path     = "output/"     # The directory for the output
```

```
def run_template( template, sql, type )                          ⟵──────────┐
  template = File.new( "#{$template_path}#{template}.template" ).read
  erb = ERb.new( template )
  flex = FlexibleSQL.new( sql, type )                                        ERb template  ❶
  varHash = { "sql" => flex.perl_sql(),                                      helper function
              "binds" => flex.perl_binds(),
              "mapped" => flex.perl_mapped() }
  erb.result( binding )
end

def tag_select( sql )                                              ❷ Function for
  return run_template( "select", sql, "select" )                     each tag type
end

def tag_select_into( sql )
  return run_template( "select_into", sql, "select" )
end

def tag_foreach( sql )
  return run_template( "foreach", sql, "select" )
end

def tag_function( sql )
  return run_template( "function", sql, "function" )
end

def tag_procedure( sql )
  return run_template( "procedure", sql, "procedure" )
end

def tag_insert( sql )
  return run_template( "insert", sql, "insert" )
end

def tag_update( sql )
  return run_template( "update", sql, "update" )
end

def handle_statement( tag, sql )
  $statement_handle = "#{$sth_prefix}#{$next_sth}"
  out = send( "tag_" + tag, sql )
  $next_sth += 1
  out
end

if ( ARGV[0] )                    ⟵── Reads the input file
  in_text = File.new( ARGV[0] ).read()
  base = File.basename(ARGV[0])
  base.sub!( /[.]\w+$/, "" )                                    Creates the output
  out_file_name = "#{$output_path}#{base}.pl"                   filename
else
  print "You must specify a psql file name as the first argument\n"
  exit
end
```

```
in_text.gsub!( /<option\s+name=\"([^"]*)\"\s+value=\"([^"]*)\"\s*>/i ) {
  name = $1
  value = $2
  name.strip!()
  value.strip!()
  $template_path = value if ( name == "template_path" )
  $database_handle = value if ( name == "database_handle" )
  $sth_prefix = value if ( name == "sth_prefix" )
  ""
}

tag_names = [ "select", "select_into", "function",
              "procedure", "foreach", "insert", "update" ]

tag_names.each() { |tag|
  in_text.gsub!( /<#{tag}>\s*(.*?)\s*<\/#{tag}>/s ) {
    sql = $1
    handle_statement( tag, sql )
  }
}

tag_names.each() { |tag|
  in_text.gsub!( /<#{tag}\s+"(.*?)\s*">/s ) {
    sql = $1
    handle_statement( tag, sql )
  }
}

print "Building #{out_file_name}...\n"
fh = File.new( out_file_name, "w" )
fh.print in_text
fh.close()
```

Handles options embedded in input file

A list of tags we handle

❸ Looks for tags that open and close

❹ Looks for standalone tags

Creates the output file

❶ This function runs the ERb template with the specified SQL from the tag. The return value is the result of the template.

❷ Each tag type has its own helper function. The name of each function is `tag_<tag-name>`. So the function that handles the select tag is `tag_select`, and so on.

❸ This regular expression pattern handles tags that both open and close (e.g., `<select>` ...`</select>`).

❹ After you have parsed the tags that both open and close, it is time to read the standalone tags (e.g., `<select ...>`).

The generator uses `FlexibleSQL` to handle the SQL statements in the `PerlSQL` class. The class creates the Perl code required for the SQL string, the bind operations, and the arguments to the DBI `execute` method. Listing 8.2 shows the code for the `FlexibleSQL` class.

Listing 8.2   The FlexibleSQL class

```
class FlexibleSQL

  def initialize( sql, type )
    @type = type                              ❶ FlexibleSQL
    @original_sql = sql                          class definition
    @perl_sql = ""
    @bound_variables = {}
    @perl_mapped = []
    parse()
  end

  attr_reader :perl_sql   # The SQL string as a Perl string   ❷ Returns the
                                                                  PerlSQL string
  def perl_binds()                    ❸ perl_binds returns a string
    str = ""                            containing DBI binding calls
    @bound_variables.keys.each() { |item|
      str += "#{$sth_prefix}#{$next_sth}->bind_param"
      str += "( \"#{item}\", #{@bound_variables[item]} );\n";
    }
    str
  end

  def perl_mapped()               ❹ perl_mapped
    @perl_mapped.join( ", " )         returns a string
  end                                 of mapped
                                      variable names
private
                                  ❺ SQL parser
  def parse()
    repIndex = 0
    @perl_sql = @original_sql.gsub( /<<\s*(.*?)\s*>>/ ) {   ❻ Handles the
      # Add a replacement bound variable                       << ... >>
      repIndex += 1                                            syntax in the
      repName = "repvar" + repIndex.to_s()                     SQL string
      @bound_variables[ repName ] = $1
      ":" + repName
    }

    @perl_sql.gsub!( /<\$\s*(.*?)\s*\$>/ ) {   ❼ Handles the
      field = $1                                   <$ ... $>
      field.strip!                                 syntax in
      name = field                                 the SQL string
      perl_name = "$" + field
      field.scan( /(\w+)\(([^)]*)\)/ )
      if ( $1 && $2 )
        name = $1
        perl_name = $2
```

```
        end
        name.strip!
        perl_name.strip!
        @perl_mapped.push( perl_name )
        name
      }

      @perl_sql.gsub!( /\*\*\s*(.*?)\s*\*\*/ ) {
        field_list = $1
        field_list.strip!()
        fields = []
        boundRealNames = []

        field_list.split( "," ).each { |field|
          field.strip!
          name = field
          perl_name = "$"+field
          md = field.scan( /(\w+)\(([^)]*)\)/ )
          if ( defined? md[0][0] && defined? md[0][1] )
            name = md[0][0]
            perl_name = md[0][1]
          end
          name.strip!
          perl_name.strip!

          repIndex += 1
          repName = "repvar#{repIndex}"
          @bound_variables[ repName ] = perl_name
          boundRealNames.push( ":" + repName )
          fields.push( name )
        }

        if ( @type == "insert" )
          fieldNames = fields.join( ", " )
          boundNames = boundRealNames.join( ", " )
          "( #{fieldNames} ) values ( #{boundNames} ) "
        elsif ( @type == "update" )
          joinedItems = []
          index = 0
          fields.each { |field|
            joinedItems.push( field + "=" + boundRealNames[ index ] )
            index += 1
          }
          joinedItems.join( ", " )
        else
          ""
        end
      }
    end
end
```

8 Handles the ** ... ** syntax in the SQL string

9 Handles either the INSERT or UPDATE path

❶ The `FlexibleSQL` class wraps an SQL string that contains special markup. The special markup specifies where variables go, or where values are to be read from, in the return stream.

❷ Using the `perl_sql` method on the object returns the SQL that should be sent to the DBI `prepare` statement.

❸ The `perl_binds` method returns a string that has Perl code in it to handle all of the required bind calls that bind variables to returned data.

❹ The `perl_mapped` method returns a string that contains the arguments given to the DBI `execute` method.

❺ This is the main method of the class. It parses the SQL and creates the Perl SQL, bindings, and mappings.

❻ The `<<variable>>` syntax indicates that the variable specified in the current scope should be inserted in this position in the SQL stream. The insertion is accomplished using bind variables so there is no problem with quoted strings or special characters. Here is an example of the use of the `<<...>>` syntax:

```
SELECT * FROM user WHERE id=<<$id>>
```

❼ The `<$ [sql_field]([perl_variable]) $>` syntax tells `FlexibleSQL` that you want the data returned for the field stored in a particular Perl variable. Here is an example:

```
SELECT <$ first_name($first_name) $> FROM user WHERE id=<< $id >>
```

In this case, you are telling `FlexibleSQL` that the field name is `first_name` and that you want the value of the `first_name` field returned from the query to go into the `$first_name` Perl variable.

❽ The `**...**` syntax is used specifically by `insert` and `update` statements. It specifies the array of SQL field names and Perl variable names that are to be inserted or updated. Here's an example of this type of statement:

```
UPDATE user SET ** first_name($first_name), last_name($last_name) ** WHERE
id=<<$id>>
```

❾ This code handles the placement of the SQL variables and their bindings, depending on whether this is an `update` or `insert` statement.

A template file is available for each of the operands supported by the PerlSQL generator (e.g., `select`, `insert`, `update`, `select_into`). This template file is used to create the Perl code that implements the `select` tag, as shown here:

```
eval {
  my <%= $statement_handle %> = <%= $database_handle %>>prepare( "<%= varH
ash['sql'] %>" );
  <%= varHash['binds'] %><%= $statement_handle %>>execute();
  my $ps_out = ();
  while( my $ps_row_ref = <%= $statement_handle %>>fetchrow_hashref() ) {
    push @$ps_out, $ps_row_ref;
  }
  $ps_row_ref;
}
```

The rest of the templates are available in the code package associated with this book (www.codegeneration.net/cgia).

8.4.5   Performing system tests

You can unit-test the PerlSQL generator by running the generator on a number of test files and then storing the output of those files as known goods after they have been inspected. After the generator is modified, you can run the test system again and compare the new output against the known good output.

To implement the system test, use the simple system test framework (described in appendix B). The definition file for the test system is shown here:

```
<ut kgdir="kg">
  <test cmd="ruby psqlgen.rb examples/test1.psql">
      <out>output/test1.pl</out>
  </test>
  <test cmd="ruby psqlgen.rb examples/test2.psql" out="output/test2.pl">
  </test>
  <test cmd="ruby psqlgen.rb examples/test3.psql" out="output/test3.pl">
  </test>
  <test cmd="ruby psqlgen.rb examples/test4.psql" out="output/test4.pl">
  </test>
  <test cmd="ruby psqlgen.rb examples/test5.psql" out="output/test5.pl">
  </test>
  <test cmd="ruby psqlgen.rb examples/test6.psql" out="output/test6.pl">
  </test>
  <test cmd="ruby psqlgen.rb examples/test7.psql" out="output/test7.pl">
  </test>
  <test cmd="ruby psqlgen.rb examples/test8.psql" out="output/test8.pl">
  </test>
  <test cmd="ruby psqlgen.rb examples/test9.psql" out="output/test9.pl">
  </test>
</ut>
```

8.5 FINDING SQL TOOLS

SQL has been embedded into a number of popular languages. It's most often bound to a particular database vendor, such as Sybase, Oracle, or Microsoft. Using the hybrid language provided by these vendors, you can avoid the maintenance and construction issues associated with building your own custom generator solution. Here are some references to some of these SQL hybrid languages:

- SQLJ is Java with embedded SQL for Oracle (www.oracle.com).
- Pro*C is C with embedded SQL for Oracle (www.oracle.com).
- ESQL/C is C with embedded SQL for Microsoft SQL Server (www.microsoft.com).
- ecpg is C with embedded SQL for Postgres (www.us.postgresql.org).

8.6 SUMMARY

Companies that provide database solutions often offer a corresponding embedded SQL technology to make it easier for engineers to write SQL access code. There are several advantages to creating a domain-specific language, such as a language with embedded SQL. However, there are some drawbacks as well. We discussed both in this chapter, and you should weigh the pros and cons when you are deciding whether to use the inline-code expansion technique.

In the next chapter, we'll talk about arguably one of the most useful types of code generation: the data-handling generator.

CHAPTER 9

Handling data

Code that reads and writes data formats can be created by code generation techniques. The up-front benefit with a generator is that you can feel confident that you won't get the keyboard entry errors that turn a `long` into an `int` and take two days to find. But the real value of using code generation for data handling is in the use of an *abstract file definition*.

From this abstract definition, you can generate code for the file format in a variety of languages and generate conversion routines, as well as documentation or test data. For example, given a single abstract definition for a file format, we could create libraries that read and write the format for C, Java, and Perl. Another example is creating data adapter code that builds data-munging code to convert data from one format to another.

In this chapter, we show you several generation strategies based on this philosophy of using an abstract definition for your file formats.

9.1   CODE GENERATION VERSUS A LIBRARY

File format reading is usually done with a library, so why use code generation? Let's start by looking at the library approach. There are two strategies for building a library to support a file format. The first is simply to write the library with the text or binary structures implicit in the code. This is by far the most common technique.

With the second technique, you have the library read in a definition of the file format and then adjust its behavior to read the incoming stream. This library has to be pretty complex to handle a range of file formats. It also locks up a lot of design in the library itself that can't be ported to other languages.

Most of the logic required to generate a file reader is available in a variety of languages. File I/O is fairly similar across the common languages. The base data types and the file I/O handling classes or routines change names, but the idea is pretty much the same.

Using a generator, you can create an abstract definition of your file format and generate implementations of that format in several languages. No single language implementation technique offers the same reward.

In the case study portion of this chapter, we'll build a generator that builds comma-separated value (CSV) readers. In addition, we cover generation data translators and binary file reader/writers.

9.2 A CASE STUDY: A SIMPLE CSV-READING EXAMPLE

Our case study generator builds a file reader that reads a list of names and ages from a CSV file. It's a simple example, but it provides a context for additional functionality as your requirements for data import, export, and translation expand. Let's start with an example of our file format:

```
"Jack","D","Herrington",34
"Lauren","C","Herrington",32
"Megan","M","Herrington,",1
```

As you can see, this file contains four fields (first name, middle name, last name, and age) separated by commas. You can use quotes in strings to avoid confusion when you have commas inside the data.

If you were to write an XML document that would describe your comma-separated format, it would look like this:

```
<spec>                                    Specifies a Reader class
  <entity   name="Name">                  to read Name objects
    <field name="first_name" type="String" user="First Name" />
    <field name="middle_initial" type="String" user="Middle Initial" />
    <field name="last_name" type="String" user="Last Name" />     Fields and
    <field name="age" type="Integer" user="Age" />                    types
  </entity>
</spec>
```

Name is the one entity defined in the file. The Name entity includes four fields: first_name, middle_initial, last_name, and age. Each field is defined with its type and username. To keep it simple, let's define the type using Java types.

In the next section, we'll look at what you can expect this generator to do for you.

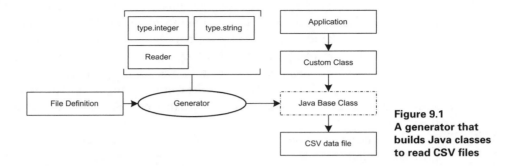

**Figure 9.1
A generator that
builds Java classes
to read CSV files**

9.2.1 Roles of the generator

Before we begin, let's list what the generator will do:

- Generate the code that will handle reading the CSV data and storing its contents in memory.
- Check errors while reading the data.
- Produce the technical documentation for any classes that are created.

The generator does not need to:

- Document the structure of the file.
- Write data in the output file format.
- Handle cross-field validation.
- Validate the entire data set.
- Validate the data set against any other internal system resource.

Now you can address the architecture of the generator that will fulfill these requirements.

9.2.2 Laying out the generator architecture

We chose to use a partial-class generator model for the CSV reader generator because we want to build classes that are designed to be extended from an abstract model of the file format. The generator takes the definition of the file format and builds a Java file that reads that format. It uses one template for the Java file and one template for each of the different field types. The output of the templates is written into the Java file to complete the generation cycle. Figure 9.1 shows the block architecture of the generator.

Next let's look at the steps this generator will go through as it executes.

9.2.3 Processing flow

Here are the process steps used by the generator:

- Reads in the file definition XML and stores it locally.
- Follows these steps for each entity:
  - Invokes the `Reader` template with the entity name, the class name, and the fields. The `Reader` template uses the type templates to build the basic processing steps for each field.
- Stores the output of the `Reader` template in the correct Java file.

Now you're ready to build the code for your generator.

9.2.4 Building the code for the CSV reader generator

The generator uses Rexml to read the description of the CSV format into memory. It then uses the ERb text-template system to build the Java classes. Listing 9.1 shows the code for the CSV reader generator.

Listing 9.1 csvgen.rb

```
require "rexml/document"                          ◁ Includes the XML parser
require "erb/erb"          ◁ Includes the ERb system
require "ftools"

Field = Struct.new( "Field", :java_name, :java_type, :user_name )    ◁ Creates the Field class ❶

def read_def_file( file_name )
  doc = REXML::Document.new( File.open( file_name ) )      ◁ Parses the input XML
  doc.root.each_element( "entity" ) { |entity _node|
    entity = entity_node.attributes[ "entity" ].to
    class_name = "#{entity}Reader"
    fields = []
    entity_node.each_element( "field" ) { |field_node|
      field = Field.new();
      field.java_name = field_node.attributes[ "name" ].to_s
      field.java_type = field_node.attributes[ "type" ].to_s      ❷ Parses the XML
      field.user_name = field_node.attributes[ "user" ].to_s
      fields.push( field )
    }

    template_result = run_template( "Reader.java.template", binding )    ◁ ❸ Runs the template

    dir = File.dirname( file_name )
    out_file_name = "#{dir}/#{class_name}.java"
    print "Creating #{out_file_name}...\n"
    fh = File.open( "#{out_file_name}", "w" )          ❹ Saves the template output
    fh.print template_result
    fh.close()
```

```
    }
  end

  def run_template( template_name, bind )        ⟵┐  ERb template
    erb = ERb.new( File.new( "templates/#{template_name}" ).read )   helper function
    return erb.result( bind )
  end

  if ARGV[0]                        ┐  Sends the command-line
    read_def_file( ARGV[ 0 ] )    ⟵┘  argument to the generator
  else
    print "Must specify an input C file\n"
  end
```

❶ The `Struct` Ruby class builds a new class with the specified fields. The fields are both readable and writable using the `.` syntax. This use of `Struct` creates a new class called `Field` that has the member variables `java_name`, `java_type`, and `user_name`.

❷ This section parses the XML into a class name, an entity name, and an array of fields where each field is specified using a `Field` object.

❸ The call to `run_template` builds the Java file using `Reader.java.template`. (This template is described in listing 9.2.)

❹ This code creates the Java file with the result of the template.

Next you build the template (listing 9.2) for the `Reader` Java class, which is used by the generator to build a CSV reader class. The template makes extensive use of iterators to create data members and handlers for all the fields.

Listing 9.2   Reader.java.template

```
import java.io.*;
import java.util.*;

/**
 * This is the base class for the CSV reader. You should derive your class
from this
 * and make any modifications you like.
 */
public class <%= class_name %> {

  /**
   * The data structure class          ❶  Shows the interior
   */                                        data structure class
  public class <%= entity %>
  {
<% fields.each { |field| %>
    /**
     * The <%= field.user_name %>
     */
```

```
      public <%= field.java_type %> <%= field.java_name %>;
<% } %>
  }

  /**
   * The input stream
   */
  private InputStream _in;
```
❷ **Shows the input stream for the CSV data**

```
  /**
   * The finished data input.
   */
  private ArrayList _data;
```
❸ **Shows the resulting output data**

```
  public <%= class_name %>( InputStream in )
```
❹ **Shows the constructor for CSV reader class**

```
  {
    _in = in;
    _data = new ArrayList();
  }

  /**
   * size returns the count of data rows found in the input.
   */
  public int size()
  {
    return _data.size();
  }

  /**
   * Returns the '<%= entity %>' object for the specified row.
   */
  public <%= entity %> get( int index )
  {
    return (<%= entity %>)_data.get( index );
  }

  /**
   * Reads in the input stream
   */
```
❺ **Reads and stores the data**

```
  public void read()
  {
    StringBuffer line = new StringBuffer();
    line.setLength( 0 );

    try {

      while( true )
      {
        int nChar;

        if ( ( nChar = _in.read() ) == -1 )
          break;

        char cChar = (char)nChar;

        if ( cChar == '' )
```

```
      {
        process_line( line );
        line.setLength( 0 );
      }
      else
      {
        line.append( cChar );
      }
    }
  }
  catch( IOException except )
  {
    if ( line.length() > 0 )
      process_line( line );
  }
}

/**
 * Processes a single input line.
 *
 * @arg line The row text
 */
protected void process_line( StringBuffer line )
{
  ArrayList fields = new ArrayList();

  boolean inQuotes = false;
  boolean escaped = false;
  StringBuffer text = new StringBuffer();

  for( int index = 0; index < line.length(); index++ )
  {
    if ( escaped )
    {
      text.append( line.charAt( index ) );
    }
    else
    {
      if ( line.charAt( index ) == '' )
      {
        inQuotes = inQuotes ? false : true;
      }
      else if ( line.charAt( index ) == '\' )
      {
        escaped = true;
      }
      else if ( line.charAt( index ) == ',' && ! inQuotes )
      {
        fields.add( new String( text ) );
        text.setLength( 0 );
      }
      else
      {
        text.append( line.charAt( index ) );
      }
    }
```

❻ Handles a single line of data

```
      }

    if ( text.length() > 0 )
      fields.add( new String( text ) );

    String strArray [] = new String[ fields.size() ];
    fields.toArray( strArray );

    process_fields( strArray );
  }

  /**
   * This is the main processor for a single row of string fields
   *
   * @arg fields The array of strings that make up the row
   */
  protected void process_fields( String fields[] )
  {
    <%= entity %> data = newRecord();
<% fields.each_index { |index| field = fields[ index ] %>
    data.<%= field.java_name %> = process_<%= field.java_name %>( fields[
<%= index %> ] );
<% } %>

    addRecord( data );
  }

  /**
   * Creates a new record
   */
  protected <%= entity %> newRecord( ) { return new <%= entity %>(); }
<% fields.each { |field| %>
  /**
   * Processes the <%= field.user_name %>
   *
   * @arg <%= field.java_name %> The <%= field.user_name %>
   */
  protected <%= field.java_type %> process_<%= field.java_name %>( String
<%= field.java_name %> ) {
    <%= run_template( "type.#{field.java_type.downcase}.template", binding
).strip! %>
  }
<% } %>

  /**
   * Adds a record to the data collection
   *
   * @arg data The new record
   */
  protected void addRecord( <%= entity %> data ) { _data.add( data ); }
}
```

7 process_fields
handles each field

8 Creates handlers
for each field

❶ This portion of the template builds the entity class that will represent one record from the data.

❷ The `_in` member variable is the input stream from which the class reads the CSV input.

❸ The `_data` member variable is an `ArrayList` that hold references to all of the entity classes created when you read the file.

❹ This code builds the constructor for this class.

❺ `read` is the main entry point for the class. It reads the file and parses the data into the data array.

❻ `process_line` handles processing one line of the CSV file. The method uses a state machine to build each field into an array of strings.

❼ `process_fields` takes the strings from `process_line` and puts them one by one into the fields of the new `entity` object. The generator creates `process` methods for all of the fields, and they populate each field stored in memory with data of the correct type. You can override these in your derived class to create custom field processing.

❽ This section of the template builds the `process` methods for each field. The template uses `run_template` to invoke the correct template for the type of the field.

Each data type has its own template to get the return value in the class. This is the template used to build the contents of the `process` method for an integer field:

```
return Integer.getInteger( <%= field.java_name %> );
```

The template for a string type is shown here:

```
return <%= field.java_name %>;
```

Next you create the Java class. It's a class called `NameReader`—the `Name` portion comes from the XML definition. Within this class is another class called `Name` that represents a single line of CSV information. The iterator in the template builds the fields within the `Name` class. The Java class definition then continues on into the heart of the reader, where you define the constructor, the I/O mechanism, and the individual handlers for each field. These handlers are built using iterators that cover each field in the definition XML. Listing 9.3 shows the generated Java class for your CSV format.

Listing 9.3   Reader.java.template output

```
import java.io.*;
import java.util.*;

/**
 * This is the base class for the CSV reader. You should derive your class
from this
 * and make any modifications you like.
 */
```

CHAPTER 9   HANDLING DATA

```
public class NameReader {

  /**
   * The data structure class
   */
  public class Name
{
/**

     * The First Name
     */
    public String first_name;

    /**
     * The Middle Initial
     */
    public String middle_initial;

    /**
     * The Last Name
     */
    public String last_name;

    /**
     * The Age
     */
  public Integer age;

  }

  /**
   * The input stream
   */
  private InputStream _in;

  /**
   * The finished data input.
   */
  private ArrayList _data;

  public Reader( InputStream in )
  {
    _in = in;
    _data = new ArrayList();
  }

  /**
   * size returns the count of data rows found in the input.
   */
  public int size()
  {
    return _data.size();
  }

  /**
   * Returns the 'Name' object for the specified row.
```

❶ The interior data structure class

❷ The new constructor

❸ The data accessor

```
    */
    public Name get( int index )
    {
      return (Name)_data.get( index );
    }

    /**
     * Reads in the input stream
     */
    public void read()
    {
      StringBuffer line = new StringBuffer();
      line.setLength( 0 );

      try {

        while( true )
        {
          int nChar;

          if ( ( nChar = _in.read() ) == -1 )
            break;

          char cChar = (char)nChar;

          if ( cChar == '\n' )
          {
            process_line( line );
            line.setLength( 0 );
          }
          else
          {
            line.append( cChar );
          }
        }
      }
      catch( IOException except )
      {
        if ( line.length() > 0 )
          process_line( line );
      }
    }

    /**
     * Processes a single input line.
     *
     * @arg line The row text
     */
    protected void process_line( StringBuffer line )
    {
      ArrayList fields = new ArrayList();

      boolean inQuotes = false;
      boolean escaped = false;
      StringBuffer text = new StringBuffer();
```

❸ The data accessor

❹ Input parsing system

```
      for( int index = 0; index < line.length(); index++ )
      {
        if ( escaped )
        {
          text.append( line.charAt( index ) );
        }
        else
        {
          if ( line.charAt( index ) == '\"' )
          {
            inQuotes = inQuotes ? false : true;
          }
          else if ( line.charAt( index ) == '\\' )
          {
            escaped = true;
          }
          else if ( line.charAt( index ) == ',' && ! inQuotes )
          {
            fields.add( new String( text ) );
            text.setLength( 0 );
          }
          else
          {
            text.append( line.charAt( index ) );
          }
        }
      }

    if ( text.length() > 0 )
      fields.add( new String( text ) );

    String strArray [] = new String[ fields.size() ];
    fields.toArray( strArray );

    process_fields( strArray );
  }

  /**
   * This is the main processor for a single row of string fields
   *
   * @arg fields The array of strings that make up the row.
   */
  protected void process_fields( String fields[] )
  {
    Name data = newRecord();

    data.first_name = process_first_name( fields[ 0 ] );

    data.middle_initial = process_middle_initial( fields[ 1 ] );

    data.last_name = process_last_name( fields[ 2 ] );

    data.age = process_age( fields[ 3 ] );

    addRecord( data );
  }

  /**
```

```
 * Creates a new record
 */
protected Name newRecord( ) { return new Name(); }

/**
 * Processes the First Name
 *
 * @arg first_name The First Name
 */
protected String process_first_name( String first_name ) {
  return first_name;
}

/**
 * Processes the Middle Initial
 *
 * @arg middle_initial The Middle Initial
 */
protected String process_middle_initial( String middle_initial ) {
  return middle_initial;
}

 /**
 * Processes the Last Name
 *
 * @arg last_name The Last Name
 */
protected String process_last_name( String last_name ) {
  return last_name;
}

/**
 * Processes the Age
 *
 * @arg age The Age
 */
protected Integer process_age( String age ) {
  return Integer.getInteger( age );
}

/**
 * Adds a record to the data collection
 *
 * @arg data The new record
 */
protected void addRecord( Name data ) { _data.add( data ); }
}
```

❺ Handlers for each field

❶ The **Name** class stores the data for each name in the CSV file.

❷ The **NameReader** constructor takes an **InputStream**, from which it will read the CSV stream.

❸ The **get** method returns the **Name** object at the specified index.

❹ The `read` method processes the data from the `InputStream` and stores it in the `_data` array.

❺ Each field has a `process` method, which you can override in a derived class to create any custom processing you may require.

The `MyReader` class derives from `NameReader` and could implement special processing for any of the fields. This example does not, however, make any changes to the field processing behaviors:

```java
import java.io.*;
import NameReader;

class MyReader extends NameReader
{
  public MyReader( FileInputStream in )
  {
    super( in );
  }
}
```

Here's the test code to use `MyReader` to read the `Name` entities from the file:

```java
import java.io.*;
import MyReader;

public class test {
  static public void main( String args[] )
  {
      FileInputStream in;        ⟵— Shows the file object
      MyReader reader;           ⟵— Shows the CSV reader

      try
      {
        in = new FileInputStream( "data.csv" );   ⟵— Opens the file

        reader = new MyReader( in );              Creates the CSV reader
        reader.read();                            and reads the file

        in.close();       ⟵— Closes the file

        for( int index = 0; index < reader.size(); index++ )    Prints the
        {                                                        first_name
          System.out.println( reader.get( index ).first_name );  field of each
        }                                                        record

      } catch( Exception except ) {

      }
    }
  }
}
```

9.2.5 Performing system tests

You can test the generator by using the simple system test framework (described in appendix B) to verify that the output of the generator is the same as the known goods that you stored when you ran the test and found the output acceptable.

Here is the input definition file for the system test framework:

```
<ut kgdir="kg">
  <test cmd="ruby -I../lp csvgen.rb examples/classes.xml" out="examples/
Reader.java" />
</ut>
```

In the next section, we look at a different kind of generator that builds code to translate existing data into a predefined format for data import.

9.3 TECHNIQUE: DATA ADAPTERS

Another common use for generation is to build adapters that read custom formats and convert the data into a form required by the target system. This is a data adapter technique because the adapter takes the data from one source and, using a set of filters and processing, adapts that data to a form suitable for a target system.

The ideal architecture has a data adapter framework into which each customized data adapter fits. Each adapter is suited to a particular input format. The framework defines the format that the adapter must match in order to bring data into the system. Let's take a look at the specific tasks we expect this generator to do.

9.3.1 Roles of the generator

Start with a set of responsibilities for the generator:

- Build the data adapter that converts the input into the form required for insertion into the database.
- Create code that embeds documentation that will be used later to generate technical documentation.

To clarify the role of the generator, you must also define what the generator will not do. In this case, our generator will not be responsible for building design documentation for the adapter or creating documentation about the input format.

With this information about the role and responsibilities of the generator clearly understood, let's examine the architecture of the generator.

9.3.2 Laying out the generator architecture

For the data adapter generator, we chose a tier-generation pattern because we want to build entire data adapters from abstract models. The generator reads the description of the data and builds the data adapter using a set of templates. You can write custom code to add fields or alter the interpretation of fields from the incoming data. The flow of input and output is shown in figure 9.2.

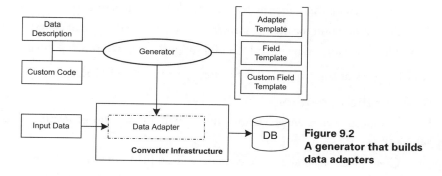

**Figure 9.2
A generator that builds
data adapters**

When you build this generator, you already know the data format requirements of the target system. The only unknown is the incoming file format. This greatly simplifies the design of the generator as compared to a generator where both the input and output formats are unknown.

9.3.3   Processing flow

Data adapter generator

This generator is very application specific. This means that customizing it for your situation may not be simple. The general processing steps are as follows:

- Reads in and stores the data description.
- Reads in the custom code and merges it into the data description.
- Creates a buffer to hold the code for all of the fields.
- Follows these steps for each field:
  - If the field is processed without customizations, uses the standard field template to build the field code.
  - If the field has customized processing, uses the custom field template and gives it the custom code and the field definition.
- Uses the adapter template to build the adapter with the field code buffer.

Finally, let's make one last data-handling generator; this one builds reader/writer code for binary files.

9.4   TECHNIQUE: BINARY FILE READER/WRITER

Proprietary binary file formats are excellent for reading and writing efficiency, but they lock customers into a file format that they cannot read without dedicated software. Using a generator to build your binary file reader/writer code has these advantages:

- The file definition is abstracted so that anyone can write a program that can read and parse the definition file.

- The generator can build support for the file format in a variety of different languages.
- Documentation for the file format can be generated automatically.
- The generator can be reused to build support for any number of binary file formats.

Now let's look at some of the specifications for this type of generator.

9.4.1   Roles of the generator

First, let's specify what the generator will and will not do. Our generator will be responsible for:

- Creating the read and write code for a given file format in one or more languages.
- Using the embedded documentation standard for the target language as you build the code for the file format handler.

The generator will not be responsible for:

- Building unit test cases for the code.
- Building design documentation for the test cases.
- Building any application logic around the file-format handler.
- Validating the input file beyond basic format size and string validation.
- Performing cross-field validation of the input file as it is read.

With these responsibilities clearly defined, you can now specify the architecture of the generator.

9.4.2   Laying out the generator architecture

The generator takes the binary file format as input and uses a set of templates—one or more per language—to develop the output reader/writer code. Figure 9.3 shows the tier-generator architecture for the binary file reader/writer generator.

9.4.3   Implementation recommendations

Here are some tips that should help you when developing this binary file reader/writer generator:

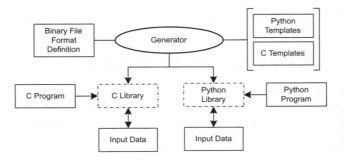

Figure 9.3
A generator that can build binary file I/O code for multiple output languages— in this case, C and Python

- This generator should not allow for custom code. Leave all of the language-specific elements of the library implementation to the templates. This ensures portability between languages.

- The generator needs to ensure that all of the default values for the fields (e.g., the type and the default value) are set within the generator itself before the templates are invoked. If the generator handles the defaults, you will not have a problem with the templates handling the interpretation of the default values in different ways.

- When you generate for multiple languages, you will have to create a set of constant types for each of the machine types. The generator leaves the interpretation of the machine types into language types up to the templates.

- Some languages (e.g., Java) have implicit big or little endian ordering to their machine types. You need to account for this in the design of your file format. Ruby and Perl allow for both endian styles when reading binary files.

9.4.4 Processing flow

Binary file reader/writer generator

Here is the basic series of steps that you can use as a starting point for your generator:

- Reads in the binary file format.
- Normalizes all of the defaults so that the templates get fully defined structures for every field.
- Runs the template for each language and stores the result.

9.5 FINDING TOOLS TO DO IT FOR YOU

The field of binary file format reader/writer generators was limited at the time of this writing. The one we could find was Flavor, which builds C++ and Java file readers for binary audio formats from an XML description (http://flavor.sourceforge.net). A handy web site for finding the format of binary files is the Wotsit archive of file formats (www.wotsit.org).

9.6 SUMMARY

Handling file formats and data conversion presents an ideal opportunity to use code generation, not only to develop the file support quickly but also to abstract the file format so that a number of different outputs can be created. This includes support for different languages, documentation, and test code.

This chapter has covered many of the key data-handling tasks with generation approaches. These tasks included reading and writing text (CSV) files, reading and writing binary files, and performing data-format conversion for input or export.

In the next chapter, we'll look at generators that create database access layers.

CHAPTER 10

Creating database
access generators

With contributions from Eric Rollins

I desperately needed a tool to make EJB development easier and less time consuming.
Ara Abrahamian (XDoclet team leader)

Teaching engineers how to use code generation for database work is my primary reason
for writing this book. This motivation comes from some personal experiences with
database work.

My first experience with generating database access code was building stored procedures for an Oracle database. I was working with a partner, a database engineer who
had already built the stored procedures for inserting, updating, and deleting records
for the first three of the 70-plus tables required in the application. To help him, I tried

a code generation approach. Two hours and 150 lines of Perl later, we were able to generate about 90 percent of the stored procedures. The other 10 percent were written by hand and wrapped the generated procedures in larger transactions.

Our generator had a simple design. The front end read the SQL generated by the ERWin schema design tool and stored all of the tables and fields. The back end used templates to build the insert, edit, and delete stored procedures from the table and field data.

We estimated that the generator saved us about a month's worth of tedious effort. In addition, the code was nearly bug-free. At the time we shipped the application, only two bugs had been logged against the stored procedures.

Later, we went on to use additional generators for the database layer. As a result of this success, we also used generators on other portions of the project, such as the user interface.

From that moment on, I was a true believer in code generation for database access, and I remain so to this day. In this chapter, we look at the high-level benefits you'll reap by using database access generators.

10.1 BENEFITS OF DATABASE ACCESS GENERATORS

Here are some of the reasons that code generation and database access are an ideal pairing:

- *It doesn't take a lot of effort to make a big impact on productivity in database work—* As I've discovered firsthand, in two hours it's possible to build a generator that can save you weeks of effort.

- *It is important to keep the design of the database abstracted from the code that implements that design*—Code generation can help achieve that goal by moving the schema into an abstract definition. In our example in the introduction, we maintained the design of the database schema in ERWin and used the output from ERWin as a data source when constructing our stored procedures. Later we added more generators that built the application code that sat on top of the tables and stored procedures. The ERWin model acted as our abstracted form of the database.

- *Database code is uniquely repetitive*—This makes database code an ideal target for generation.

- *The database is at the core of the system*—When you have generated the database and the surrounding access code, they will have a consistent design and interface. This means that it becomes easy to generate the layers that sit on top of the database. If the database is hand-coded, then the layers above it will need table-specific code to handle the design of a particular table or group of tables.

- *The complete system is often spread across several systems and languages*—In our example, the stored procedure layer was the second of three database access components required for the production system. The first was the database physical schema, written in Oracle SQL. The stored procedure layer itself was written in Oracle PL/SQL. The third layer was the application's database access layer, written in Perl. If your applications have a similar architecture, maintaining these three layers and keeping them synchronized is best done by an automated system, such as a code generator.

In the next section, we show you the database access generator at the core of the original case study.

10.2 THE BIG PICTURE

The case study in chapter 1 was a database application, and as such the database was at the core of the architecture. Figure 10.1 shows the database generator in the larger topology of the case study.

In the case study, the database generator was the first generator built. It created the core system components, such as the schema, the EJB code, and deployment descriptors, from a schema definition. The generator also built a database API definition file, which we used as input to other generators. These included the user interface, unit tests, and RPC generators.

In this chapter we present another database generator case study. This new generator will be capable of performing all of the actions described in the original study. In addition, we introduce alternative generator designs for platforms other than J2EE.

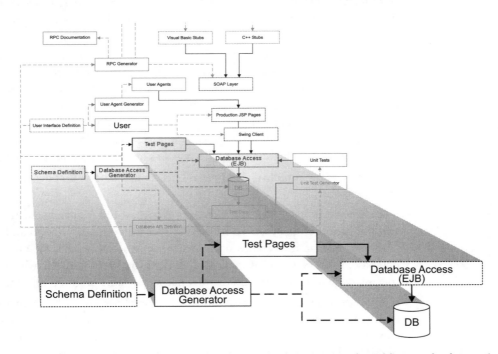

Figure 10.1 The database generator at the center of the case study architecture in chapter 1

We also offer some suggestions for off-the-shelf generators that you can use to generate database access layers.

Before we get into the specifics of these solutions, let's define some terms that we'll use frequently.

10.2.1 Terminology

Take a moment to familiarize yourself with the nomenclature used throughout this chapter:

- *Field*—The basic unit of data stored within the database. Example fields are first name, zip code, or salary.
- *Field definition*—The meta-attributes associated with a field. This includes, for example, the type, the size, and the name.
- *Row*—A single block of fields within a table. A table can have any number of rows. All rows in the same table contain the same fields.
- *Table definition*—A named grouping of field definitions. The Person *table definition* would include *fields* for the first name, middle name, and last name.
- *Table*—An associated grouping of data in rows. For example, the Person table includes the rows of data for the first name, middle name, and last name fields.
- *Primary key*—A key that consists of one or more fields from a table. It is guaranteed to be unique, and searching on the primary key retrieves only a single record for a given key.
- *Foreign key*—A field that holds the value of a primary key in another table.
- *Relationship*—The binding between tables using primary key and foreign key fields.
- *Database*—The sum of all of the tables.
- *Schema or schema definition*—The sum of all of the table and relationship definitions.
- *Query*—An SQL SELECT statement.
- *Query result*—The rows returned from a query. One SQL query might return all of the names in the Person table. Another might return just a single name based on the primary key field in the Person table.
- *Database operation*—An abstract term for any operation performed against a database; for example, SELECT, INSERT, UPDATE, and DELETE.
- *Transaction*—A set of database operations that are bound together as a unit. If any operation fails, the entire transaction is undone. Transactions preserve the integrity of the relationships within the database.
- *Entity*—In this chapter, the term *entity* refers to a single row within a table. Other books use the term *entity* to refer to a collection of data from multiple tables. In this chapter, we use the former, a one-to-one relationship between entity classes and tables.

10.2.2　Integration with existing tools

Three types of programming and design tools will affect the design of your generator and how you use the generator during development. Let's take a look at these tools.

Database wizards

Database wizards are tools integrated within integrated development environments (IDEs) that build database access classes from information entered into dialog boxes. A tier generator, such as the one we present in this case study, will not integrate with an IDE wizard. This is because the generator takes exclusive responsibility for the database tier, including the application server code and the database code. If you share the responsibility across tools, there is a possibility that the business logic and the schema could get out of synchronization.

E/R diagramming tools

ERWin (www.ca.com/products/alm/erwin.htm) is an example of an entity-relationship diagramming tool used by database architects to create both logical and physical schemas. ERWin can output a database schema in SQL that you can use as the definition file for your generator.

You should decide which source—either the E/R diagramming tool document or the database access definition file—contains the true design of the database schema. The generator should be a downstream mechanism for the E/R tool, or the output from the generator should be a schema file readable by the E/R tool.

Modeling tools

You can use modeling tools such as Rational Rose (www.rational.com/products/rose) to develop the semantic model for your application. These tools can output the model as XML, which the generator can use as a definition file.

AndroMDA (see section 10.11) uses XML output from Rational Rose to generate EJB classes.

10.2.3　Working with other generators

The database access code generator has stewardship of two extremely valuable pieces of information. First, it maintains the *schema*, so it has detailed information on all the table definitions, field definitions, and relationships. Second, it maintains the *database access* API, so it has full knowledge of the architecture of the interface, as well as specific knowledge of the interfaces of each of the database access classes.

This information can be valuable to upstream components such as the business logic or user interface layers. The case study in chapter 1 showed a database generator that fed many downstream generators. This is advantageous for a number of reasons:

- There is no higher quality information about an API than what can be created by the generator that builds the API.

- Using information provided by the generator reduces redundant data entry.

- Generator-provided information can be used for compile-time checking against the interface.

Before you get started building the database access generators, let's look at some arguments you're likely to come up against when advocating this kind of generation to your team.

10.3   PREPARING FOR COMMON CONCERNS

In this section, we examine commonly held concerns about using code generation to create database access layers. Some of these concerns result from a fear of the unknown; others are well-founded technical issues. Engineers are skeptical and some of that healthy skepticism is, well, healthy. All of these issues will doubtless come up to some degree as you design, implement, and deploy the tool, and you should be prepared to address them.

10.3.1   The code is going to be out of control

This is also known as the "I'm going to push a button and a lot of code is going to come out that I don't understand" concern. In *The Pragmatic Programmer* (Addison-Wesley, 1999), Andrew Hunt and Dave Thomas recommend that you "never ship wizard code you don't understand." This is excellent advice. You should fully and completely understand the tools you are using to build your application.

This is particularly relevant to SQL code created by a database access generator. You should make sure that the SQL and its surrounding infrastructure code matches your quality guidelines.

Once you fully understand the function of the generator, you will be in complete control of your system.

10.3.2   I'm going to be the only one who knows what's going on

Being the sole developer on a generator can leave you with the impression that if you were to leave the team the generator would never be used. This is a legitimate concern that deals mainly with the culture of your company and your development team. The lead engineer for the generator needs to be both advocate and educator. Chapter 2 deals with these cultural issues and provides you with some techniques to ensure that the generator is deployed successfully.

10.3.3   Our application semantics aren't well defined yet

The decision about when to bring in a generator can be a tough one. To get the best results from generation, you should have a clear idea of the application semantics. A well-written generator is flexible enough to change as your understanding of the application changes.

You don't want to use the generator as a hammer. "I'll write the generator when you finish the specification to my satisfaction," is a counter-productive attitude that will give the generator (and you) a bad name. An alternative is to use the generator to build what is known and to demonstrate that output to show positive progress. Then, use that progress to motivate your coworkers to get busy creating the extra definition required to complete the project. This technique is also valuable because running the generator against your design as it unfolds is a quick way of double-checking your understanding about what additional information is required from the project specifications.

10.3.4 This is going to take all the joy out of coding

Generators take the grunt work out of the coding schedule and leave you free to concentrate on more interesting problems. If redundant code writing is what you consider fun, then you may find a generator is not for you.

Building a generator is an interesting problem, and the technical issues that the generators don't cover are usually interesting problems. Believe me, when the generators are done with their work there will always be plenty of "fun" work left to do.

Developing the database schema and application semantics from the customer's requirements is difficult enough. Once you've done that, why not make your implementation easier by using a code generator that can turn your design into high-quality code?

10.3.5 The database design is too complex to be generated

Even with the most complex schemas, there is almost always some code that can be generated that will offload a few of the more repetitive tasks. The majority of the time, however, the database schema itself is not that complex. The complexity lies within the application semantics. In this case, you should see whether you can separate the generation of the persistence layer from the implementation of the application semantics in the business logic layer.

Either way, you should be able to find elements of your technology stack that are amenable to code generation.

10.3.6 The generated SQL SELECT statements will be rubbish

SQL SELECT statements tend to fall into two categories: simple SELECTs (to get the related data normalized across multiple tables) and complex report queries (which contain nested SELECTs or complex where clauses).

Related data-gathering SELECT statements can be generated without much worry about efficiency. A handwritten five-table join is going to be just as inefficient as a generated five-table join. When you are using a lot of joins to get a single block of data, your problem is with the schema and not with generation. You should consider building materialized views or de-normalizing your schema.

Complex reporting queries are another matter. It is my experience that these queries are best handwritten and tweaked directly in SQL for efficiency. The generator can still provide value by building the infrastructure around the query to plug it into your application architecture.

A valuable middle-of-the-road alternative is to make the generator build all of the queries in your application but to allow for augmentation of the definition file with an optional, custom query in place of the generated query. Using this approach maintains the productivity benefits of SQL generation, while allowing runtime efficiency tweaking with customized SQL.

10.3.7 The up-front development cost is too high

The return on investment from a database generator is proportional to the size and complexity of the database schema. For small schemas, a generator might be overkill. However, a generator provides consistency, quality, productivity, and abstraction benefits that cannot be achieved with hand-coding. This should tilt the scale toward generation when the direct schedule impact favors neither approach.

10.3.8 I don't have all of the prerequisite skills

Building a database access generator for web applications that provides end-to-end coverage (a database schema for testing web pages) requires:

- Use of command-line tools and shell scripts (for running the generator and unit tests)
- Unit-test framework experience
- Expertise in the implementation language of the generator
- Experience with the language of the definition files
- Knowledge of the target language and database access framework
- Experience with the web page server language and HTML
- SQL knowledge for creating schemas, designing efficient database operations, and structuring queries

Do you need to understand all of these technologies? Yes. Think of it this way: This knowledge is valuable and should help you across the duration of your career. Most important for building efficient database access layers for production systems is a good knowledge of SQL. All of the object frameworks in this chapter eventually boil down to making SQL operations and queries; knowledge of SQL is critical to understanding why your database access is slow and how it can be optimized.

Do all of the members of your generator team have to understand these technologies? Again, the answer is yes. In order to maintain and extend the generator, each team member has to be familiar with the construction of the generator as well as the code the generator builds.

10.3.9   The information here is centered around web applications; what about client/server?

The chapter focuses on generating a database abstraction layer for any type of application. The decision to develop the example architectures around web applications is arbitrary. The database access layer architectures are all amenable to integration within a web application, a client/server application, or a standalone application.

10.3.10   My application doesn't use a database

Many applications built today do not require access to a database, but some have no structured storage requirements whatsoever. This chapter concentrates on database access, but the fundamentals apply to any data storage and query applications.

In the next section, we look at the workflow of a database access generator, and then we begin building some case study generators.

10.4   WORKFLOW COMPARISON

As we've mentioned before, the standard engineering workflow is edit, compile, and test. If the code displays an error, you repeat the process until it's working correctly. Generating a database access tier adds a few extra steps to the standard workflow. Along with the standard edit-compile-test or edit templates-generate-compile-test cycles, you must perform two additional steps between the compile and test cycles: deployment to the server and initialization of the database with any schema or test data alterations. Figure 10.2 shows the entire workflow.

At this point, you're ready to start building your first database access generator— we begin with one that generates EJB.

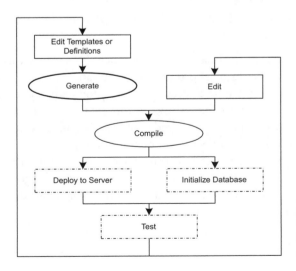

Figure 10.2
The edit, compile, test workflow when you are using the database generator

10.5   *A CASE STUDY: EJB GENERATION*

The database access object protocol within the Java J2EE standard is called Enterprise JavaBeans (EJB). The EJB standard is complex, and a variety of Java object types and XML standards are required to build EJBs. Designing, building, deploying, and testing an EJB-based application can be a multiyear effort.

We chose EJB for this case study because the complexity of the standard makes this project ideal for automated generation. Although the case study centers around building code to the EJB standard, the core concepts, techniques, and flow are applicable to building any form of database access layer. The templates may change, but the concepts remain the same.

10.5.1   The architecture of the EJB database access layer

We chose a subset of the EJB architecture that we believe creates an architecture that is reliable and production ready. This does not imply that the architecture of the EJB we present is right for your application. You should first develop your EJB architecture without thinking about code generation and then build your generator to enforce that structure.

To aid in explaining the database architecture, we selected the real-world example of a small book collection database. The entities within the database are what you would expect: authors, books, and publishers. *Entity* is the term that is used within the EJB architecture to connote one business-level object within the system. In this case study, the *entity* classes directly map one to one to tables; thus, the term entity refers to a single object, such as a single book, publisher, or author.

Our approach is to use the EJB entity bean structure to edit or update a single entity, and then use the JDBC direct database access system to run queries to retrieve large blocks of data. For example, one of the EJB entity beans that you'll build updates the name of a particular author. You'll use JDBC and a direct SQL query to the database to search for all of the books by a particular author.

For this project, we believe this EJB/JDBC structure provides the correct balance between a solid object-oriented approach and runtime efficiency.

10.5.2   EJB options

You have several options from which to choose when you build an EJB-based application. One of the most important decisions you'll make is choosing between *container-managed persistence* (CMP) and *bean-managed persistence* (BMP). In CMP the application server itself (the *container*) handles the adding, updating, and deleting of records from the database. In the BMP model, each bean handles its own adding, updating, and deleting directly using JDBC. For this case study, we elected to use CMP.

We chose not to use container-managed relationships (CMR) in this example. The schema.xml definition file contains a complete foreign key relationship map. If you intend to use CMR in your application, we suggest that you use code generation techniques to build the complex XML deployment descriptors that are required with that option.

Section 10.5.12 includes a number of web links and books that explain the merits of the EJB deployment options.

10.5.3 The schema

You need a schema to model the book collection for the sample project. This schema contains three tables: Book, Author, and Publisher. The central table is Book. Each row in Book represents a book with its title, ISBN, status, and a count of the number of copies available. In addition, each row relates to an author and a publisher. An author has a name and a pen name. A publisher has a name. The relationships between the tables are straightforward. Each book has one author and one publisher. Figure 10.3 shows the tables and the relationships between the tables. In the figure, the acronym *PK* stands for primary key and *FK* stands for foreign key.

Now let's look at the different EJB classes and interfaces that are output by the generator.

Entities

Several objects and interfaces within the EJB framework are responsible for modeling a single entity. For example, the Book entity is handled by:

- The entity interface
- The entity bean
- The entity home
- The stateless session interface
- The stateless session bean
- The stateless session bean home
- The value object

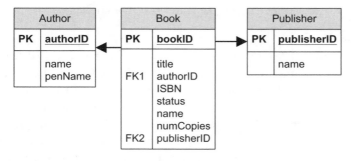

Figure 10.3   The book database schema

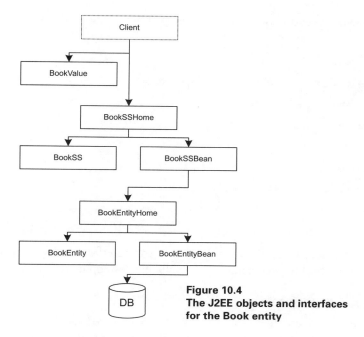

Figure 10.4
The J2EE objects and interfaces
for the Book entity

In addition, any queries associated with the entity will have their own value object types, with instance variables specific to the expected result of the query. Figure 10.4 shows the relationship between these classes and interfaces.

These objects are broken into two layered groups: the entity layer and the session layer. The stateless session layer acts as a library for interaction with the entity beans. This "stateless session facade" is mainly there for efficiency reasons. The facade adds, updates, and deletes entities using value objects, which are simple structures represented as classes. The facade then uses the entity beans to implement the entity maintenance. The value of the facade lies in its transactional binding. Two advantages to having the stateless session facade layer are:

- Because access to the interface uses large blocks of data (value objects), the API is efficient across the network using either RMI or SOAP.

- The facade layer protects the business logic of the record because the entire record must be updated by passing all of the values and not just single values.

Both the session facade and the entity beans are arranged into groups of three related objects. Each layer has a home, an interface, and a bean. The *home* is used to find the beans. The *interface* is for remote access, although we are using a local object in the case study to provide better performance. The *bean* is the actual implementation of the entity-specific functionality for the tier.

The following pseudo-code fragment shows how a new entity is created within the server:

```
// From the page:
  ValueObject valueObject = new ValueObject()
// ... Fill the value object ...
  SSHome ssHome = jndi lookup("SS path")
  SS ss = ssHome.create()
  ss.add(valueObject)
// Inside Stateless Session Bean on server:
  EntityHome entityHome = jndi lookup("Entity path")
  Entity entity = entityHome.create( params, copied, from, value, object )
```

With a requirement to build five-plus classes and two interfaces for every entity in your application, you'll find the generator to be a valuable development tool.

Deployment descriptors

In addition to the beans, the application server needs XML deployment descriptors. These deployment descriptors tell the application server details about the application, such as what beans are available, what type of persistence they use, and their transactional requirements.

Because the generator builds all of the beans, it is easy for it to create the deployment descriptors for the beans as well. This is important because these descriptor files can be complex and difficult to maintain by hand. In addition, deployment descriptors have vendor-specific elements that could be maintained at the generator level, which allows for portability to other application servers.

Now you're ready to define the responsibilities of your case study generator.

10.5.4   Roles of the generator

For this project, your database generator should maintain all of the persistence and query logic as well as the business logic. This means that the database generator takes responsibility for these tasks:

- All database operations, including all UPDATE, INSERT, and DELETE statements.
- All queries against the database.
- The business logic.
- The physical schema of the database.
- Any stored procedures used to implement the database operations or queries.
- Testing systems to support the testing of the database access layer.

The generator will not handle the following:

- Storage of any preferences associated with a single session with the application interface.
- Export of the data to other systems or import of data from other systems (though import/export code will make extensive use of the database code).
- The user interface validations or the workflow patterns for usability.

Of course, the list of responsibilities will vary for each generator.

Some architectures will separate the persistence function from the business logic. This is a valid approach, and if you use it, you should make sure that you have designated which portions of the code the generator is responsible for before design and construction of the generator begins.

Whether you buy a generator or use an open source generator, you should make sure that the role of the generator is clear and well understood.

10.5.5 Laying out the generator architecture

Our case study generator is called EJBGen (not to be confused with the EJBGen currently in the public domain). The generator takes three definition files as input. The first is the schema.xml file, which contains the definition for all of the tables, fields, and the relationships within the schema. The next file is extensions.xml, which contains extra queries and custom business logic. These extra queries can be used as the back end for specialized reports. The third is samples.xml, which contains sample data used to pre-load the database through the database access layer. Figure 10.5 shows the inputs and outputs to the EJB generator.

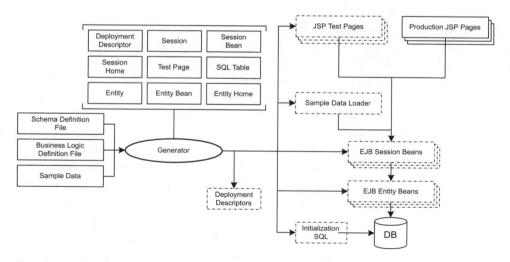

Figure 10.5   The generator builds the EJB code, schema, and deployment descriptors for a Java database tier.

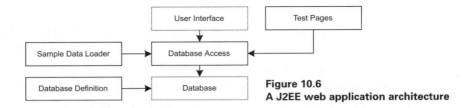

Figure 10.6
A J2EE web application architecture

As you can see, the outputs and their corresponding templates are numerous. Figure 10.6 shows where the outputs from the generator sit within the full architecture of a web application.

In the figure, the solid bordered boxes are the domain of the EJB generator. Central to the output is the database access layer that sits between the user interface layer and the database. The database server could be any modern relational database, such as SQLServer, Oracle, MySQL, or PostgreSQL.

We decided to use an all open source EJB solution to build the case study. The architecture uses Tomcat as the web server, JBoss as the application server, and PostgreSQL as the database engine.

Let's take a look at the outputs:

- *EJBs*—The primary output of the generator is the set of EJBs that represent the entities in your book database. These EJBs provide both database persistence and business logic. In some architectures, a business logic layer sits between the user interface and the database access layer. With this generator, the business logic is folded into the database access layer by use of the extensions.xml definition file described in section 10.5.8.

- *SQL definition file*—One of the key advantages of the case study generator is the synchronization of the physical schema in the database to the field and object definitions in the application. To make that happen, the generator needs to build the SQL table construction code. In this case study, the generator creates a single SQL command file that builds the tables, creates any sequence generators, and then constructs any relationships between the tables.

- *Deployment descriptors*—As you'll recall, one of the responsibilities of the generator is to maintain these XML deployment descriptor files. The deployment descriptors bind the beans to the application server. These files are tedious to maintain by hand, so there is real value in the generator's ability to maintain these files.

- *Test JSPs*—Nothing is complete until you can test it, so the first step in this case is to actually see the data appear on the web server using JSPs. To that end, you can have the generator build, add, delete, and update pages for each entity type. In addition, you can create simple reports that list all of the entities within the system, as well as create display pages for any custom queries that you generate.

- *Sample data import through the stateless session facade*—In addition to creating end-user test pages with the JSPs, you can create a set of routines that will load the database using your EJB layer. Using the EJBs to add new data to the database is a first-level check that your EJBs are working and that the database is responding the way you want. The presence of known sample data in the system will also allow you to create end-to-end system tests for your database access layer.

10.5.6   Processing flow

EJB generator

The case study EJB generator follows the tier generator model that reads a definition file and uses templates to build a number of output files. The generator follows this process flow:

- Reads the schema file and stores it internally.
- Creates the SQL schema file.
- Reads the extensions file.
- Reads the sample data.
- For each table follows these steps:
- Builds the entity, entity bean, and entity home.
- For each value object follows these steps:
    - Builds the value object Java file.
    - Builds the test JSP file.
- Creates the stateless session, stateless session bean, and stateless session home.
- Creates the add, update, and delete JSP files for testing.
- For each query creates a JSP file.
- Creates the index JSP file, which points to all of the test pages.
- Creates the stateless session factory class.
- Creates the deployment descriptors.
- Creates the sample data loader.

Whenever the process indicates that we are creating a file, you use a template to build the output file. This use of templates keeps the logic code for the generator separate from the formatting of the output code.

A key aspect of this generator is that the templates are merely output handlers. The brains of the generator are in the core Ruby code. This centralization of knowledge is important to ensure that all of the templates are given the correct interpretation of the definition files. If the interpretation of the definition files were left to each of the templates (as is the case in other generators in this book), then two templates could interpret field definitions differently, causing disparity across the output files.

10.5.7   The schema definition

Three definition files (schema, extensions, and sample data) go into the generator. The central definition file is the schema file, which contains the table definitions, the field definitions, and the table relationship specifications. Here is the schema definition for this case study:

```
<schema package="gen" jndi-prefix="gen">                    ❶ The main
                                                                schema node
  <table name="Book">
    <column name="bookID" datatype="integer" not-null="true"      The Book ❷
      primary-key="true" />                                          table
   <column name="title" datatype="varchar" length="80" not-null="true" />
    <column name="ISBN" datatype="varchar" length="80" not-null="true"
      unique="true" />
    <column name="authorID" datatype="integer" not-null="true" />
    <column name="publisherID" datatype="integer" not-null="true" />
    <column name="status" datatype="integer" not-null="true" />
    <column name="numCopies" datatype="integer" not-null="true" />
  </table>

  <table name="Author">                                       The Author ❸
    <column name="authorID" datatype="integer" not-null="true"    table
      primary-key="true" />
    <column name="name" datatype="varchar" length="80" not-null="true"
      unique="true" />
    <column name="penName" datatype="varchar" length="80" />
  </table>

  <table name="Publisher">
    <column name="publisherID" datatype="integer" not-null="true"
      primary-key="true" />
    <column name="name" datatype="varchar" length="80" not-null="true"
      unique="true" />                                              The  ❹
  </table>                                                       Publisher
                                                                   table
  <foreign-key>
    <fk-table>Book</fk-table>
    <fk-column>authorID</fk-column>
    <fk-references>Author</fk-references>          Relationship ❺
  </foreign-key>                                   between books
                                                    and authors
  <foreign-key>
    <fk-table>Book</fk-table>
    <fk-column>publisherID</fk-column>
    <fk-references>Publisher</fk-references>       Relationship ❻
  </foreign-key>                                   between books
                                                   and publishers
</schema>
```

❶ The schema tag defines the Java package name and the prefix for use with JNDI. Inside the schema tags are all of the table tags, which define the different tables, and the foreign-key tag, which defines the relations between each table.

② This block of XML defines the Book entity. The `BookID` field is the primary key for the table. The fields of the table are `title`, `ISBN`, `status`, and `numCopies`. The author of the book and the publisher are defined through relations to the Author and Publisher tables through `AuthorID` and `PublisherID`.

③ The Author table is defined in this block of XML. It contains the primary key field `AuthorID`, as well as fields that store the author's name and pen name.

④ This XML block defines the Publisher table, which contains two fields: the `PublisherID` field, which is the primary key, and the name field, which stores the name of thepublisher.

⑤ The `foreign-key` tag defines a relationship between two tables. In this case, we are relating the Book table to the Author table through the `AuthorID` field.

⑥ This block relates the Book table to the Publisher table through the `PublisherID` field.

10.5.8 The extensions definition file

The basic schema and its entity objects are never enough to implement a production system of any complexity. You also need custom queries and customized business logic. The case study generator uses an extensions file:

```
<extensions>

  <value-object name="BookWithNamesValue" base-table="Book">
    <add-column table="Author" column-name="name" />
    <add-column table="Author" column-name="penName" />
    <add-column table="Publisher" column-name="name" />
  </value-object>

  <sql-query-method name="getAllByTitle" value-object="BookWithNames
Value" >
    <parameter name="title" java-type="String" />
    <where>Book.title = ?</where>
  </sql-query-method>

  <sql-query-method name="getAllByAuthorName" value-object=
"BookWithNamesValue"
    <parameter name="authorName" java-type="String" />
    <where>Author.name = ?</where>
  </sql-query-method>

  <finder-method name="findAllByPublisherID" table="Book">
    <parameter name="publisherID" java-type="java.lang.Integer" />
    <ejb-ql>SELECT OBJECT(o) FROM Book o WHERE o.publisherID = ?1</ejb-ql>
  </finder-method>

  <custom-method name="updateStatusByPublisher" table="Book"
returntype="void" >
    <parameter name="publisherID" java-type="Integer" />
    <parameter name="newStatus" java-type="Integer" />
```

The BookWith-NamesValue value object **①**

The getAll-ByTitle definition **②**

The getAllByAuthor-Name definition **③**

The findAllBy-PublisherID definition **④**

The update StatusBy-Publisher method **⑤**

```
  <body>
    BookEntityHome home = BookEntityBean.getHome();
    Collection coll = home.findAllByPublisherID(publisherID);
    for(Iterator i = coll.iterator(); i.hasNext(); ){
      BookEntity book = (BookEntity)i.next();
      book.setStatus(newStatus);                    The update Status-  ⑤
    }                                               ByPublisher method
  </body>
</custom-method>

</extensions>
```

❶ The `BookWithNamesValue` object defines the fields that are returned from an SQL query. There is a big efficiency improvement with this technique instead of using Enterprise JavaBeans Query Language (EJB/QL). The `BookWithNamesValue` structure is specified first by using the Book table as the base set of fields, then using `add-column` tags to include additional fields that will be returned by the query.

❷ The `getAllByTitle` query is defined by specifying the `where` tag that creates the SQL `where` clause and the `BookWithNamesValue` object as the output. By using the `base-table` attribute that is referred to by the `value-object`, the generator can build the query and add the `where` clause to get the correct data from the database.

❸ The `getAllByAuthorName` query is defined using a similar method. In this case, the query gathers all of the authors that match a particular name.

❹ The `findAllByPublisherID` query is an EJB finder that is specified by the `finder-method` tag. This query will find all of the books published by a particular publisher. It is implemented using the EJB/QL functionality, which queries the local object store instead of the database.

❺ The `updateStatusByPublisher` query shows how you can implement custom business logic in this generator. In this case, you are attaching the method to the `Book` class. The `return-type` attribute tells the generator the return type of the method. The `parameter` tags specify the arguments to the method and their types. The `body` tag defines the Java for the method. It is important for the generator to understand the input arguments and output type so that the generator can marshal the method through the rest of the technology stack.

10.5.9 Sample data definition

This case study EJB generator also builds Java code that will preload the database with sample data through the EJB layer. The data is organized into rows that have a table specification attached. Within each row are data elements organized into column tags. Each column has a name that corresponds to the field in the row and a value, which is the sample data value.

Here is an example set of data:

```
<samples>
  <row table="Author">
    <column name="authorID" value="100" />                    Sample
    <column name="name" value="Conway" />                     author record
  </row>
  <row table="Author">
    <column name="authorID" value="101" />
    <column name="name" value="Tate" />
  </row>
  <row table="Publisher">
    <column name="publisherID" value="100" />                 Sample
    <column name="name" value="Manning" />                    publisher record
  </row>
  <row table="Book">
    <column name="bookID" value="100" />
    <column name="title" value="Object Oriented Perl" />
    <column name="ISBN" value="1-884777-79-1" />              Sample
    <column name="authorID" value="100" />                    book record
    <column name="publisherID" value="100" />
    <column name="status" value="3" />
    <column name="numCopies" value="1" />
  </row>
  <row table="Book">
    <column name="bookID" value="101" />
    <column name="title" value="Bitter Java" />
    <column name="ISBN" value="1-930110-43-X" />
    <column name="authorID" value="101" />
    <column name="publisherID" value="100" />
    <column name="status" value="5" />
    <column name="numCopies" value="1" />
  </row>
</samples>
```

10.5.10 Implementation

The central ejbgen.rb file uses the functions defined in ejbgenRead.rb to read the XML definition files. ejbgenRead.rb in turn creates classes that are defined in ejbgenDefs.rb. Process flow returns to ejbgen.rb, which then invokes the templates that build the target output files. The templates access the data from the definition files by accessing the classes defined in ejbgenDefs.rb. Figure 10.7 is a block diagram of the generator Ruby code, broken into three files. Figure 10.8 shows a UML diagram that represents the classes defined in the ejbgenDefs.rb file.

To learn more about this generator and its templates, see appendix C.

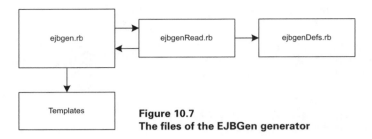

Figure 10.7
The files of the EJBGen generator

10.5.11 Performing system tests

The first set of system tests run against the generator uses the system test framework described in appendix B. This system test runs the generator and stores the output files as known goods. Then, at any time you can rerun the test and compare the current output against the known goods to see if any changes have been made to the output. The system test definition file is included on the book's web site at www.codegeneration.net/cgia.

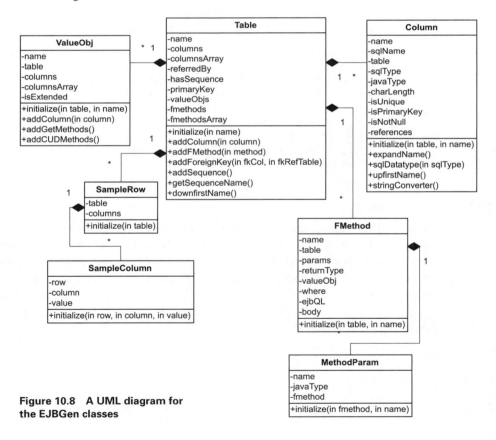

Figure 10.8   A UML diagram for
the EJBGen classes

The second unit test is the sample data loader that uses the EJB entity classes created during generation to load the data into the database. This data-loading test is developed as a primary output of the generator. For more details, see the code in appendix C.

This twofold approach to unit testing provides excellent coverage of the system. First, the output of the generator is checked directly, and then the function of the output code is checked.

You can also check the result through the web server using the test pages.

10.5.12 J2EE developer resources

If you want to become more familiar with J2EE and EJB, try some of the resources listed here:

- The official Sun J2EE site (http://java.sun.com/j2ee/) is the source for Java development kits as well as a resource for developer documentation.
- Sun's J2EE Patterns page (http://developer.java.sun.com/developer/technicalArticles/J2EE/patterns/) contains pragmatic advice on using J2EE in your enterprise application.
- The Server Side (www.theserverside.com) has articles and example code for developers building Java web applications.
- JBoss (www.jboss.org) is the application server used in our case study. This site has downloads and documentation for the application server.
- Tomcat (http://jakarta.apache.org/tomcat/index.html) is the web server and JSP infrastructure used in the case study to serve the web pages.
- PostgreSQL (www.postgresql.com/) is the free database server used in the case study.
- The official site for the JUnit testing framework is www.junit.org.
- The Struts Model-View-Controller framework (http://jakarta.apache.org/struts/index.html) is used for connection pooling in the case study.
- *Web Development with JavaServer Pages, 2nd Edition*, by Duane K. Fields, Mark A. Kolb, and Shawn Bayern (Manning, 2001), covers the JSP front-end portion of the server stack.
- *Java Development with Ant*, by Erik Hatcher and Steve Loughran (Manning, 2002), contains a section on generation with XDoclet.
- *Enterprise JavaBeans*, by Richard Monson-Haefel (O'Reilly, 2001), covers the EJB architecture in depth.
- *SQL in a Nutshell*, by Kevin Kline, with Daniel Kline (O'Reilly, 2002), discusses using SQL for database access.
- *Java Enterprise in a Nutshell*, by David Flanagan, Jim Farley, William Crawford, and Kris Magnusson (O'Reilly, 2002), is a reference guide for the J2EE API.

10.5.13 Generators for J2EE

Here are some generators that build classes and interfaces for the J2EE architecture:

- sql2java creates Java classes that map to a database schema (http://sql2java.sourceforge.net/).
- Jenerator is a generator for J2EE (www.visioncodified.com).
- AndroMDA is a model-driven generator that builds EJBs, Struts, deployment descriptors, and database code (http://andromda.sourceforge.net/). AndroMDA is the successor to UML2EJB. AndroMDA is designed to conform to the Object Management's model-driven architecture (MDA) standard. This is a standard for code generation from UML.
- EJBGen 2.0 generates EJBs from an XML description (http://sourceforge.net/projects/ejbgen/).
- Jaxor uses XML as a definition file format to create plain old Java objects (POJOs) for database access (http://jaxor.sourceforge.net/features.htm).
- JBossDruid creates EJB/CMP beans from a database physical schema (http://jbossdruid.sourceforge.net).
- ArcStyler (www.arcstyler.com) from IO is an application-building generator that handles database access as part of its role. ArcStyler is an MDA generator that builds Java code from UML.

10.6 TECHNIQUE: GENERATING JDBC

Before EJB arrived, Java developers were using a three-tier architecture based on JSP and JDBC, where the JDBC code was wrapped in plain old Java objects (POJOs). This technique is still valuable, and we've included a generator architecture to provide an alternative to database access with Java using EJB.

In this section, we describe the List/Entity architecture shown in Figure 10.9. We used this architecture with the database generators in the sections that follow. The List/Entity architecture is a simplified database architecture that uses two classes for access to each table as opposed to five with EJB.

10.6.1 Roles of the generator

As with the case study generator, it is important to first declare in a straightforward manner what the generator will and will not do. Let's start with what the generator will handle:

- All database operations, including all UPDATE, INSERT, and DELETE statements.
- All queries against the database.
- The physical schema of the database.
- Any stored procedures used to implement the database operations or queries.
- Testing pages to support the testing of the database access layer.

The generator will not handle the following:

- The business logic, which will be handled by a layer above the database access layer.
- Storage of any preferences associated with a single session with the application interface.
- Export of the data to other systems, or import of data from other systems (this code will make extensive use of the database code).
- The user interface validations or the workflow patterns for usability.

With this list of responsibilities in hand, you can now determine the architecture of the generator.

10.6.2 Laying out the generator architecture

The architecture is three-tiered, just as in the EJB example: the user interface talks to a business logic layer, which in turn talks to the database access layer, which performs the persistence role. The test pages talk directly to the database access layer. The sample data loader also uses the database access layer. The database is initialized via a generated database definition.

Figure 10.9 shows a high-level architecture for a web server that uses persistence based on direct connectivity with JDBC. The difference between this model and the J2EE model in the case study is the structure of the database access layer. Instead of having five classes (and two interfaces) to represent a single entity within the database, you have two: entity and list.

The Entity/List model

From the client perspective, there are two main use cases. The first we will call *entity access*. In this case, we want to create, update, or delete a single record in the database. The second case we'll call *list access*. This time we'll make a query against the database, which will return a large block of structured data.

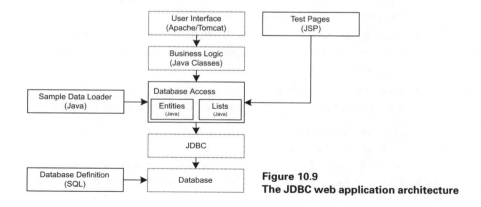

Figure 10.9
The JDBC web application architecture

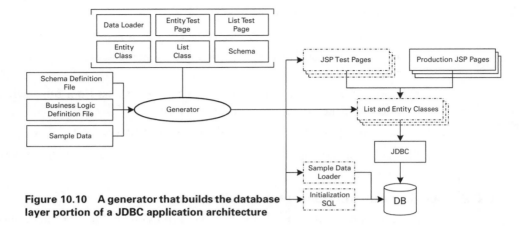

Figure 10.10   A generator that builds the database layer portion of a JDBC application architecture

Using the database from the case study, the entity access path is ideal for adding Book records or editing a Publisher record. You'll use list access when you're presenting a list or a report, such as a list of all of the publishers.

You provide access to entities by creating a single `Entity` class for each entity in the database (e.g., Book, Author, Publisher). The `Entity` class has two constructors. The basic constructor creates an empty `Entity` object with only default values. The other constructor takes a primary key and constructs the `Entity` object using the data for that primary key in the database. The `Entity` has `set` and `get` methods for each field, as well as an `update` method, which either creates or updates an object depending on whether it already exists in the database.

The `List` class implements the list access path. This object is a library, and each of its methods is a static method that performs a query. The result of each query can be one of the options shown here:

- *A single value*—An example is querying for the user ID from a user login name.
- *An array of single values*—An example is returning the user IDs from all of the users whose name matches a given criterion.
- *A single hash table*—This is used when the query is designed to get back a single structured response. An example is a query that gets all of the user information for a single user ID.
- *An array of hash tables*—This is used for reporting. An example is a query that returns all of the user information for all of the users matching a particular name.

The generator should either choose the correct result type for a given query or allow the engineer to define the return type manually.

As with the case study architecture, the input in this generator is a schema definition. The outputs are the `Entity` and `List` classes as well as the schema for the database, the database loader, and the test pages. The generator for this architecture is shown in Figure 10.10.

Now let's step through the processes that this generator performs.

10.6.3 Processing flow

JDBC generator

Here are the steps that the JDBC generator follows:

- Reads in the definition file and stores it locally.
- Creates the schema SQL file based on the definition file.
- Creates the sample data loader, which uses SQL to load data into the database.
- For each entity, follows these steps:
  - Creates the entity Java file.
  - Creates the test pages for the `Entity` class.
- For each list follows these steps:
  - Initializes a cache of methods.
  - For each query:
    - Decides the return type and invokes the proper template, and then adds the output to the method cache.
    - Creates the test page for this query.
- Creates the `List` class Java with the method cache.

10.6.4 JDBC developer resources

Here are some resources for JDBC development:

- Sun's official JDBC page (http://java.sun.com/products/jdbc/) contains the JDBC API documentation and other JDBC-related resources.
- *Java Server Pages, 2nd Edition*, by Hans Bergsten (O'Reilly, 2002), is an excellent book on JSP development.
- *Database Programming with JDBC and Java, Second Edition*, by George Reese (O'Reilly, 2000), covers using the JDBC interface within Java.

10.7 TECHNIQUE: GENERATING DATABASE ACCESS LAYERS FOR ASP

Active Server Pages (ASP) was Microsoft's first web application server model. The basics of the model are fairly simple. IIS, Microsoft's web server, runs ASP pages, which in turn call COM objects written in either Visual Basic or C++ to read and persist data from the database. This section discusses the architecture for an ASP generator.

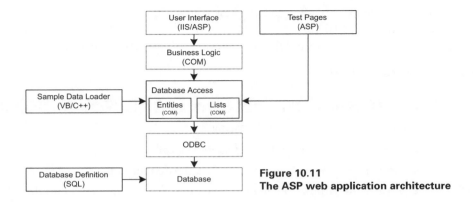

Figure 10.11
The ASP web application architecture

10.7.1 Roles of the generator

The roles of this generator are the same as those of the JDBC generator described in section 10.6.1.

10.7.2 Laying out the generator architecture

Our recommended ASP architecture is similar to the JDBC model, but we've changed the names of the components. We are using IIS instead of Apache and ASP instead of Tomcat and JSP. On the back end, we are using ODBC instead of JDBC. Figure 10.11 shows the high-level architecture.

The architecture of the database access layer follows the Entity/List model described earlier in section 10.6.

The design of the tier generator is shown in Figure 10.12. The generator creates a set of database COM controls and ASP pages from an abstract definition of the code that will be generated.

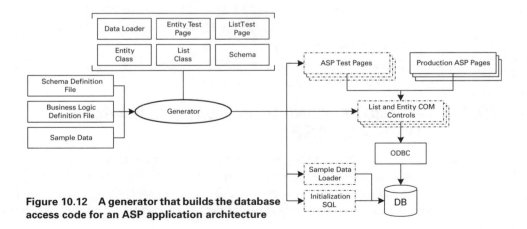

Figure 10.12 A generator that builds the database access code for an ASP application architecture

Using templates, the generator turns a schema definition into these outputs:

- A set of `List` and `Entity` classes that wrap the database schema
- A schema definition suitable for use by the database
- A data loader that uses the `Entity` classes to populate the database with the test data
- Test pages that layer on top of the `List` and `Entity` classes to expose the interface

This generator can work with either C++ or VB as the COM control language. In this section, we refer to the controls as simple COM controls or COM classes.

10.7.3   Processing flow

ASP generator

The generator follows these steps:

- Reads in the definition file and stores it locally.
- Creates the schema SQL file based on the definition file.
- Creates the sample data loader, which uses SQL to load data into the database.
- For each entity follows these steps:
  - Creates the `Entity` COM class.
  - Creates the test ASP pages for the `Entity` COM class.
- For each list follows these steps:
  - Initializes a cache of methods.
  - For each query:
    - Decides the return type and invokes the proper template, then adds the output to the method cache.
    - Creates the test page for this query.
- Creates the `List` COM class with the method cache.

10.7.4   ASP developer resources

Here are some important resources for ASP developers:

- You'll find the original Duwamish online application architecture at http://msdn.microsoft.com/library/default.asp?url=/library/en-us/dnduwon/html/d5ntierarch.asp.
- *ASP in a Nutshell, 2nd Edition: A Desktop Quick Reference*, by A. Keyton Weissinger (O'Reilly, 2000), examines the building of ASP pages for IIS.
- *Developing ASP Components, 2nd Edition*, by Shelley Powers (O'Reilly, 2001), discusses the development of COM components for IIS.

10.8 TECHNIQUE: GENERATING DATABASE ACCESS LAYERS FOR ASP.NET

ASP.NET is Microsoft's update to its web application server platform, ASP. It is similar to ASP, but there is a new page layer—ASP.NET—as well as a business logic model called "code-behind." Microsoft has also included a new database access technology called ADO.NET, and a new programming language, named C#, that is a programming model similar to Java. Components, now called *assemblies*, can be built in a number of languages including VB.NET, C++, J#, and C#.

In this section, we describe the architecture for an ASP.NET generator.

10.8.1 Roles of the generator

The roles of this generator are the same as those of the JDBC generator described in section 10.6.1.

10.8.2 Recommended architecture

Figure 10.13 shows a three-tier web application architecture built using Microsoft's .NET toolkit. This architecture is very similar to the ASP architecture. The key difference is the addition of a SOAP access point as a peer to the user interface. The SOAP layer acts as the *web services* entry point.

The SOAP layer provides Remote Procedure Call (RPC) access to the database access layer, so the adventuresome engineer might want to consider using the SOAP layer as a data loader, providing an end-to-end test of the entire technology stack.

The database access layer will use the Entity/List model presented in section 10.6.

10.8.3 Laying out the generator architecture

The generator takes the schema definition, business logic definitions, and sample data as input and uses a set of templates, much like our case study, to generate the entity and list assemblies as well as the schema, the data loader, and a set of ASP.NET test

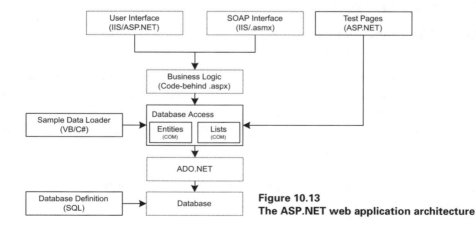

Figure 10.13
The ASP.NET web application architecture

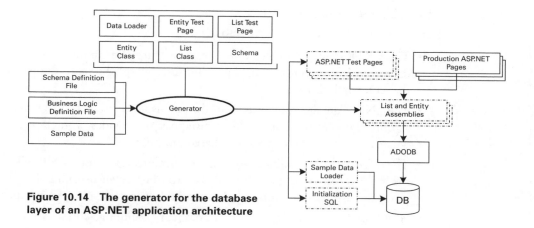

Figure 10.14   The generator for the database layer of an ASP.NET application architecture

pages that test access to the database access layer. Figure 10.14 shows the tier generator for this model.

Assemblies can be built in a variety of languages. This generator architecture assumes no particular language for assembly construction.

10.8.4   Processing flow

ASP.NET generator

The generator follows these steps:

- Reads in the definition file and stores it locally.
- Creates the schema SQL file based on the definition file.
- Creates the sample data loader, which uses SQL to load data into the database.
- For each entity follows these steps:
  - Creates the entity assembly.
  - Creates the test ASP.NET pages for the entity assembly.
- For each list follows these steps:
  - Initializes a cache of methods.
  - For each query:
    - Decides the return type and invokes the proper template, adds the output to the methods cache.
    - Creates the test ASP.NET page for this query.
- Creates the list assembly with the method cache.

10.8.5   ASP.NET developer resources

Here are some important ASP.NET resources:

- The ADO.NET architecture guide (http://msdn.microsoft.com/library/default.asp?url=/library/en-us/dnbda/html/daag.asp) discusses the proper use of the ADO architecture.
- The .NET architecture roadmap (http://msdn.microsoft.com/library/default.-asp?url=/library/en-us/dnbda/html/distapp.asp) provides a high-level view of Microsoft's design for applications based on .NET.
- The Duwamish online application architecture for ASP.NET (http://msdn.microsoft.com/library/default.asp?url=/library/en-us/dnbda/html/bdasam-pduwam7.asp) is an example application built using the .NET framework.
- *ADO.NET Programming*, by Arlen Feldman (Manning, 2002), covers programming to Microsoft's ADO standard.
- *ASP.NET in a Nutshell*, by G. Andrew Duthie and Matthew MacDonald (O'Reilly, 2002), examines building web pages with Microsoft's ASP.NET technology.
- *Programming C#, 2nd Edition*, by Jesse Liberty (O'Reilly, 2002), explores the C# programming language.
- *Programming .NET Web Services*, by Alex Ferrara and Matthew MacDonald (O'Reilly, 2002), discusses adding SOAP interface layers to .NET web applications.

10.8.6   Generators for .NET

The following are resources for ASP developers:

- C# Data Tier Generator builds SQL and C# from a database (http://csharpdatatier.sourceforge.net).
- DeKlarit (www.deklarit.com) is a commercial product that builds database access and user interface code for C# and the .NET framework.

10.9   TECHNIQUE: GENERATING DATABASE ACCESS CLASSES FOR PERL DBI

Perl has been used to build dynamic web sites since the introduction of CGI. Both Amazon and Yahoo! have used Perl on their web servers. An Apache server using `mod_perl` to run Perl in-process with the server can be as efficient as .NET or J2EE.

In this section, we examine the architecture for a generator that builds a Perl DBI database access layer and its ancillary files.

10.9.1   Roles of the generator

The roles of this generator are the same as those of the JDBC generator described in section 10.6.1.

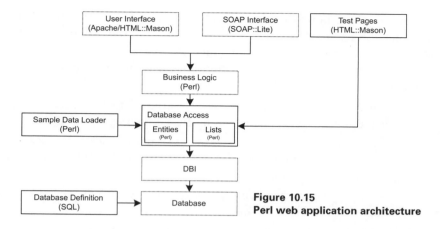

Figure 10.15
Perl web application architecture

10.9.2 Laying out the generator architecture

Our Perl application server uses an all open source technology stack. Figure 10.15 shows a block diagram for the three-tier architecture.

The three main entry points to this application server are:

- The HTML user interface, which runs on Apache and uses HTML::Mason as the page markup language. This layer talks to the business logic layer.

- The SOAP layer that is built using the SOAP::Lite module from CPAN. This layer talks to the business logic layer.

- A set of database access test pages, which also use HTML::Mason as the page markup language. This layer talks to the database access layer and is generated along with the database access classes.

The database access layer follows the Entity/List architecture. Entities and lists are built as Perl classes. These classes use Perl's DBI layer to run operations and queries against the database.

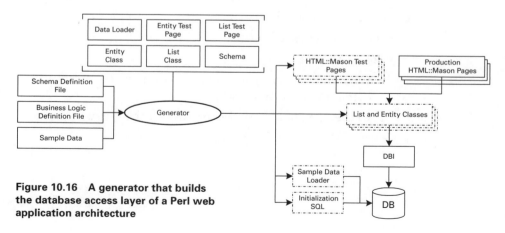

**Figure 10.16   A generator that builds
the database access layer of a Perl web
application architecture**

Figure 10.16 shows the block architecture of the tier generator. This generator takes an abstract architectural definition as input and builds Perl classes for database access and test pages using a set of templates.

The generator takes the schema definition and sample data as input and builds the following outputs:

- *Entity Perl classes*—`Entity` classes represent each table in the schema and provide the ability to create, edit, and update each entity.

- *List Perl module*—`List` functions are used for bulk queries against the database. The queries are implemented as functions within Perl modules, which are grouped together by their primary tables.

- *Schema*—The physical schema for the database is implemented as a series of SQL commands stored in a text file.

- *Sample data loader*—This is a set of sample data that is implemented as a series of SQL commands that loads the SQL schema.

- *Test HTML::Mason pages*—These pages provide a rudimentary interface to the entity and list functionality created by the generator.

10.9.3   Processing flow

Perl DBI generator

The generator follows these steps:

- Reads in the definition file and stores it locally.
- Creates the schema SQL file based on the definition file.
- Creates the sample data loader, which uses SQL to load data into the database.
- For each entity follows these steps:
  - Creates the `Entity` class.
  - Creates the test HTML::Mason page for the `Entity` class.
- For each list follows these steps:
  - Initializes a cache of functions.
  - For each query:
    - Decides the return type and invokes the proper template, then adds the output to the function cache.
    - Creates the test HTML::Mason page for this query.
- Creates the list module with the functions cache.

CHAPTER 10   CREATING DATABASE ACCESS GENERATORS

10.9.4 Perl/DBI developer resources

We've listed some Perl resources for your convenience:

- The HTML::Mason site (www.masonhq.com) is a resource for developers who use the Mason component framework to build web pages.
- The Comprehensive Perl Archive Network (CPAN, at www.cpan.org) is the central resource for Perl development. It is an archive of Perl modules that cover every conceivable requirement.
- You'll find the home page for DBI at http://dbi.perl.org/. The FAQ is at http://dbi.perl.org/doc/faq.html.
- *Web Development with Apache and Perl*, by Theo Petersen (Manning, 2002), examines building web applications with Perl.
- *Object-Oriented Perl*, by Damian Conway (Manning, 1999), is an excellent book on building Perl classes.
- *Programming the Perl DBI*, by Alligator Descartes and Tim Bunce (O'Reilly, 2000), covers using the DBI to query and operate on a database.
- *Programming Perl, 3rd Edition*, by Larry Wall, Jon Orwant, and Tom Christiansen (O'Reilly, 2000), is the classic Perl book by Larry Wall, the creator of Perl.
- *Embedding Perl in HTML with Mason*, by Dave Rolsky and Ken Williams (O'Reilly, 2002), discusses using HTML::Mason to build dynamic web pages.

10.10 *TECHNIQUE: GENERATING DATABASE ACCESS CLASSES FOR PHP*

PHP is a powerful and robust page markup language now in its fifth release. With a clean object model and the Pear portable database access layer, PHP is an excellent choice for web application development. In this section, we'll look at creating a generator in PHP that accesses a database.

10.10.1 Roles of the generator

The roles of this generator are the same as those of the JDBC generator described in section 10.6.1.

10.10.2 Laying out the generator architecture

Our PHP architecture recommendation is a classic three-tier technology stack. The user interface, implemented in PHP on top of Apache, calls a set of business logic objects, also implemented in PHP. These in turn talk to the generated database access layer with its entity/list objects implemented in PHP. The database access objects talk to the database through the Pear portable database access layer. Figure 10.17 shows the block diagram.

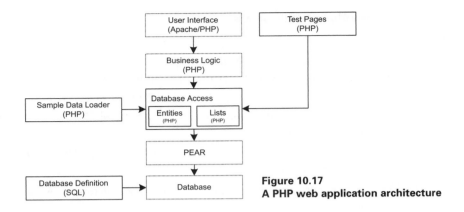

Figure 10.17
A PHP web application architecture

The architecture for the database access layer is the Entity/List model described in section 10.6.

Figure 10.18 shows the tier generator for this PHP architecture. This generator builds a set of PHP classes and pages from an abstract definition of the system that will be built.

The generator takes the schema definition file and the sample data as input and produces, through the use of templates, these outputs:

- *Entity PHP classes*—The `Entity` classes provide the create, edit, and update functionality for each table.

- *List PHP classes*—The `List` classes provide access to queries for reports and list pages.

- *Schema*—The physical schema for the database is implemented as a series of SQL commands stored in a text file.

- *Sample data loader*—This is a set of sample data that is implemented as a series of SQL commands that loads the SQL schema.

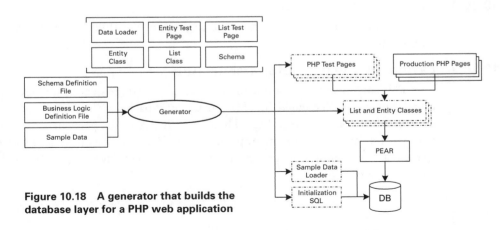

Figure 10.18   A generator that builds the database layer for a PHP web application

- *Test PHP pages*—These pages provide a rudimentary interface to the `Entity` and `List` classes created by the generator.

10.10.3   Processing flow

PHP generator

The generator follows these steps:

- Reads in the definition file and stores it locally.
- Creates the schema SQL file based on the definition file.
- Creates the sample data loader, which uses SQL to load data into the database.
- For each entity follows these steps:
  - Creates the `Entity` class.
  - Creates the test PHP page for the `Entity` class.
- For each list follows these steps:
  - Initializes a cache of functions.
  - For each query:
    - Decides the return type and invokes the proper template, then adds the output to the function cache.
    - Creates the test PHP page for this query.
- Creates the `List` class with the functions cache.

10.10.4   Generators for PHP

Several PHP code generators are available off-the-shelf. Some of them use an existing database schema as the input source to build corresponding PHP database access wrappers and pages. We've listed a couple of these tools for you:

- PHPBuns is an open source database access and web page generator for PHP (http://phpbuns.sourceforge.net).
- PostgresPHPGenerator builds PHP from a Postgres physical schema (http://sourceforge.net/projects/pgphpgenerator/).

10.10.5   PHP developer resources

Here are some PHP developer resources:

- The PHP home page (www.php.net) is the central source for all things PHP.
- The PHP page on O'Reilly's OnLAMP site (www.onlamp.com/php/) is an excellent source for articles on PHP.
- PHP Freaks (www.phpfreaks.com) is a PHP community site with code, tutorials, and articles.

- The Pear home page (http://pear.php.net/) is the source for documentation on the Pear database interface layer.
- *Web Database Applications with PHP & MySQL*, by Hugh E. Williams and David Lane (O'Reilly, 2002), covers building web applications using PHP.
- *Programming PHP*, by Rasmus Lerdorf and Kevin Tatroe (O'Reilly, 2002) is a reference manual for the PHP programming language.
- *PHP Cookbook*, by Adam Trachtenberg and David Sklar (O'Reilly, 2002) is a set of useful recipes to make programming PHP easier.

In the next section, we look at ways to generate models of database access apps off the shelf using AndroMDA.

10.11 OFF-THE-SHELF: ANDROMDA

Model-driven generation uses the UML generated by a modeling tool, such as Rational Rose, as the abstract definition source for the generation of production code. This generation from a graphical abstraction can be extremely appealing—it is much easier to read a picture of the schema than an XML representation.

The Object Management Group (http://www.omg.org) has defined the MDA (Model Driven Architecture) standard. This standard defines how UML can be *compiled* using code generators into executable code. AndroMDA, ArcStyler, and Optimal J are all examples of MDA generators. These use an abstact UML definition as input and build one or more tiers of code. We will concentrate on how AndroMDA, an open source generator, uses a cartridge model to build J2EE database access code. Changing cartridges will allow you to build code for other technologies.

In the next section, we describe what the generator will and will not do.

10.11.1 Roles of the generator

The AndroMDA generator has one main responsibility: creating the EJBs that represent the entities specified in UML form.

Here's what it doesn't take responsibility for:

- The schema in the database
- Business logic code that sits on top of the EJB layer
- The user interface validations or the workflow patterns for usability

With that in mind, let's look at the architecture of the AndroMDA generator.

10.11.2 Laying out the generator architecture

To generate a model using AndroMDA, you can use Rational Rose to export an XML rendition of the current model. The generator reads this model and, using a variety of XSLT templates, builds Struts pages, session and entity beans, deployment descriptors,

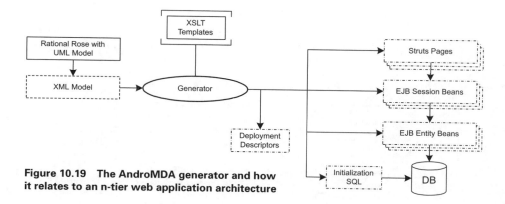

**Figure 10.19 The AndroMDA generator and how
it relates to an n-tier web application architecture**

and SQL to initialize the database. Figure 10.19 shows the block architecture for
AndroMDA, an open source model-driven generator.

10.11.3   Developer resources

Here are resources for AndroMDA:

- The official home page for AndroMDA is http://andromda.sourceforge.net/.
- Poseidon (www.gentleware.com) is an open source UML modeling tool you can
  use if you plan to go with a model-driven generation approach based on UML.
- ArcStyler from Interactive (http://www.arcstyler.com/) Objects is an MDA generator that builds both .NET and J2EE code.
- OptimalJ (http://www.optimalj.com/) is an MDA generator from Compuware
  that generates full applications on the J2EE technology stack.

10.12 *OFF-THE-SHELF: XDOCLET*

XDoclet (http://xdoclet.sourceforge.net) is a code-munging generator for Java that has
a devoted and growing following. The generator uses JavaDoc comments (via the
Doclet API) to invoke modules that build a variety of different output files. The standard purpose is to build the infrastructure beans around handwritten entity beans,
thus offloading a lot of typing from the engineer. In this section, we cover what the
generator will and will not do.

10.12.1   Roles of the generator

The XDoclet generator has one main responsibility: creating the entity and session
bean infrastructure around a set of existing beans.

It does not take responsibility for:

- The schema in the database
- Business logic code that sits on top of the EJB layer
- The user interface validations or the workflow patterns for usability

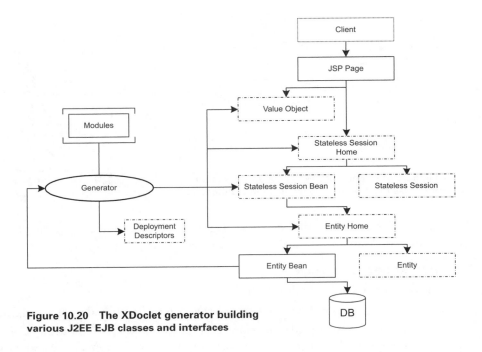

**Figure 10.20   The XDoclet generator building
various J2EE EJB classes and interfaces**

Let's look at the architecture of the XDoclet generator.

10.12.2   Laying out the generator architecture

The entity bean is the starting point for this generator. The bean acts as input to the generator, which parses out the JavaDoc comments and, using a set of modules, builds almost all of the surrounding infrastructure for the bean. Figure 10.20 shows the block architecture for XDoclet as it is used to build a J2EE server stack.

At the time of this writing, XDoclet did not generate a schema to initialize the database server.

10.13   *DESIGN TIPS*

You can make some application architecture decisions before you begin building your generator, which will simplify the resulting design. Here are some suggestions:

- Unify your schema generation. Don't use one tool to build the schema and then generate code to that schema. A generator that builds both the physical schema and the database access objects assures synchronization between the two.

- Also, your application semantics may require additional supporting tables to back up the original set of entity tables, such as transaction logging tables. These types of structural tables are easily built by a generator while leaving the abstract definition clear of this type of information.

- If possible, you can simplify both the database access layer and the generator design by using a one-to-one mapping between entities and tables.
- You should spend design time on the fields of the tables and the general relationships between those tables. The implementation of the infrastructure elements of the tables, such as primary and foreign keys, history tables, and the relationships between tables, should be handled by the generator. This ensures that the generator will be able to build efficient queries and will be portable between database servers.

10.14 FINDING A TOOL TO DO IT FOR YOU

Database access is easily the most popular form of code generation. You can find generators for almost every conceivable platform and to suit every need. Here are just a few:

- EJBGen (www.beust.com/cedric/ejbgen/) is similar to XDoclet in using JavaDoc to define beans and deployment descriptors. It does not generate the SQL schema for deployment in the database.
- Ironspeed (www.ironspeed.com/products.asp) generates complete web application stacks (database definition, business logic, and interfaces) based around Microsoft's technologies.
- Codecharge (www.codecharge.com/index2.html) presents an IDE for developing web applications, which are then generated into J2EE, ASP, ASP.NET, PHP, Perl, or ColdFusion.
- TierDeveloper by AlachiSoft (www.alachisoft.com/product.htm) can generate to both J2EE and ASP.NET. It builds middle-tier database objects as well as documentation.
- Proc-Blaster from LockwoodTech (www.lockwoodtech.com) generates database access code and stored procedures for Microsoft technologies.
- ER/Studio (www.embarcadero.com/products/erstudio/index.asp) is an excellent alternative to ERWin.

10.15 SUMMARY

In database applications, the database is the foundation of the application. The strength of the foundation always determines the stability of the surrounding code. This chapter has shown that generation is the best technique for building strong database code and, by extension, a strong foundation for your application. If you generate only one section of code in your application, it should be the database code.

In the next chapter, we look at generators that build web services layers.

CHAPTER 11

Generating web services layers

A web services layer exposes the business logic of your application to the outside world. If your business logic and security layers are well defined, the task of exporting them through web services requires some simple code to interface your API to the RPC layer and to marshal the data between the two. This process involves building a remote-access layer that is a peer of the user interface. You can use several RPC standards for this purpose. In this chapter, we concentrate on XML-RPC and SOAP, both of which are based on XML and provide tools and support across a wide variety of operating systems and programming languages.

This is just the type of work for which code generation was invented. We show you not only how to create the RPC layers for an application using a generator, but also how to build stub code for the client—in Visual Basic, Perl, Java, or C#—that will make your interface easy to use.

11.1 THE BIG PICTURE

The case study in chapter 1 used an RPC generator to build an external interface for the application. RPC layers are, by definition, multicomponent affairs. A server portion sits as a peer to the user interface on the server side. Corresponding to the server portion are one or more client portions, which act as stubs for the procedures implemented in the server portion. You can build multiple client portions—one for each of the possible client languages. For example, you can deliver stub APIs in Visual Basic, C++, and Java—if your customer base requires that type of diversity in language selection—by simply including additional templates in the generator. The generator and the system components it creates are shown in figure 11.1.

In this chapter, we present a case study XML-RPC generator that builds both server and client code. Later, in section 11.3, we introduce a similar generator design, this one for the SOAP architecture.

11.1.1 Providing security and authentication

If your server offers weather information, you probably don't need to worry about authenticating your clients. But more complex services are likely to need a method for determining who is accessing the server and making sure that users are who they claim to be.

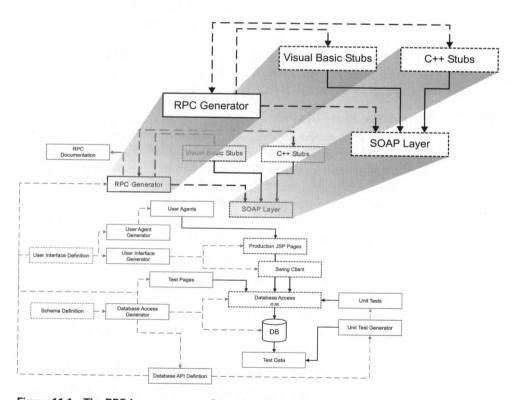

Figure 11.1 The RPC-layer generator from the original case study

Authentication of the user of the web services interface is complicated by the fact that both XML-RPC and SOAP are completely *stateless*. This means that every call to the interface is its own complete transaction. There is no way to bundle a set of method invocations together into a single transaction.

The two basic approaches to handling authentication in a stateless environment are:

- *Using tickets*—In this model, the client first requests a ticket from the server using a specific method. The request contains the user's authentication information (i.e., the login and password). The client then sends the ticket along with all subsequent requests.

- *Authenticating on each request*—In this model, the client sends authentication information (i.e., the login and password) with each request.

Code generation is useful in either approach. The generator that builds the client and server portions of the RPC code can hide from client users both the implementation of the authentication model as well as the target API on the server.

On the client side, the generated API can have a login method that takes and stores the authentication information. Then the API can either request a ticket or send the information on each request. In this way, client code can remain the same even if the authentication scheme changes.

On the server side, the set of authenticated logins can be cached locally within the generated interface. Alternately, the authentication system in the business logic layer or application server can be used, if such a system exists.

11.1.2 Why not use a library?

A library is often a valid approach to exporting a web services layer, so why generate the layer? For C and C++, a library uses a set of structures to define a mapping layer, which in turn defines the functions that are to be exported and their arguments. Other languages, such as Java and C#, support *reflection*, which is a way of identifying the methods of an object at runtime. RPC libraries make use of reflection by adjusting their interfaces on the fly to match the methods of the exported objects.

Generation provides advantages in both environments:

- When using a static-mapping library for C or C++, the maps still need to be maintained and synchronized with the application code. This type of maintenance is an ideal task for code generation.

- A reflection library may not be compatible with your business logic interface. A generator can work in conjunction with the reflection library to create a compatible, intermediate layer.

In either case, the library will not supply you with client-side stub code that is tailored to the web services interface you provide. The generators shown in this chapter represent examples not only of building the marshalling code for the server, but also of building the client-side stubs at the same time so that the two interfaces—client and server—are kept perfectly in sync.

11.2 A CASE STUDY: GENERATING XML-RPC FOR JAVA

XML-RPC is an RPC layer on top of XML. It's often compared to SOAP. Generally, XML-RPC is considered to be of lighter weight and simpler than SOAP.

The case study generator exports a simple library of functions through XML-RPC using the Java XML-RPC library from Apache. We chose XML-RPC for the case study because the implementation is generally smaller. However, the generation concepts are portable between the two.

Here are some terms specific to this case study and XML-RPC that you should become familiar with:

- *Target*—This term applies to both classes and methods. The `target` class provides the web services that are exported through the XML-RPC layer. The `target` class is used as input to the generator to create the `handler` and `stub` classes.

- *Handler*—The `handler` class wraps the `target` class and has a set of `handler` methods that map one to one with the exported methods of the target.

- *Stub*—The `stub` class contains all of the methods exported by the `target` class. Each of these `stub` methods calls through the XML-RPC layer to talk to the `target` class on the server. The value of a `stub` class is that it looks and acts like a local class even though the implementation of the methods is on the server.

- *Client*—The client makes use of the `stub` class to call target methods on the server.

Our sample `target` class is fairly rudimentary. The class provides functions to add numbers, subtract numbers, add strings, and perform other transformations that are meant to test all of the types that can be exported through XML-RPC.

None of these methods holds any state. Neither XML-RPC nor SOAP provides a mechanism for managing state across a session with the server. Every procedure call is considered atomic. If your business logic layer requires managing state across several method invocations to accomplish a single task, you will need to create an additional layer that provides a set of methods to accomplish each task in a completely stateless manner.

Listing 11.1 contains the code for the test service.

Listing 11.1   Test.java

```java
import java.util.*;

public class Test
{
    /**
     * @rpcgen export
     */
    public double add( double a, double b ) { return a+b; }

    /**
     * @rpcgen export
     */
    public double subtract( double a, double b ) { return a-b; }

    /**
     * @rpcgen export
     */
    public boolean invert( boolean b ) { return ( b ? false : true ); }

    /**
     * @rpcgen export
     */
    public int add_int( int a, int b ) { return a+b; }

    /**
     * @rpcgen export
     */
    public int subtract_int( int a, int b ) { return a-b; }

    /**
     * @rpcgen export
     */
    public String add_string( String a, String b ) { return a+" "+b; }

    /**
     * @rpcgen export
     */
    public double add_array( Vector a )
    {
        double total = 0.0;

        for( int index = 0; index < a.size(); index++ )
        {
            total += ((Double)a.get( index )).doubleValue();
        }

        return total;
    }

    /**
     * @rpcgen export
     */
```

❶ Markup for the generator

❷ Web service methods

```
   public String get_name( Hashtable ht )
      return (String)ht.get( "name" );
   }
}
```

❶ Adding the `@rpcgen` marker to the JavaDoc tells the generator that this method should be exported by the XML-RPC handler.

❷ The methods in this class are the "services" our server will provide.

11.2.1 The XML-RPC message flow

First, the client initiates a call to the server by calling the `add` method on the `stub`. The `stub` in turn calls the `test.add` method on the server. Next, the XML-RPC server invokes `add` on the `handler` object. The `handler` object creates an instance of the `target` object and invokes `add`. The return value is then sent back to the `client` class as the transaction unrolls. You can see this message flow between client and target in figure 11.2.

Now let's look at what you can expect this generator to do.

11.2.2 Roles of the generator

Before you build the generator, you need to specify its responsibilities. You should also define the functions for which the generator is not responsible.

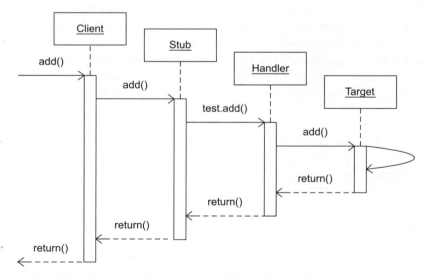

Figure 11.2   The XML-RPC flow for the add method

The generator should create the following:

- The RPC layer, which includes:
  - The server code that will handle the incoming XML-RPC methods and dispatch those requests to the correct application code.
  - Stub client code that will be used by engineers building another system that talks to our system.
- The technical documentation for the stub client code.
- Authentication of the client.
- Session management with the client.

The generator does not need to handle:

- Design documentation for the application or the external RPC layer.
- Any functionality in the application layer.

The case study generator does not address authentication and session management directly. These functions are application specific. I mention them here because authentication and session management comprise the role of the RPC layer.

At this point, you can define the architecture of the generator.

11.2.3 Laying out the generator architecture

Your generator will build code for both the client and the server. On the server side, you create handler code that will be used by XML-RPC to handle each message. On the client side, you create stub code that will look like the `target` class to the engineer but that will internally call to the server for every method.

For this generator, we chose to use a code munger model. The Java class should have JavaDoc markup in it to tell you which methods require export. The generator will read and analyze the Java file and create the appropriate handler and stub code.

Figure 11.3 shows the block architecture for the generator.

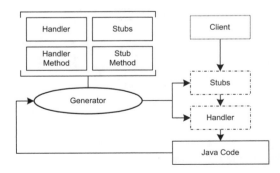

Figure 11.3
The XML-RPC generator builds stubs and handlers from Java code with JavaDoc markup.

In this architecture, the Java code acts as both input to the generator and as the final target of the XML-RPC system. The generator uses a set of templates to build the handler and stub Java code.

For this case study, you are only creating Java stubs. Keep in mind, though, that there is no reason your generator couldn't build stubs in a variety of languages.

Now let's look at the steps the generator will go through as it runs.

11.2.4 Processing flow

XML-RPC generator

Here is the process flow of the generator, in high-level steps:

- Reads the specified Java file.
- Tokenizes the Java text.
- Parses the Java text.
- Creates a buffer that will hold both the client and stub methods text.
- For each method, follows these steps:
  - Inspects the JavaDoc for the `@rpcgen` tag. If it has the tag, then it follows these steps:
    - Uses the `StubMethod` template to build the stub method and adds it to the buffer.
    - Uses the `HandlerMethod` template to build the handler method and adds it to the buffer.
- Using the stub template and the stub method buffer, builds the Java class for the stubs, and writes the result of that template to a Java file.
- Using the handler template and the handler method buffer, builds the Java class for the handler and writes that to the appropriate Java file.

11.2.5 Building the code for the XML-RPC generator

Now you're ready to start writing the code for the generator. Listing 11.2 shows the Ruby code for this generator.

Listing 11.2   rpcgen.rb

```
require "CTokenizer"
require "JavaLanguageScanner"

require "erb/erb"
require "ftools"

def read_java_file( file_name )

  print "Parsing #{file_name}...\n"
```

1 Imports Java tokenizer classes

2 Includes the ERb system

3 Main generator entry point

```
fh = File.open( file_name )
in_text = fh.read()                              Reads the
fh.close()                                       Java file

tokenizer = CTokenizer.new( )                    Tokenizes
tokenizer.parse( in_text )                       Java
                                                          Parses tokens
languagescanner = JavaLanguageScanner.new()
languagescanner.parse( tokenizer.tokens )
                                                          Removes the
file_prefix = file_name.sub( /[.]java$/, "" )             Java extension
class_name = File.basename( file_name )          Uses the filename
class_name.sub!( /[.]java$/, "" )                 as the class name

handler_methods = ""                             Creates the stub
stub_methods = ""                                and handler buffer
languagescanner.classes.each { |jclass|
  jclass.methods.each { |proto|
    next unless proto.javadoc != nil
    next unless proto.javadoc.tags[ '@rpcgen' ]   != nil
    next unless proto.javadoc.tags[ '@rpcgen' ] =~ /export/
    method_name = proto.method_name
    method_type = proto.method_type       Iterates each class and builds  ❹
    arguments = proto.arguments               server and stub code
    handler_methods += run_template( "HandlerMethod.java", binding )
    stub_methods += run_template( "StubMethod.java", binding )
  }
}

handler_name = "#{file_prefix}Handler.java"
print "Creating #{handler_name}\n"                Creates the handler  ❺
fh = File.open( handler_name, "w" )                   Java file with
methods = handler_methods                            server methods
fh.print run_template( "Handler.java.template", binding )
fh.close()

stubs_name = "#{file_prefix}Stubs.java"
print "Creating #{stubs_name}\n"                    Creates the client  ❻
fh = File.open( stubs_name, "w" )                     stubs file with
methods = stub_methods                                stub methods
fh.print run_template( "Stubs.java.template", binding )
fh.close()
                        ❼ Returns the corresponding
end                        RPC type for the Java type

def rpc_type( type )
  return "Double" if ( type == "double" )
  return "Integer" if ( type == "int" )
  return "Boolean" if ( type == "boolean" )
  return type
end                                              Calls an ERb wrapper
                                                 to run a template
def run_template( template_name, bind )
  erb = ERb.new( File.new( "templates/#{template_name}" ).read )
  return erb.result( bind )
end
```

```
if ARGV[0]
  read_java_file( ARGV[ 0 ] )                    ◁— Sends the command
else                                                  line to the generator
  print "Must specify an input C file\n"
end
```

❶ You use `CTokenizer` and `JavaLanguageScanner` to tokenize the Java file and then parse it to find the JavaDoc comments.

❷ You use ERb to invoke the templates that build the Java code.

❸ `read_java_file` is the main entry point for the generator. It reads in a Java file and builds the stub and handler code.

❹ This code builds the handler and stub methods. It iterates through each of the methods in the class and checks to see if the JavaDoc contains the `@rpcgen` tag. If it does, the templates are added for both the handler and the stub.

❺ This code uses `Handler.java.template` to build the handler Java file. The template requires the class name and the methods.

❻ This code uses `Stubs.java.template` to build the stubs Java file. The template requires the class name and the methods.

❼ `rpc_type` returns the XML-RPC wrapper type for the given Java type.

For each method, you want to export a corresponding handler method. To automate this, create the template HandlerMethod.java, which builds a handler method (listing 11.3).

Listing 11.3   HandlerMethod.java

```
<%
out_type = rpc_type( method_type )              ❶ Gets the correct Java type
                                                   for the RPC type
args = []
call_args = []                                  ❷ Interprets
arguments.each { |arg|                             arguments to
                                                   the function
  type = arg.type

  name = arg.name

  args.push( "#{type} #{name}" )
  call_args.push( "#{name}" )                                    Creates the
}                                                                Java method
%>                                                               signature ❸
  public <%= out_type %> <%= method_name %>( <%= args.join( ", " ) %> ) ◁—
  {
    <%= class_name %> obj = new <%= class_name %>();      Builds the
                                                       ❹ server class
    return new <%= out_type %>( obj.<%= method_name %>( <%= call_args.join
( ", " ) %> ) );
  }
```

❶ This template needs to create a method of the type that you are wrapping, then call a method on it and return the output value. The out_type is the XML-RPC return type.

❷ In this section, you are creating two sets of arguments. The args array contains the arguments for this method, and call_args is the array of arguments that you will send to the method of the type you are wrapping.

❸ This code builds the method signature.

❹ This code creates the object of the type that you are wrapping, and then calls the target method and sends back the return value.

Once you have all of the handler methods, put them into a class container. Listing 11.4 contains the class container template.

Listing 11.4   Handler.java.template

```
import java.util.*;

/**
 * XML-RPC wrapper for the <%= class_name %> class.
 */
public class <%= class_name %>              ◁─┐ Creates the proper
{                                              class name
<%= methods %>                              ◁─┐ Adds
}                                              methods
```

Listing 11.5 shows the final output of the generator using the handler method and handler container templates.

Listing 11.5   TestHandler.java output

```
import java.util.*;

/**
 * XML-RPC wrapper for the Test class.
 */
public class TestHandler
{
  public Double add( double a, double b )         ◁─┐  ❶ Shows the new
  {                                                       double handler
    Test obj = new Test();
    return new Double( obj.add( a, b ) );        ◁─┐  ❷ Creates the original server class

  }                                                    ❸ Invokes the original
  public Double subtract( double a, double b )          class method
  {
    Test obj = new Test();
    return new Double( obj.subtract( a, b ) );
  }
```

```
public Boolean invert( boolean b )
{
  Test obj = new Test();
  return new Boolean( obj.invert( b ) );
}

public Integer add_int( int a, int b )
{
  Test obj = new Test();
  return new Integer( obj.add_int( a, b ) );
}

public Integer subtract_int( int a, int b )
{
  Test obj = new Test();
  return new Integer( obj.subtract_int( a, b ) );
}

public String add_string( String a, String b )
{
  Test obj = new Test();
  return new String( obj.add_string( a, b ) );
}

public Double add_array( Vector a )
{
  Test obj = new Test();
  return new Double( obj.add_array( a ) );
}

public String get_name( Hashtable ht )
{
  Test obj = new Test();
  return new String( obj.get_name( ht ) );
}

}
```

❶ This is the signature that the XML-RPC library looks for when choosing methods to export. If you use `Double` instead of `double`, the method will not be exported by the XML-RPC server. The generator handles marshalling between `Double` and `double` as well as the other types.

❷ Because you are wrapping a class type, you first have to create an instance of that class.

❸ Now you invoke the corresponding method on the instance of the class.

You need one stub method for each corresponding handler method that calls the server with the appropriate arguments and handles the return value. Listing 11.6 shows the template that generates the stub code.

Listing 11.6   StubsMethod.java

```
<%args = []

elements = []

arguments.each { |arg|          ❶ Handles the arguments
  type = arg.type                  to the method
  rtype = rpc_type( type )
  name = arg.name

  args.push( "#{type} #{name}" )

  if ( rtype != type )

    elements.push( "new #{rtype}( #{name} )" )

  else

    elements.push( name )        ◁— Gets the correct Java type
                                    for the RPC type
  end
}
%>
  public <%= method_type %> <%= method_name %>( <%= args.join( ", " ) %> )
  throws XmlRpcException, IOException
  {
    Vector params = new Vector();          ❷ Marshals each
<% elements.each { |elem| %>                 argument into
    params.addElement( <%= elem.to_s %> );<% } %>   the vector

    Object result = _client.execute( "<%= class_name %>.<%= method_name %>
", params );      ❸ Executes the method on the server
<% if ( method_type != rpc_type( method_type ) ) %>  ❹ Handles the return values
    return ((<%= rpc_type( method_type ) %>)result).<%= method_type %>();
<% else %>
    return (<%= method_type %>)result;
<% end %>
  }
```

❶ This code builds the marshalling code that uses temporary variables to set up the parameters for the XML-RPC request. `type` is the type that the user wants, and `rtype` is the equivalent XML-RPC type. `args` is the array of incoming arguments to this method. `elements` is the set of new Java calls that create the marshalling objects.

❷ XML-RPC uses a `Vector` of arguments to send an XML-RPC message.

❸ This line runs the XML-RPC request.

❹ This code marshals the return value.

The stub methods are placed inside the **Stubs** container class, shown in listing 11.7.

```
import org.apache.xmlrpc.*;
import java.util.*;
import java.io.*;

/**
 * Stub class to talk with the <%= class_name %> XML-RPC web service.
 */
public class <%= class_name %>              <--| Inserts the
{                                              | class name

  private XmlRpcClient _client;

    /**
    * Constructs the stub class.
    *
    * @arg client The XmlRpcClient connection to the server.
    */
  public <%= class_name %>( XmlRpcClient client )    <--| Creates the
  {                                                     | constructor
      _client = client;
  }                                        | Inserts the
<%= methods %>                            <--| methods text
}
```

Listing 11.8 shows the output of the stub method and stub container templates.

```
import org.apache.xmlrpc.*;
import java.util.*;
import java.io.*;

/**
 * Stub class to talk with the Test XML-RPC web service.
 */
public class TestStubs
{
  private XmlRpcClient _client;

    /**
    * Constructs the stub class.
    *
    * @arg client The XmlRpcClient connection to the server.
    */
```

```
    public TestStubs( XmlRpcClient client )
    {
        _client = client;
    }
```

❶ **Generated client class with stubs**

```
    public double add( double a, double b ) throws XmlRpcException, IOExcep-
tion
    {
      Vector params = new Vector();

      params.addElement( new Double( a ) );
      params.addElement( new Double( b ) );
      Object result = _client.execute( "Test.add", params );

      return ((Double)result).doubleValue();

    }
```

❷ **Marshalling the param- eters into the Vector**

❹ **Handling the result**   **❸** **Calling the server**

```
    public double subtract( double a, double b ) throws XmlRpcException, IOEx-
ception
    {
      Vector params = new Vector();

      params.addElement( new Double( a ) );
      params.addElement( new Double( b ) );

      Object result = _client.execute( "Test.subtract", params );

      return ((Double)result).doubleValue();

    }

    public boolean invert( boolean b ) throws XmlRpcException, IOException
    {
      Vector params = new Vector();

      params.addElement( new Boolean( b ) );

      Object result = _client.execute( "Test.invert", params );

      return ((Boolean)result).booleanValue();

    }

    public int add_int( int a, int b ) throws XmlRpcException, IOException
    {
      Vector params = new Vector();

      params.addElement( new Integer( a ) );
      params.addElement( new Integer( b ) );

      Object result = _client.execute( "Test.add_int", params );

      return ((Integer)result).intValue();

    }

    public int subtract_int( int a, int b ) throws XmlRpcException, IOExcep-
tion
    {
```

```
      Vector params = new Vector();

      params.addElement( new Integer( a ) );
      params.addElement( new Integer( b ) );

      Object result = _client.execute( "Test.subtract_int", params );

      return ((Integer)result).intValue();

   }

  public String add_string( String a, String b ) throws XmlRpcException,
IOException
   {
      Vector params = new Vector();

      params.addElement( a );
      params.addElement( b );

      Object result = _client.execute( "Test.add_string", params );

      return (String)result;

   }

  public double add_array( Vector a ) throws XmlRpcException, IOException
   {
      Vector params = new Vector();

      params.addElement( a );

      Object result = _client.execute( "Test.add_array", params );

      return ((Double)result).doubleValue();

   }

  public String get_name( Hashtable ht ) throws XmlRpcException,
IOException
   {
      Vector params = new Vector();

      params.addElement( ht );

      Object result = _client.execute( "Test.get_name", params );

      return (String)result;

   }

}
```

❶ The `stub` class holds a reference to **XmlRpcClient** to make it easy to call the methods once the **stub** class is created.

❷ The first step in invoking XML-RPC is to create the argument **Vector** and to populate it with the arguments.

❸ The next step is to execute the specified function on the server.

❹ The final step is to marshal the return value.

To serve up the `TestHandler`, create a simple server, as shown in listing 11.9.

Listing 11.9   Server.java

```
import java.io.IOException;
import org.apache.xmlrpc.*;
import TestHandler;

public class Server
{
    public static void main( String[] args )
    {
        try {
          WebServer server = new WebServer( 8081 );          Creates the
                                                              server object
          server.addHandler( "Test", new TestHandler() );    Adds the test
        }                                                     web service
        catch( IOException e ) {
        }
    }
}
```

The Client.java file is a test file that uses your generated stub class to make calls to the server. Listing 11.10 contains the code for the client test class.

Listing 11.10   Client.java

```
import java.io.IOException;
import org.apache.xmlrpc.*;
import java.util.*;

public class Client
{
    public static void main( String args[] )
    {
        try                                                    Creates the
        {                                                      connection to
                                                               the server   ❶
          XmlRpcClient client = new XmlRpcClient( "http://localhost:8081" );

          TestStubs stubs = new TestStubs( client );      ❷  Creates the
                                                              local stub class
          System.out.println( "add 10, 20 = " + stubs.add( 10.0, 20.0 ) );    ❸
          System.out.println( "add 40, 100 = " + stubs.add( 40.0, 100.0 ) );
        System.out.println( "subtract 20, 10 = " + stubs.subtract
( 20.0, 10.0 ) );
          System.out.println( "invert true = " + stubs.invert( true ) );
          System.out.println( "invert false = " + stubs.invert( false ) );
          System.out.println( "add_int 20, 10 = " + stubs.add_int( 20, 10 ) );
          System.out.println( "subtract_int 20, 10 = " + stubs.subtract_int(
20, 10 ) );
          System.out.println( "add_string a, b = " + stubs.add_string( "a",
"b" ) );
```

```
                Vector da = new Vector();
                da.addElement( new Double( 10.0 ) );
                da.addElement( new Double( 20.0 ) );
                da.addElement( new Double( 30.0 ) );
                System.out.println( "add_array 10, 20, 30 = " + stubs.add_array(
    da ) );

                Hashtable na = new Hashtable();
                na.put( "name", "Jack" );
                na.put( "last_name", "Herrington" );
                System.out.println( "get_name (na) = " + stubs.get_name( na
    ).toString() );
            }
            catch( Exception e )
            {
                System.out.println( e.toString() );
            }
        }
    }
}
```

❶ This code creates the `XmlRpcClient` code, which connects you to the target server.

❷ The next step is to create the `stub` object. You give it a reference to the `client` object so that it can communicate with the server.

❸ Invokes methods on local stubs: from here on, the code tests the various methods on the server.

11.2.6   Performing system tests

To make sure the XML-RPC generator is functioning properly, let's use the system test utility (see appendix B). Here is the configuration file for the unit test system:

```
<ut kgdir="kg">
  <test cmd="ruby -I../lp rpcgen.rb examples/Test.java">
    <out>examples/TestHandler.java</out>
    <out>examples/TestStubs.java</out>
  </test>
</ut>
```

The test will run the generator on Test.java and then inspect the TestHandler.java and TestStubs.java files that are generated.

11.2.7   XML-RPC resources

At the time of this writing, I couldn't find any generators that build XML-RPC code. Instead, I have included some resources that will provide more information about the XML-RPC protocol:

- You can find the Apache library used in this case study at http://xml.apache.org/xmlrpc/.

- www.xmlrpc.org is the official XML-RPC home page.

- *Programming Web Services with XML-RPC*, by Simon St. Laurent, Joe Johnston, and Edd Dumbill, (O'Reilly, 2001), is an excellent book on programming both client and server code for the XML-RPC protocol.

11.3   *TECHNIQUE: GENERATING SOAP*

XML-RPC and SOAP are remote procedure call layers built on top of XML. XML-RPC is generally considered a simpler approach, while SOAP has wide industry backing from Sun, Microsoft, and IBM.

SOAP has related standards in addition to the RPC standard. One of the most important is the Web Service Definition Language (WSDL). WSDL describes your web service to the outside world. A WSDL description of your service is a valuable tool for the client, but it is a pain to maintain manually. Thus, another output of the SOAP generator should be the WSDL description of the service. In this section, we discuss how the architecture for a generator builds a web services layer based on the SOAP protocol.

11.3.1   Roles of the generator

The roles of the SOAP generator are the same as those of the XML-RPC generator described in 11.2.3.

11.3.2   Laying out the generator architecture

Our SOAP generator follows the tier generator model. As input, the generator takes an interface specification. This specification defines what classes and methods you want to export. Using a set of templates, the generator builds the WSDL file as well as the server code and client stubs. Figure 11.4 shows the architecture of the SOAP generator.

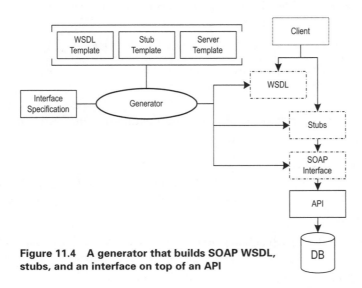

Figure 11.4   A generator that builds SOAP WSDL, stubs, and an interface on top of an API

Now let's look at the steps the SOAP generator will take as it executes.

11.3.3 Processing flow

SOAP generator

Here are the high-level steps for the process flow of the generator:

- Reads the interface specification and stores it locally.
- Builds the WSDL file using the WSDL template.
- For each class in the interface specification, follows these steps:
  - o Builds the SOAP server class using the server template.
  - o Builds the `stub` class using the stub template.

At this point the generator will have built both the server and client code for the SOAP layer.

11.3.4 SOAP resources

We've listed a few SOAP resources to help you learn the fundamentals of the SOAP protocol and web services programming:

- You can learn about Apache SOAP at http://xml.apache.org/soap/index.html.
- *Java and SOAP,* by Robert Englander (O'Reilly, 2002), covers both client and server coding for the SOAP protocol.
- *Programming Web Services with SOAP,* by James Snell, Doug Tidwell, and Pavel Kulchenko (O'Reilly, 2001), covers both client and server aspects of the SOAP protocol with a number of languages.

11.4 DESIGN TIPS

Here are some tips that will make it easier for you to generate the web services layer:

- *Keep the API atomic*—The "O" in SOAP stands for Object, but neither SOAP nor XML-RPC is in fact object-oriented. Both layers are strictly function based and are completely stateless. No session state is held between calls. If your business logic layer is completely stateless, you should have few issues exporting it as a web service.
- *Design a consistent API*—An API that uses consistent method and variable naming is significantly easier to parse with a generator because it reduces the number of special cases that have to be handled.

11.5   FINDING A TOOL TO DO IT FOR YOU

Example generators that build SOAP for C++ and Java include:

- gSOAP generates SOAP layers for C++ (http://gsoap2.sourceforge.net/).
- XDoclet has modules for generating SOAP methods for Java (http://xdoclet.sourceforge.net).

11.6   SUMMARY

A web services layer is another way of exporting the functions that the business logic layer already provides. This export layer mapping and the stub code for clients can easily get out of sync with each other or with the application layer if they are maintained by hand. Generation provides a solution that creates a consistent, well-maintained web services layer as well as stubs for the client. Using a generator can save you time and money and give your engineers the freedom to work on business-critical features.

In the next chapter, we look at generators that can build the business logic layer for you.

CHAPTER 12

Generating business logic

Business logic is the area of an application with the most edge cases and custom behaviors. For this reason, you may think that code generation cannot be used to build business logic. And it's true that you probably won't be able to generate *all* of the business logic code, but in this chapter you'll see some creative uses of code generation that should help you automate portions of it, which will speed your development greatly.

We've provided some examples of generators that can be used to make building portions of an application's quality business logic code easier. We start with a generator that aids in building the equation code that is commonplace in scientific and business applications but that can be difficult to build by hand in Java.

12.1 A CASE STUDY: GENERATING JAVA BUSINESS EQUATIONS

If you can't generate all of the business logic code, you can at least lessen the burden by building some of the tougher parts. Take, for example, writing equations for business applications in Java. Java's `Double` class can hold a lot of precision for numeric values, but if you want to avoid overflows on really large sums you should use the `BigDecimal` class to hold your values.

251

The problem is that Java doesn't support operator overloading. To add two Big-Decimal objects together, you need to use the add method on BigDecimal as shown here:

```
BigDecimal v1 = new BigDecimal( 1.0 );
BigDecimal v2 = new BigDecimal( 2.0 );
BigDecimal v3 = new BigDecimal( 0 );
v1.add( v2 );
```

This simple code adds 1 plus 2 using BigDecimal. It's not hard to imagine how complex the Java code could become for large or complex equations.

The generator should allow you to specify an equation using standard postfix notation (e.g., a = b + c) and then create the equation implementation for you. Listing 12.1 shows the example input file for the generator.

Listing 12.1   Test1.java

```
import java.math.*;

public class Test1
{
  static public void main( String args[] )
  {
    BigDecimal a;
    double b = 4.0;
    double c = 6.0;

// bdgen_start <a=b+c>          Equation to be
// bdgen_end                    implemented

    System.out.println( "Correct = 10" );
    System.out.print( "Output = " );
    System.out.println( a );
  }
}
```

The output file for the generator is also the input file. Listing 12.2 shows the output from the generator.

Listing 12.2   Test1.java after generation

```
import java.math.*;

public class Test1
{
  static public void main( String args[] )
  {
    BigDecimal a;
    double b = 4.0;
    double c = 6.0;
```

```
// bdgen_start <a=b+c>
BigDecimal v1 = new BigDecimal( b );
BigDecimal v2 = new BigDecimal( c );        Implemented equation
BigDecimal v3 = new BigDecimal( 0 );        with comments preserved
v3 = v1.add( v2 );
a = v3;
// bdgen_end

    System.out.println( "Correct = 10" );
    System.out.print( "Output = " );
    System.out.println( a );
  }
}
```

The comment is preserved for two reasons. First, this allows engineers to see the equation at the high level. Second, the generator finds these comments the next time it runs and uses them as prompts to rebuild the equation.

12.1.1 Roles of the generator

Before describing the architecture of the generator, it's important to understand what the generator handles as opposed to what other system components (or engineers) handle. The generator has one main responsibility: replacing the equation specification with implementation code for the equation.

The generator leaves these tasks to other systems (or people):

- Documenting the equation.
- Ensuring that the input or output variable types are correct.

Now that you understand the role of the generator within the larger system, you can define the architecture of the generator itself.

12.1.2 Laying out the generator architecture

The generator reads a Java file as input. It then takes the text and augments the equation comments with equation implementations. Next, it backs up the original file and replaces it with the new file that contains the equation implementations. Figure 12.1 shows the block architecture for the mixed-code generator that builds the `BigDecimal` equations.

Now let's look at the steps this generator will go through as it runs.

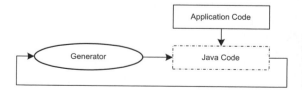

Figure 12.1
A generator that takes equations embedded in Java code comments and implements them with Big-Decimal classes

12.1.3 Processing flow

Here is the high-level process flow for the equation generator:

- Reads in the Java file.
- Finds each equation comment and follows these steps:
  - Tokenizes the equation.
  - Converts the tokens to a binary tree representation of the equation.
  - Walks the tree and creates Java code that builds variables and invokes methods to implement each node.
- Rebuilds the comment with the equation in the middle.
- Backs up the original file.
- Replaces the original file with the new text.

Now you're ready to start building the actual code for the generator.

12.1.4 Building the code for the equation generator

Listing 12.3 contains the Ruby code for the `BigDecimal` equation generation.

Listing 12.3   bdgen.rb

```
require "ftools"                     ❶ Initializes the global
                                        variable index
@@vindex = 0        ◄─┘

class EqNode                         ❷ Implements the
  def initialize( str )                various types
    @str = str                         of nodes
  end
  def to_s()
    @str
  end
end

class Variable < EqNode
end

class Operand < EqNode

  def initialize( str, func = nil )
    super( str )
    @op = str
    @left = nil
    @right = nil
    @function = func
  end

  attr_accessor :left    # The left node in the binary tree
```

```ruby
  attr_accessor :right  # The right node in the binary tree
  attr_reader :function # The name of the function

  def op()
    @function ? @function : @op
  end

  def to_s()
    if ( @left || @right )
      if ( @function && @left )
        "<op:#{op}><#{@left}>"
      elsif ( @function && @right )
        "<op:#{op}><#{@right}>"
      else
        "<#{@left}>#{@str}<#{@right}>"
      end
    else
      super()
    end
  end
end

class TokenStream < Array
  def add_literal( str )
    push( Variable.new( str ) )
  end

  def add_op( str, func )
    push( Operand.new( str, func ) )
  end

  def to_s()
    str = ""
    each { |node| str += node.to_s() }
    str
  end
end

def build_tokens( eq )
  tokens = TokenStream.new()
  specials = { '=' => 1, '(' => 1, ')' => 1, '+' => 1, '-' => 1, '*' => 1,
'/' => 1 }
  eq.gsub!( /\s+/, "" )

  token = ""
  eq.each_byte { |ch| ch = ch.chr()
    if ( specials[ ch ] )
      if ( ch == "(" && token.length > 1 )
        tokens.add_op( ch, token )
      else
        tokens.add_literal( token ) if ( token.length > 0 )
        tokens.add_op( ch, nil )
      end
      token = ""
```

❸ Represents an array of Tokens

❹ Builds tokens from equations

```
        else
          token += ch
        end
    }

    tokens.add_literal( token ) if ( token.length > 0 )
    tokens
  end

  def relate_tokens( eq, start = 0 )
    ( ( eq.length - start ) - 1 ).times { |index|
      ind = ( start + 1 ) + index
      if ( eq[ ind ].to_s == "(" )
        relate_tokens( eq, ind )
      end
    }

    if ( eq[ start ].to_s == '(' )
      relate_tokens( eq, start + 1 )
      if ( eq[ start ].function )
        eq[ start ].right = eq[ start + 1 ]
        eq.delete_at( start + 1 )
      else
        eq.delete_at( start )
      end

      ( eq.length - start ).times { |index|
        if ( eq[ start + index ].to_s == ")" )
          eq.delete_at( start + index )
          break
        end
      }
    else

      found = true
      operators = [ '/', '*', '+', '-' ]
      while( found )
        found = false
        operators.each { |op|
          ( eq.length - start ).times { |index|
            node = eq[ start + index ]
            break if ( node.to_s == ")" )
            next unless ( node.is_a?( Operand ) )
            if ( node.to_s == op )
              left = eq[ ( start + index ) - 1 ]
              right = eq[ ( start + index ) + 1 ]
              node.left = left
              node.right = right
              eq.delete_at( ( start + index ) + 1 )
              eq.delete_at( ( start + index ) - 1 )
              found = true
              break
            end
```

5 Turns the token array into a token tree

```
        }
      }
    end
  end
end

def new_varname()                    ◁— Shows utilities for
  @@vindex += 1                          building the Java
  "v#{@@vindex}"
end

def new_equate_command( commands, token )        ❻ Creates new variables in Java
  var = new_varname()
  commands.push( "BigDecimal #{var} = new BigDecimal( #{token} );" )
  var
end
                                                    ❼ Creates the final Java
def final_equate_command( commands, var1, var2 )       to output the result of
  commands.push( "#{var1} = #{var2};" )                the equation
end

def new_op_command( commands, op, var1, var2 )    ❽ Handles operands
  var = new_varname()                                (plus, minus, divide,
  if ( op.length > 1 )                               multiply)
    if ( var1 && var2 )
      commands.push( "BigDecimal #{var} = #{op}( #{var1}, #{var2} );" )
    elsif ( var1 )
      commands.push( "BigDecimal #{var} = #{op}( #{var1} );" )
    elsif ( var2 )
      commands.push( "BigDecimal #{var} = #{op}( #{var2} );" )
    end
  else
    if ( op == "/" )
      str = "BigDecimal #{var} = new BigDecimal( 0 );\n"
      str += "#{var} = #{var1}.divide( #{var2}, BigDecimal.ROUND_DOWN );"
      commands.push( str )
    else
      method = "add" if ( op == "+" )
      method = "subtract" if ( op == "-" )
      method = "multiply" if ( op == "*" )
      str = "BigDecimal #{var} = new BigDecimal( 0 );\n"
      str += "#{var} = #{var1}.#{method}( #{var2} );"
      commands.push( str )
    end
  end
  var
end

def create_commands( commands, token )       ❾ Recursively
  if ( token.is_a?( Variable ) )                builds Java for
    new_equate_command( commands, token )       operations
  else
    v1 = token.left ? create_commands( commands, token.left ) : nil
    v2 = token.right ? create_commands( commands, token.right ) : nil
```

```
      new_op_command( commands, token.op, v1, v2 )
    end
  end

  def parse_equation( eq )                 ⑩  Handles equations in Java
    tokens = build_tokens( eq )

    raise( "Invalid equation" ) if ( tokens.length <= 2 )
    raise( "Invalid equation" ) unless ( tokens[0].is_a?( Variable ) )
    raise( "Invalid equation" ) unless ( tokens[1].is_a?( Operand ) &&
  tokens[1].to_s == "="   )

    output_name = tokens.shift.to_s
    tokens.shift
    tokens_left = true

    while( tokens_left )
      relate_tokens( tokens )
      tokens_left = false
      tokens.each { |tok|
        next unless ( tok.is_a?( Operand ) )
        tokens_left = true unless ( tok.left || tok.right )
      }
    end

    out_var = nil
    commands = []

    tokens.each { |tok|
      next unless ( tok.is_a?( Operand ) )
      if ( tok.left || tok.right )
        out_var = create_commands( commands, tok )
      end
    }

    final_equate_command( commands, output_name, out_var )

    commands.join( "\n" )
  end

  def process_java_file( file_name )       ⑪  Main generator
                                              entry point
    fh = File.open( file_name )
    text = fh.read()
    fh.close()
```
Searches for
equations
```
    count = 0
    text.gsub!( /\/\/\s+bdgen_start\s+<(.*?)>(.*?)\/\/\s+bdgen_end/m ) {  ←┘
      eq = $1
      count += 1
      out = "// bdgen_start <#{eq}>\n"
```
Builds final
comments with
embedded Java
```
      out += parse_equation( eq )
      out += "\n// bdgen_end"
      out
    }
```
Backs up the
Java file
```
    File.copy( file_name, "#{file_name}.bak" )
```

```
    File.open( file_name, "w" ).write( text )                    ⟵┐  Creates a
    print "Built #{count} equations in #{file_name}\n"           │  new file
end

if ( ARGV[0] )                                        Sends a command-
  process_java_file( ARGV[ 0 ] )               ⟵┘    line argument
else
  print "Usage: bdgen myfile.java\n"
end
```

❶ vindex is a global that stores the ordinal number for the next temporary variable. Each time you create a new temporary BigDecimal object, you bump this value so that there is no possibility of a variable name collision.

❷ When you parse the equation into a tree, it will consist of EqNode objects. Each of these nodes is either a value or an operand. Variable objects represent values and operand objects represent operands (e.g., +, -, *, /). Both derive from EqNode. Variable is a specialization of EqNode. It doesn't define any new functionality, but the equation parser uses the type to decide what to do with the node.

❸ TokenStream represents a set of tokens that make up an equation. For more about tokenizing, refer to the language parser toolkit documentation in chapter 3. This TokenStream class derives from the standard Ruby Array and adds helper methods for adding literals (variable names and constants) and operands.

❹ build_tokens reads an equation and tokenizes it.

❺ relate_tokens turns a flat array of tokens into a tree of equation nodes.

❻ new_equate_command creates Java to build a BigDecimal with a constant value.

❼ final_equate_command creates Java to assign the output of the equation to the local variable that is supposed to hold the output.

❽ new_op_command builds Java to implement plus, minus, multiply, or divide operations, or to call a method.

❾ create_commands walks the hierarchy and uses the Java building functions to create the Java that implements the equation.

❿ parse_equation joins together the text parsing and the Java creation. It takes the string of the equation and returns a string of Java that implements the equation.

⓫ process_java_file reads the Java text file, reads the comments, and replaces them with implementation. It then backs up and replaces the original file.

12.1.5   Performing system tests

To test the equation generator, use the system test (see appendix B), which compares the current output of the generator against a set of known goods. Here is the definition file for the generator:

```
<ut kgdir="kg">
  <test cmd="ruby bdgen.rb examples/Test1.java" out="examples/Test1.java" />
  <test cmd="ruby bdgen.rb examples/Test2.java" out="examples/Test2.java" />
  <test cmd="ruby bdgen.rb examples/Test3.java" out="examples/Test3.java" />
  <test cmd="ruby bdgen.rb examples/Test4.java" out="examples/Test4.java" />
</ut>
```

Next we'll look at a type of generator that automates the building of reports.

12.2   *A CASE STUDY: THE REPORT LOGIC AND INTERFACE GENERATOR*

Chapter 10, "Creating database access generators," covered generation for the data entry and editing portions of an application. A major portion of any database application consists of the reports the system generates. In this section, we explain how you can apply code generation to building report generation.

Efficient reporting means using block requests of the database by creating custom queries that sum and group the data. The reporting system back end handles querying the database and getting the data into a form suitable for easy display. All of the math for the report must be done on the back end. The reporting system front end formats the output for the presentation medium.

This factoring of the business logic in the report back end from the display on the front end means that the report back end can be reused by any number of front-end mechanisms. These mechanisms could include:

- A batch report email sender
- A notification system based on the reporting values
- The exporting of report values through SOAP or XML-RPC
- The display of the report through multiple output mediums (e.g., HTML or client/server)

To demonstrate how a generator can be applied to this problem, let's pick a Java web application as our target architecture. On the back end, we use custom POJOs (plain old Java objects) to query the database through JDBC. On the front end, we use JSP to build HTML from the report results.

12.2.1   Roles of the generator

The report generator is a key component of any business system. It's also a component that frequently will have responsibilities added to its domain over time, which can cause it to become obfuscated. To avoid that feature creep, you should specify in clear terms what the system is responsible for and what it is not. Because the generator builds the reports, its responsibilities within the system are similar to the reporting engine itself. Let's look at the specific responsibilities of this generator:

- Translating abstract requirements of fields and sorting them into a report.
- Creating the reporting layer of the application, which includes:
  - The low-level reporting API that reads data from the database and massages it into a form appropriate for presentation.
  - The presentation layer for each report.
  - Technical documentation for the report.
  - Rudimentary end-user documentation for the report.

The generator is not responsible for creating:

- Ad-hoc reports.
- Query criteria other than the criteria defined by the report.
- Design documentation for the reports built by the system.

With this in mind, you can now define the architecture of the generator.

12.2.2 Laying out the generator architecture

The generator takes a report description and an interface description and, using a set of templates, builds the JSP pages and POJO objects. Custom code can also be input to alter the behavior of the back-end report builder. Figure 12.2 shows the block architecture for the tier generator.

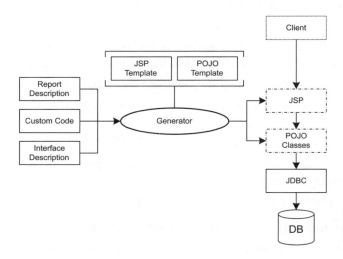

Figure 12.2
A generator that builds JSP and report logic classes for a web application

The report description and interface description files are central to this generator. The report description includes:

- Arguments for the report query
- SQL for the query
- All of the fields returned from the query and their types
- The data to be grouped, sorted, and summed
- References to the custom code that handle various custom field behaviors

The interface description includes:

- Formatting for each of the fields of the display
- Arguments for the report, the locations from where those arguments came, and the controls that should be used to show the value of the argument

12.2.3   Processing flow

Report logic and interface generator

This section shows a list of processing steps for the generator. They are just a starting point; your report system generator will have custom requirements that alter this design.

- Reads the report description and stores it.
- Reads the interface description and stores it.
- Populates any default values in the interface description with the values from the report description.
- Creates a buffer to hold the field processing methods.
- For each field, follows these steps:
  o If the field has custom code, uses the custom code template to build the field logic; otherwise, uses the standard field template to build the field logic.
- Uses the query template to build the JDBC access code.
- Merges the field code and the query code into a single POJO using a container template.
- Stores the output of the template as the report POJO.
- Invokes the interface template to build the JSP report page. This report page uses the POJO object to query the data.
- Stores the output of the template as the report JSP.

12.2.4   A report logic and interface generator alternative

An alternative to building a single generator is to build two generators that cascade. The first builds the report logic and the second builds the interface. Figure 12.3 shows the block architecture diagram for two cascading generators.

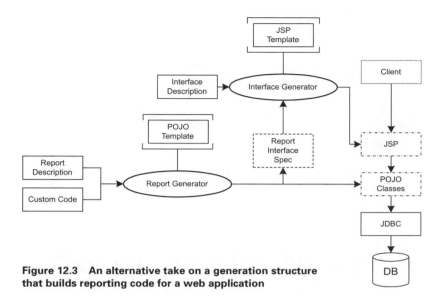

Figure 12.3   An alternative take on a generation structure that builds reporting code for a web application

The report logic generator uses the report description to build the POJO classes. In addition, the generator produces a report interface specification that feeds into the interface generator. The interface generator uses the interface description in combination with the report interface specification to build JSPs that provide an interface for the reports.

This approach is preferred because you can reuse both the report generator and the interface generator. The report generator can be used to create customized report queries, which are used outside a user interface. You can reuse the interface generator to display data from any service that produces a report-style interface.

12.2.5   Report logic generation tools

Tools that build report generators include the following:

- DataVision is an open source reporting tool (http://datavision.sourceforge.net/).
- JRPT is a Java report engine generator (http://sourceforge.net/projects/jrpt/).

12.3   SUMMARY

Business logic layers are usually hand coded, but that doesn't mean you can't find ways to use generation. All it takes is a little creativity and you should be able to apply code generation to speed your development.

The next chapter provides smaller code generation solutions for a number of common software engineering problems.

C H A P T E R   1 3

More generator ideas

Generators do not need to be large and elaborate affairs. This final chapter is intended to give you some ideas for creating small generators that can help you on a day-to-day basis. The examples we present take only a day or so to write but can reduce your workload by days or even weeks, depending on the generator's target.

13.1 TECHNIQUE: MAINTAINING HEADER FILES

One reason to choose Java over C++ is its simple maintenance of the header file. Maintaining the header file may seem trivial, but if you've ever had to recompile a huge project because you forgot to add one small method, you'll appreciate this feature. The generator we describe in this section makes life easier on C++ engineers by creating and maintaining C++ header files derived from the implementation files.

Let's look at what this type of generator does.

13.1.1 Roles of the generator

The header generator is responsible for:

- Creating headers for classes contained entirely in single implementation files and including some extra markup to define fields.

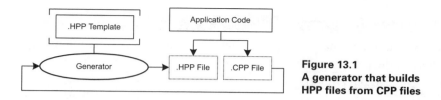

Figure 13.1
A generator that builds HPP files from CPP files

The generator does not take responsibility for these tasks:

- Building C++ templates.
- Building technical or design documentation for the classes.

Now let's look at the architecture for the generator.

13.1.2   Laying out the generator architecture

The generator reads in the CPP file and then either reads and alters or creates the new HPP file directly. This, among other reasons, makes the tool ideal for integrating into an IDE. When using an IDE, you can run this generator as an external tool whenever you add a method to the CPP file. The generator receives the pathname of the current file automatically, scans the file, and then adds the method to the HPP file. After it alters the HPP file, the generator prints a short report detailing the number of methods that it added to the HPP file; this report appears in the output window. Figure 13.1 is a block-flow diagram of this simple generator.

Now let's look at the high-level process steps this generator runs through.

13.1.3   Processing flow

C++ header generator—from scratch

Two program flows are possible. The first is when you just rebuild the HPP file from scratch each time. In that case, the generator follows these steps:

- Reads the CPP file.
- Tokenizes the code.
- Parses the code tokens to find the method signatures and the comments for additional information, such as public, private, protected, and default values.
- Builds the new HPP contents using the HPP template.
- Backs up the original HPP file.
- Creates the new HPP with the new contents.
- Prints the results of the generation cycle.

13.1.4 Processing flow

C++ header generator—with existing methods

If you decide to merge in the new methods with the existing methods, the generator follows these steps:

- Reads the CPP file.
- Tokenizes the code.
- Parses the code tokens to find the method signatures and uses the comments for additional information, such as public, private, protected, and default values.
- Reads the HPP file.
- Tokenizes the code.
- Parses the code tokens to find all of the method signatures.
- Compares each code signature against the signature in the CPP file to see if any alterations or additions occurred.
- In the case of alterations, the generator builds the signature, uses it as a search in a regular expression to find the original, and replaces it with the new signature.
- In the case of additions, the generator finds special comments that denote the public, protected, and private portions of the class definition and adds the method directly after the comments.

C++ header generators

An example generator for C++ header generation and maintenance is ClassCreator, which builds C++ implementation files from headers (http://sourceforge.net/projects/classcreator/).

13.2 TECHNIQUE: CREATING DLL WRAPPERS

A classic method of writing reusable code under Windows is to create DLLs with your C++ code. The problem is that the DLL interface is a functional and not an object-oriented interface. This requires the object interface to be *flattened* into a procedural interface.

For each method on the object you want to export, you create a function in the DLL interface. The first argument to the function is the object pointer; the rest are the arguments for the method. The body of the function casts the object pointer to the object type and invokes the method call; it then sends back the value returned by the method.

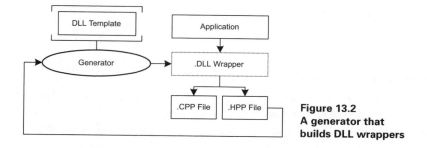

Figure 13.2
**A generator that
builds DLL wrappers**

13.2.1   Roles of the generator

Before developing the architecture for the DLL wrapper generator, you need to specify the role that the generator will play within that architecture. This generator will be responsible for:

- Managing the DLL interface for specific classes that are to be exported from the DLL. These classes must follow the class design style required by the generator.

This generator does not take responsibility for:

- Exporting templates, C functions, or C++ classes that do not follow the class construction guidelines.
- Merging the DLL interface from the class with any other interfaces.
- Creating technical or design documentation for the interface.

With these responsibilities in hand, you can define the architecture of the generator.

13.2.2   Laying out the generator architecture

The generator takes the HPP file for the target class as input and generates the DLL wrapper using a wrapper template. Figure 13.2 shows a block input/output flow for the DLL wrapper generator.

13.2.3   Processing flow

DLL wrapper generator

Here are the process steps for the DLL wrapper generator:

- Reads the HPP file.
- Tokenizes the class definition.
- Parses out the public methods. Optionally, it uses comments to define which constructor to use and what public methods are to be exported.
- Passes the exported methods on to the DLL template.

- Uses the output of the DLL template to create the wrapper .c and .h files. Depending on how you design your layer, you may also want to create a DLL descriptor file.

Generators for building DLL wrappers

General-purpose DLL wrapping generators are still somewhat rare. An important one is the Simplified Wrapper and Interface Generator, or SWIG (www.swig.org), which can be used to wrap DLL wrappers around C++ classes under Windows.

In the next section, we look at generators that wrap scripting languages.

13.3 TECHNIQUE: CREATING WRAPPERS FOR EXTERNAL LANGUAGES

One of the great things about scripting languages is that whenever you get a performance bottleneck you can migrate a portion of functionality into C and then use the functions as an external library to the scripting language. Each scripting language has a different way of doing this, but all are somewhat cumbersome. The generator you'll build next solves this issue by reading the engineers' existing interface files and creating the wrappers automatically.

13.3.1 Roles of the generator

The role of the wrapper generator is similar to the DLL interface generator in section 13.2. This generator has one main responsibility: managing the wrapper for specific classes that are to be exported. These classes must follow the class design style required by the generator.

Here's what the generator doesn't do:

- Export templates, C functions, or C++ classes that do not follow the class construction guidelines.
- Merge the wrapper generated for the classes with any other interface wrappers.
- Create technical or design documentation for the interface.

Let's now turn our attention to the architecture.

13.3.2 Laying out the generator architecture

This architecture closely resembles the generator architecture for the DLL wrapper generator. Figure 13.3 shows the input and output flow of the language interface generator.

The generator takes the HPP or .h file for the target code as input and, using one or more templates, builds the wrapper for the external language.

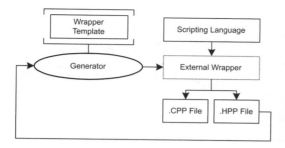

Figure 13.3
A generator that builds the external wrappers that sit between scripting languages and C++ code

13.3.3   Processing flow

External language wrapper generator

The process flow is fairly language-specific. However, we have included a simple skeleton flow here so that you can see the general steps, regardless of your chosen language:

- Reads the HPP file.
- Tokenizes the class definition.
- Parses out the public methods. Optionally, the generator uses comments to define which constructor to use and what public methods are to be exported.
- Passes the exported methods on to the templates.
- Uses the output of the templates to create the output files.

Generators for building wrappers for external languages

The Eiffel Wrapper Generator, or EWG (http://sourceforge.net/projects/ewg) is the only example we could find of a generator that builds external language wrappers. The tool builds glue code between Eiffel and C libraries.

13.4   *TECHNIQUE: CREATING FIREWALL CONFIGURATIONS*

Firewalls from different vendors have different configuration options and syntax. If you could maintain your firewall rules at an abstract level, then when the hardware changes, you could change your generator to implement the new rules on the new hardware without having to modify the rules. In this section, we build a firewall configuration generator.

13.4.1   Roles of the generator

You begin by defining the roles of the generator. This generator has one main responsibility: creating the complete firewall configuration file.

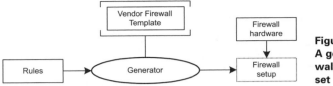

**Figure 13.4
A generator that builds firewall definition files from a set of rules in XML**

The generator is not responsible for:

- Documenting the configuration.
- Deploying the configuration.
- Configuring devices outside firewalls.
- Building non-firewall configuration files within a firewall device.

Next you need to define the architecture of the firewall generator.

13.4.2   Laying out the generator architecture

The firewall generator reads in the rules for the firewall from an XML description and builds setup files using a set of vendor-specific templates. If your network setup is complex, you may want to have another file that defines your network devices so that the generator can determine the templates it should use for the individual rules. Figure 13.4 shows the block architecture for the firewall configuration generator.

Now let's walk through the steps this generator takes as it does its work.

13.4.3   Processing flow

Firewall configuration generator

Here is the process flow for the generator:

- Reads in the rules from the XML file and stores them locally.
- Normalizes the rules internally and replace any defaults with their real values.
- Invokes the vendor-specific template files and passes them the rules.
- Stores the output of the generator into the setup text files.

In the next section, you'll see a simple generator that saves time by creating lookup tables for you.

13.5 TECHNIQUE: CREATING LOOKUP FUNCTIONS

There are times when you can improve the performance of your application dramatically by trading space for time. One technique is to create precompiled lookup tables.

For example, suppose you need a `sin()` lookup table function. You can easily create a function that locates a requested value in a table containing the values of `sin()` at a specific granularity.

The input C file for this generator, shown in listing 13.1, resembles the input for the system test from appendix B.

Listing 13.1 lookup_function_example.c

```
// <lookup_func name="sin" count="1000" start="0" step="0.0001"
equation="sin(x)">                    Specifies the
// </lookup_func>                     lookup table


int main( int argc, char *argv[] )
{
  printf( "sin(0.0) = %d\n", sin_lookup( 0.0 ) );
  printf( "sin(0.5) = %d\n", sin_lookup( 0.5 ) );      Tests the new
  printf( "sin(1.0) = %d\n", sin_lookup( 1.0 ) );      lookup function
}
```

The generator looks for the XML comments in the input .c or CPP file and creates a new function for matching the specifications. Here's an example result:

```
// <lookup_func name="sin" count="1000" start="0" step="0.0001"
equation="sin(x)">
static double sin_lookup( double value )
{
  double dValues = { 0.0, ... };            Implements the
  return dValues[ int( value * 1000 ) ];    lookup function
}
// </lookup_func>

int main( int argc, char *argv[] )
{
  printf( "sin(0.0) = %d\n", sin_lookup( 0.0 ) );
  printf( "sin(0.5) = %d\n", sin_lookup( 0.5 ) );
  printf( "sin(1.0) = %d\n", sin_lookup( 1.0 ) );
}
```

As you can see, the comment is preserved, but now there is an interior to the comment: the new `sin_lookup` function, which takes a `double` as input and returns a `double` as output. The `double` is multiplied by the count, and the static array of values, `dValues`, is indexed to obtain the correct output value.

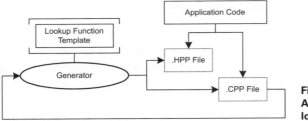

Figure 13.5
A generator that builds look-up functions for C++

13.5.1 Roles of the generator

We can distill the active role of the lookup function generator into one main item: decomposing the functions specified in abstract form into executable code. The generator will not take responsibility for these tasks:

- Technical or design documentation for the functions.
- Unit tests for the functions.
- Input validation.
- Parameter sanity checking for the functions—whether the functions are in the right state, or they have the proper arguments, or they're called in the correct order, and so forth.

Knowing what the generator will and will not do aids you in defining the architecture, which is the next step.

13.5.2 Laying out the generator architecture

The generator takes the CPP or .c file as input and then uses templates to build the new output for the CPP file (and the HPP file, if the lookup function is to be externally visible). Figure 13.5 shows the block diagram for the lookup function generator.

Next let's look at the process flow for this generator.

13.5.3 Processing flow

Lookup function generator

The processing steps for the lookup function generator are:

- Reads the CPP file.
- Each time it finds special comment code, the generator follows these steps:
  o Parses out the attributes of the function.
  o Runs the equation internally to build the lookup table. This is where a self-interpreting language such as Ruby, Perl, or Python can really come in handy.
  o Invokes the lookup function template with the attributes and the lookup values.
  o Builds the new contents for the output file from the results of the template.

- Inserts the result back into the original text.
- Backs up the original file.
- Creates the new .CPP or .c file.

The final example generator in our book is a helpful utility for using precompiler macros in C and C++.

13.6 *TECHNIQUE: CREATING MACRO LOOKUP TABLES*

Both C and C++ support constants using precompiler macros. The problem with these macros is that when you are debugging you cannot see the name of the symbolic constant; instead, all you see is the constant value. It would be convenient to have a tool that takes the value of a symbolic precompiler macro and returns its name. In this section, we show you how to build a lookup table generator.

13.6.1 Feeding code to the generator

The code in listing 13.2 includes a few `#define` macros and a comment that says where the lookup table function should go.

Listing 13.2   lookup_table_example.c

```
#define IDOK 2                    #define
#define IDCANCEL 3                macros

// <lookup_table>               Location for the
// </lookup_table>              lookup function

int main( int argc, char *argv[] )
{
  printf( "%d - %s\n", IDOK, define_lookup( IDOK ) );        Code that tests
  printf( "%d - %s\n", IDCANCEL, define_lookup( IDCANCEL ) );  the lookup
}                                                              function
```

The code would look like this after the generator runs:

```
#define IDOK 2
#define IDCANCEL 3

// <lookup_table>
static char *define_lookup( int value )
{
  if ( value == IDOK ) return "IDOK";              The lookup
  if ( value == IDCANCEL ) return "IDCANCEL";      function
  return "";
}
// </lookup_table>

int main( int argc, char *argv[] )
{
```

```
    printf( "%d - %s\n", IDOK, define_lookup( IDOK ) );
    printf( "%d - %s\n", IDCANCEL, define_lookup( IDCANCEL ) );
}
```

13.6.2 Roles of the generator

The lookup table generator is very simple and has just one main responsibility: building the lookup table functions within an implementation file. The generator will not take responsibility for documenting the lookup function, either on a technical or a design level.

13.6.3 Laying out the generator architecture

As input, the generator takes the HPP or CPP files that contain the pre-processor macros. Then, using a set of templates, the generator builds the lookup table function. The output of the template is then stored in a target CPP file. Figure 13.6 shows the block architecture for the lookup table generator.

Now let's look at the steps the generator goes through as it executes.

13.6.4 Processing flow

Lookup table generator

Here is the step-by-step process flow for this generator, which builds the code in the example from listing 13.2:

- Reads the CPP file.
- Parses out and creates a catalog of the **#define** macros.
- Creates the lookup table function using the lookup table template.
- Finds and replaces the **lookup_table** tag comments with the new code.
- Makes a backup of the CPP file.
- Replaces the CPP file with the new text.

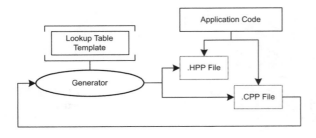

**Figure 13.6
A generator that builds
lookup tables for C++**

13.7 SUMMARY

As we stated in the introduction, the generators in this chapter are very simple; with the right tools they should only take a day or so to build, but they will repay you immeasurably in saved time and trouble over the long run. These examples are just the edge of the spectrum of practical code generation techniques.

Throughout this book, you have seen examples of where and how code generation can be applied. It is our hope that you will customize and apply these techniques to your own problems and your specific architecture. We hope we have convinced you that code generation yields benefits in the areas of quality, consistency, and productivity—benefits that you can reap in every level of your application development.

APPENDIX A

A brief introduction to Ruby

In this appendix, we provide a brief overview of the basics of the Ruby language.

Ruby programs and scripts are simple text files that have the filename extension *.rb*. To execute a Ruby program, you simply type

```
ruby file_name.rb
```

where *file_name* represents the name of the Ruby file you wish to run.

Ruby is an imperative language, and as such, a program file consists of a set of linear command invocations similar to C, C++, Perl, or Java. The Hello World application in Ruby is simply

```
print "Hello World\n"
```

Carriage returns are used to delineate commands. For example,

```
print "This is "
print "a test\n"
```

prints "This is a test" on a single line by calling `print` twice. You can use a semicolon if you prefer more compact code. The previous example would look like this:

```
print "This is "; print "a test\n"
```

A.1 RUBY FUNDAMENTALS

The sections that follow provide information on the basics of Ruby. Readers already familiar with Ruby should skip ahead to section A.2, which discusses more advanced Ruby features.

Using comments

Comments in Ruby start with a hash (#) character. Here is an example:

```
# This is a comment
print "Hello"   # Here is another comment
```

Variables

In Ruby, all variables are objects. Here are some example variable declarations in Ruby:

```
anInteger = 42
aFloatingPoint = 3.141519
myString = "Hello"
anotherString = 'Goodbye'
myBoolean = true
anArray = ["First", "Second", 3 ]
aHash = { 'first_name' => 'Jack', 'last_name' => 'Herrington' }
```

This is the basic set of types. You never need to define a variable as a specific type; Ruby is latently typed, like Perl and Python. This means that you are not required to explicitly set the type of a variable. A set of operations is available that you can use to inspect the type of any variable, but that discussion is beyond the scope of this appendix and those operations are usually not required for everyday applications.

Global variables

You can define a global variable by using the $ prefix. Ruby includes a few standard global variables. Some examples are $stderr, $stdout, and $stdin (standard error, standard out, and standard in, respectively).

Math operations

Mathematical operations are what you would expect; here's a simple formula:

```
money = 100.0
tax = money * 0.08
```

In this example, you're calculating the amount of tax on $100 at an 8 percent tax rate.

Conditionals

Ruby sports the standard set of Boolean logic conditional operators, including `if`, `else`, and `elsif`. In addition, it allows for the Perl-style `unless`, which is an inverted `if`. An example `if` statement is:

```
if ( x > 0 )
   print "Positive"
end
```

In this example, you're checking to see if x is greater than zero. If it is, the code prints `Positive`. The following code snippet checks various weight classes using `elsif`:

```
if ( x > 0 )
   print "Positive"
elsif ( x < 0 )
   print "Negative"
else
   print "Zero"
end
```

This code uses a cascading series of `if` and `elsif` statements to check the value of x. Given a value of x, the code prints `positive`, `negative`, or `zero`.

An alternative to `if` is the `unless` keyword, which is just an inverted `if`. An example `unless` statement is:

```
unless ( broken )
   print "Everything is ok"
end
```

In this case, the string `"Everything is ok"` is printed unless the variable `broken` evaluates to `true`.

Conditionals can also include `and` and `or` statements using the C standard `&&` and `||`, respectively. The `!` operator also works for `not`.

Loops and iterators

Ruby supports a number of looping conventions. Let's start with this simple `while` statement:

```
while ( <conditional> )
   … do some stuff
end
```

In addition to the standard imperative looping operators (`while`, `for`, `until`, etc.), Ruby supports safe iterators. For example:

```
myArray = [ 1, 5, 10 ]

myArray.each { |value|
   print "#{value}\n"
}
```

The each method calls the block that is presented to it for each of the values in the array. The block is passed the current value, which is placed into the variable value. This value is then printed. This example also shows a method of including a variable in a print format statement using the #{<varname>} syntax.

You may notice that the times iterator is used throughout the book. The code

```
5.times { print "Hello\n" }
```

prints "Hello" five times. We can apply the times method to 5 because all variables in Ruby, even simple values like 5, are objects. For a more detailed explanation of the block style of invocation—where a method can take a portion of code to yield to as an argument—see section A.2.

Using functions

Defining a function is simple:

```
def addTen( aNumber )
   aNumber + 10
end

print addTen( 20 )
```

The function addTen takes a number and returns its value plus 10. return is implied because the plus operation is the last operation in the function. Of course, you can add return to your code if you wish.

Classes

Defining a class is also straightforward:

```
class Cat
   def initialize( name )
      @name = name
   end
   def say_something()
      print "Meow, my name is #{@name}\n"
   end
end

myUsul = Cat.new("Usul" )
myUsul.say_something()
```

In this example, you're defining a new class called Cat that contains a name. Instance variables are prefixed with the @ sign. In addition to having a constructor (initialize), this class offers a method called say_something, which tells Cat to say something, whereupon it "speaks" its name.

The code that uses the class creates a new Cat with the name Usul and then invokes the say_something method on the class.

Deriving one class from another is supported. Multiple inheritance is not supported, but Ruby does allow support for "mix-ins," whereby the implementation of one class can be imported into another. These features are not extensively used in this book; you should consult a Ruby book for further details (see section A.3).

Using accessors

Creating read and write methods for member variables is good practice—it keeps others from writing to public member variables and allows you to trace who is getting and setting values. To make it easy to create accessors (read and write methods), you can use the `attr_reader`, `attr_write`, and `attr_accessor` keywords.

Here is an example:

```
class Cat
    def initialize( name )
        @name = name
    end

    attr_reader :name

    def say_something()
        print "Meow, my name is #{@name}\n"
    end
end

myUsul = Cat.new("Usul" )
print myUsul.name
```

The `name` method is created automatically by the `attr_reader` keyword. The `attr_writer` keyword creates a method that allows you to specify

```
myUsul.name = 'Joe'
```

The `attr_accessor` keyword builds both the reader and writer methods.

The eval keyword

Ruby is an *interpreted* language, which means that it is compiled at runtime and the compiled op-codes are then run against a virtual machine. This means that you can generate new code on the fly and present it for compilation and execution during the execution of a host script. You accomplish this by using the `eval` keyword. For example:

```
while( true )
    print "Equation > "
    equation = readline()
    print "#{equation.chomp} = #{eval(equation)}\n"
end
```

This code snippet shows a number of things. First it illustrates the use of `readline` to read standard input. Second, it shows that you can put any expression in the `#{...}` portion of a print statement, including complex ones like `eval`. Third, it shows using the `chomp` method on a string to "eat" the trailing carriage return. Fourth, and most important, it shows how you can use the `eval` keyword to run an arbitrary string and execute that string as Ruby code.

If you run this program and type `1+2` followed by a return, you get the following:

```
Equation > 1+2
1+2 = 3
Equation >
```

`eval` is at the core of the ERb template-handling package. ERb reads in the templates and turns them into Ruby code. It then runs `eval` on that code at runtime to "execute" the template.

Regular expressions

Regular expressions are invaluable to code generation and text handling in general. A complete treatise on regular expressions is well beyond the scope of this book, but you should get a sense of how Ruby handles regular expressions in the syntax.

You can define a regular expression using operators or objects. The operators are merely shorthand for the object versions. A simple matching expression using operators is shown here:

```
myString = "My dog has fleas"
if ( myString =~ /dog/i )
    print "Dog is in string '#{myString}\'\n"
end
```

Here you are checking for the existence of the pattern `dog` in a string using the `=~` operator. This more complex search example extracts substrings from a string using a pattern:

```
myString = "key:value"
if ( myString =~ /(\w+):(\w+)/ )
    print "#{$1} => #{$2}\n"
end
```

Here you apply the regular expression `(\w+):(\w+)` to the string. The parentheses delineate elements of the string that are to be extracted. These extracted substrings are stored as the special values `$1`, `$2`, and so forth in the order of their appearance in the regular expression.

Another common use of regular expressions is to replace substrings within a string with new values. Here is an example substitution in Ruby:

```
myString = "My dog has fleas"
myString.sub!( /dog/, "cat" )
print "#{myString}\n"
```

Here you are replacing an occurrence of `dog` with `cat`. You do this using the `sub!` method on the `String` class. The use of the `!` symbol at the end of the method is a Ruby convention that implies that the change will be made in place. The `sub` method (without the !) does not change the string but instead returns a new string with the altered value.

You can find more information about regular expressions in *Mastering Regular Expressions*, by Jeffrey Friedl (O'Reilly, 2002).

A.2   AN ADVANCED RUBY PRIMER

In this section, we examine more advanced Ruby topics, including exception handling, file input/output, the p operator, and the yield keyword.

Exception handling

In Ruby, exception handling is built into the base language. To wrap some code in an exception handler, you use the begin and rescue keywords, as shown here:

```
begin
    ... some risky stuff ...
rescue => myErr
    print "Ran into some trouble:\n\n#{myErr}\n"
end
```

In this case, if any uncaught exceptions are thrown within the execution of the risky stuff, they are caught in the rescue statement and an error is printed. Ruby supports specification of the exception type in the rescue handler as well as the subclassing of existing exception types.

File I/O

File I/O in Ruby is really simple. Ruby has a built-in File class that works across various platforms and is easy to use. Here is an example of reading a file:

```
fh = File.open( "test.txt" )
print fh.read
fh.close()
```

Here you are opening the file using the open class method on the File class. The variable returned is a File object handle. You then call the read function, which reads all of the contents of the file. The contents are then printed and the file is closed.

Here is a slightly more Ruby-like style of reading the same file:

```
File.open( "test.txt" ) { |fh|
    print fh.read
}
```

This is the same example as the previous one, with the exception that here the read is performed only if the file is opened. Also, there is no requirement to have a close method call because the file is closed automatically at the end of the block execution.

To open a file for writing, you use an optional second argument on the `open` method, as you can see in this example:

```
File.open( "test.txt", "w" ) { |fh|
   fh.print "Hello\n"
}
```

Again, the block is run only if the file is successfully opened, and the file is closed automatically at the end of the execution of the block.

The p operator

Ruby has a clever operator named p, which can print to standard output a text version of whatever object it is presented with. This comes in very handy when you are debugging and you don't know the variable's value. For example, the code

```
myArray = [ 1, 5, "hi", "there" ]
p myArray
```

prints this to the standard output:

```
[1, 5, "hi", "there"]
```

The yield keyword

Iterators, like `each` and `times`, are not built into Ruby. These iterators are built in Ruby using the `yield` keyword. Here is an example of an iterator that presents to the block all of the odd numbers in a given range:

```
def myIterator( startValue, endValue )
   curValue = startValue
   while( curValue < endValue )
      if ( curValue % 2 == 1 )
         yield curValue
      end
      curValue += 1
   end
end

myIterator( 10, 20 ) { |value| print "#{value}\n" }
```

Running this Ruby code prints the values 11, 13, 15, 17, and 19, just as it should. The real trick is in the `yield` invocation in the middle of the `while` loop. `yield` takes the supplied arguments and presents them to the block that was given to the function. This block of code

```
{ |value| print "#{value}\n" }
```

then takes the value and prints it. If the block returns a value, it becomes the return value of `yield`. Using an iterator/yield pattern, you can build a data filter, with your code block not only receiving values but generating new values as well.

The generators in this book use `yield` to build specialized iterators that allow templates to easily generate similar code for multiple items. An example is generating the column definitions for all of the columns in a table. The column definitions are XML objects and the block code is actually an ERb template, but the resulting implementation is very clean because of the use of the `yield` keyword.

A.3   LEARNING MORE ABOUT RUBY

Ruby is a language worth exploring. It has a clean syntax and is easy to read. It is purely object-oriented, while at the same time being simple and fun to use. Here are some references where you can learn more about Ruby:

- *Programming Ruby,* by Dave Thomas and Andrew Hunt (Addison-Wesley, 2000), is the definitive work on Ruby and is commonly known as the "pick-axe" book in the Ruby community. This book goes into detail on every aspect of Ruby, from its syntax and operators to its class libraries. It also shows you how to embed Ruby in other languages.
- *Ruby in a Nutshell,* by Yukihiro Matsumoto (O'Reilly, 2001), is a quick-reference book for the Ruby enthusiast written by the master himself.
- *The Ruby Way,* Hal Fulton (Sams, 2001), is another good reference work on Ruby. This book focuses more on programming style and method, as opposed to being a strict reference.

In addition to these books, you can check out these online resources:

- Ruby Central (www.ruby-lang.org) is the central site for all things Ruby. It features links to other Ruby resources and serves as a good jumping-off point.
- The Ruby Application Archive (http://raa.ruby-lang.org/) is Ruby's answers to Perl's CPAN. Here you can find modules and libraries to use with Ruby.
- Ruby Garden (http://www.rubygarden.org/) is Dave Thomas's Wiki dedicated to Ruby. It is an invaluable technical and community resource for Ruby programmers.

The simple system test framework

System tests are particularly important when you are generating lots of code quickly. One small bug in the generator can cause a lot of bad code to be generated. That is why all of the case studies in this book include a section showing you how to use a system test framework to test the generator.

You can find test frameworks for Ruby at these sites:

- RubyUnit (http://homepage1.nifty.com/markey/ruby/rubyunit/index_e.html)
- Test::Unit (http://testunit.talbott.ws/)

The system test framework we describe in this appendix is not meant to replace any of these utilities. Our goal is to show you a convenient example of building a simple framework to test command line-based code generators.

B.1 THE BASIC DESIGN

This simple system test runs command-line programs and compares the output of the program against a stored known goods file. You specify the command lines through an XML file that contains both command lines for running and naming the file or files that are output from the command line. In this section, we'll take a look at the basic design of this system.

B.1.1 Processing flows

There are two processing flows for the system test. The first is for building the known goods, and the second is for testing against the known goods.

Building known goods

The processing flow for building the known goods is shown here:

- Reads the XML file and builds the internal representation.
- For each test follows these steps:
  - Runs the command line.
  - For each output file, makes a copy of that file in the known goods directory.

Testing against the known goods

Here's the processing flow for testing against the known goods:

- Reads the XML file and builds the internal representation.
- Initializes a list of test failures.
- For each test, follows these steps:
  - Runs the command line.
  - For each output file, compares it against the corresponding file in the known goods directory. If the two files are not identical, then it adds this test to the failure list. If there is no known goods file, then it adds this test to the failure list.
- Prints a list of test failures.

B.1.2 The input file format

As we mentioned earlier, you specify the list of tests using XML. An example XML definition is shown here:

```
<ut kgdir="kg">
  <test cmd="ruby uigen.rb definitions/form1.def" out="output/form1.jsp" />
  <test cmd="ruby uigen.rb definitions/form2.def" out="output/form2.jsp" />
  <test cmd="ruby uigen.rb definitions/table1.def" out="output/table1.jsp" />
</ut>
```

The <ut> tag specifies the known goods directory using kgdir and contains all of the tests. Tests are specified using the <test> tag. Each <test> tag specifies a command line using the cmd attribute and an output using the out attribute.

A test can also specify multiple output files for a single command-line test, as shown here:

```
<ut kgdir="kg">
  <test cmd="ruby -I../lp rpcgen.rb examples/Test.java">
      <out>examples/TestHandler.java</out>
      <out>examples/TestStubs.java</out>
```

```
    </test>
</ut>
```

You can expand the `<test>` tag to include multiple `<out>` tags. Each `<out>` tag contains the name of the output file as text. In the previous example, the one invocation of `ruby -I../lp rpcgen.rb examples/Test.java` creates both examples/TestHandler.java and examples/TestStubs.java.

B.1.3   The ut1.rb code

Here's the code for our simple system test framework:

```
require 'rexml/document'
require 'getoptlong'
require 'ftools'
require 'ostruct'

@@xml_file = ""                          ❶ Parses out the
@@is_making = false                        command line

begin

  opts = GetoptLong.new(
    [ "--test", "-t", GetoptLong::NO_ARGUMENT ],
    [ "--make", "-m", GetoptLong::NO_ARGUMENT ],
    [ "--file", "-f", GetoptLong::REQUIRED_ARGUMENT ]
  )

  opts.each_option do |name, arg|
    @@xml_file = arg if ( name == "--file" )
    @@is_making = true if ( name == "--make" )
  end

rescue

  print "ut1 usage:\n";
  print "  ruby ut1.rb -f xml_def_file - To run the tests against the known
goods\n"
  print "  ruby ut1.rb -m -f xml_def_file - To regenerate the known goods\n"
  exit

end

begin
                                                              Reads the
  doc = REXML::Document.new( File.open( @@xml_file ) )    ⤶   XML file

rescue

  print "Could not open or parse #{@@xml_file}"
  exit

end
                                                          Gets the known goods
kgdir = doc.root.attributes[ 'kgdir' ]                ⤶   directory name

unless kgdir

  print "No known good directory defined on the 'ut' tag.\n"
```

```
      exit

  end

  tests = []
```
Iterates through
each test XML node
```
  doc.root.elements.each( "test" ) { |test_node|

    files = []
```
❷ **Gets all of the output filenames**
```
    files.push( test_node.attributes[ 'out' ] ) if ( test_node.attributes-
  [ 'out' ] )

      test_node.elements.each( "out" ) { |out_node|
        out = out_node.text.strip
        files.push( out ) if ( out )
      }

      tests.push ( OpenStruct.new( {
        'command' => test_node.attributes[ 'cmd' ],
        'output_files' => files
      } ) )
```
❸ **Adds the test to
the list of tests**
```
  }
```
**Initializes a list
of test failures**
```
  failures = []
```
**Iterates through
each test**
```
  tests.each { |test|

    print "#{test.command}\n"
    system( test.command )
```
**Runs the
command**

**Builds a name
for the known
goods file**
```
    test.output_files.each { |file|

      known_good_name = kgdir + "/" + File.basename( file )

      begin
        current_result = File.open( file ).read()
      rescue
```
**Reads in the
known goods**
```
        print "Failure: No output file - #{file}\n"
        next
      end
```
**Switches on testing or
makes known goods**
```
      if ( @@is_making )
        print "Storing #{file} to #{known_good_name}\n"
        File.syscopy( file, known_good_name )
        print "Known good #{known_good_name} stored\n"
      else
```
**Copies the out-put file
to the known goods file**
```
        print "Checking #{file} against #{known_good_name}\n"
        begin
          good_result = File.open( known_good_name ).read()
          if ( good_result != current_result )
            print "Failure: Known good comparison failed\n"
            failures.push test.command
          end
        rescue
          print "Failure: No known good file - #{known_good_name}\n"
          failures.push test.command
        end
```
**Reads the
output file**

❹ **Checks output
against the
known goods**

```
      end
    }
    print "\n"
  }

  unless ( @@is_making )
    if ( failures.length > 0 )
      print "\n\nTests failed:\n\n"
      failures.each { |test| print "  #{test}\n" }
      exit -1
    else
      print "\n\nNo test failures\n"
    end
  end
```

Prints out test failures

❶ The output of the command-line processing section is the name of the input XML file and the flag that defines whether you are testing against the known goods or creating the known goods. The XML filename is stored as the global `@@xml_file`, and the `@@is_making` flag is set to true when you are building the known goods.

❷ In this section, you look for both the `out` attribute on the test node and any `out` nodes for populating the `files` array. The `files` array stores the names of all the out-put files.

❸ You use `OpenStruct` to create an object for storing the test command and the test out-put files. `OpenStruct` takes a hash table of values and creates a new object that supports the `.` syntax for the field names. In this case, if you have a reference to one of these `OpenStruct` objects, you can use the `obj.command` method to return the command name and `obj.output_files` to get the array of output files. Without `OpenStruct`, you would use the regular hash table syntax of `hash['command']` and `hash['output_files']`.

❹ This code does a byte-by-byte comparison of the output file against the known goods file. In some cases, this may be too sensitive. The addition of some white space, for example, can have no semantic effect, yet it could cause a failure of the system test.

You may want to change the way the comparison is done in order to lessen the sensitivity of the test. One possibility is to remove all white space before the comparison. Although some errors may be overlooked, it is far more likely that common white-space issues (e.g., extra returns) will be ignored and not result in a test failure.

If that solution is too drastic, you may want to go with a multistage test, whereby the test with whitespace comparisons disabled can produce failures and a byte-by-byte comparison can produce only warnings.

EJBGen code and templates

In this appendix, we describe all of the code and templates for the EJBGen generator. We show the output using the example definition files in the EJBGen case study (chapter 10, section 10.5). You can find code that is not included here on the book's web site (www.codegeneration.net).

C.1   THE GENERATOR CODE

The next three sections examine the code for the EJBGen generator.

C.1.1   ejbgenRead.rb

The file in listing C.1 contains the code for reading the three input files: schema, extensions, and samples. The schema file contains XML that describes all of the tables and their relationships. The extensions file includes any extra data transfer object, query, or custom method definitions. As you'd expect, the samples file contains sample data that we want to load into the database to test the database access layer code.

Listing C.1   ejbgenRead.rb

```
def getXMLAttr( elem, attrName )                    ⟵┐ Gets an XML attribute
  attr = elem.attributes[attrName]                    │ from a node
  if !attr
    raise "ERROR:  missing attribute [#{attrName}]"
  end
  return attr
end                                                 ┐ Gets the text from
                                                    │ within a node
def getXMLElemText( baseElem, elemName )            ⟵┘
  elem = baseElem.elements[ elemName ]
```

```
    if !elem
      raise "ERROR:  missing element [#{elemName}]"
    end
    elemText = elem.text
    if !elemText
      raise "ERROR:  element [#{elemName}] empty"
    end
    return elemText
  end

  def readSchema()            ◁— Reads the schema.xml file
    $stderr.print "processing #{SCHEMA_FILE}...\n"
    doc = REXML::Document.new( File.open(SCHEMA_FILE))
    doc.elements.each("schema") { |schema|
      $package = getXMLAttr(schema, "pacage")        ◁— Gets the package
      $jndiPrefix = getXMLAttr(schema, "jndi-prefix")   ◁— Gets the JNDI prefix
    }

    doc.elements.each("schema/table") { |table|      ◁— Parses each table definition
      tableName = getXMLAttr(table, "name")        ◁— Gets the name of the table
      tbl = Table.new(tablName)                    | Creates the value
      val = ValueObj.new(tbl, tableName + VALUE_SUFFIX)  | and table objects

      table.elements.each("column") { |coumn|      | Gets information
        columnName = getXMLAttr(column, "name")    | for each column
        col = Column.new(tbl, columnName)
        val.addColumn(col)
        dataType = getXMLAttr(column, "datatype")
        col.setDatatype(dataType)
        col.charLength = column.attributes["length"]
        col.isNotNull = TRUE if column.attributes["not-null"]
        col.isPrimaryKey = TRUE if column.attributes["primary-key"]
        col.isUnique = TRUE if column.attributes["unique"]
      }

      tbl.addSequence          | Sets up the table
      val.addGetMethods        | and value objects
      val.addCUDMethods
    }
    doc.elements.each("schema/foreign-key") { |fk|    ◁┐ Iterates through
                                                      | the foreign keys
      fkTableName = getXMLElemText(fk, "fk-table")    ◁┐ Gets and checks
      fkTbl = $tables[fkTableName]                    | the table

      if !fkTbl
        raise "ERROR:  foreign-key fk-table [#{fkTableName}] not found"
      end

      fkColumnName = getXMLElemText(fk, "fk-coumn")   ◁┐ Gets and checks
      fkCol = fkTbl.columns[fkColumnName]             | the column name

      if !fkCol
        raise "ERROR:  foreign-key fk-table [#{fkTableName}] " +
          "does not contain fk-column [#{fkColumnName}]"
      end
```

```
      fkReferencesName = getXMLElemText(fk, "fk-refeences")     ◁─┐  Gets and
      fkRef = $tables[fkReferencesName]                            │  checks the
                                                                   │  references
      if !fkRef                                                    │  table
        raise "ERROR:  foreign key fk-table [#{fkTableName}] " +
          "fk-column [#{fkColumnName}] fk-references [#{fkReferencesName}] " +
          "table not found"
      end

      fkTbl.addForeignKey( fkCol,fkRef )     ◁─  Adds the foreign key to the table
    }

  end

  def loadParams( elem, fmethod )
    elem.elements.each("parameter") { |param|
    name = getXMLAttr(param, "name")
      javaType = getXMLAttr(param, "java-type")
      p = MethodParam.new(fmethod, name)
      p.javaType = javaType
    }
  end

  def readExtensions()     ◁─  Reads extensions.xml                Reads the
    $stderr.print "processing #{EXTENSIONS_FILE}...\n"            extensions file
    doc = REXML::Document.new( File.open(EXTENSIONS_FILE))  ◁─┐   Iterates
    doc.elements.each("extensions/value-object") { |valueOject| ◁ through the
      name = getXMLAttr(valueObject, "name")                 ◁─  value objects
      baseTableName = getXMLAttr(valueObject, "base-table")
      baseTable = $tables[baseTableName]                          Gets the name
      if !baseTable                                               and base table
        raise "ERROR:  value-object [#{name}] base-table [#{baseTableName}] " +
          "not found"
      end
      val = ValueObj.new(baseTable,name)     ◁─  Creates the new value object

      baseTable.columnsArray.each { |c|
        val.addColumn(c)
      }
                                                                  Handles the add-
      valueObject.elements.each("add-column") { |column|  ◁─┘   column tags
        tableName = getXMLAttr(column, "table")
        table = $tables[tableName]
        if !table
          raise "ERROR:  add-column table [#{tableName}] not found"
        end
        columnName = getXMLAttr(column, "column-name")
        col = table.columns[columnName]
        if !col
          raise "ERROR:  add-column column [#{columnName}] of table " +
            "[#{tableName}] not found"
        end
        newCol = col.clone
        newCol.expandName
        val.addColumn(newCol)     ◁─  Adds the column to the value object
```

```
      }
    val.addGetMethods          ⟵ Adds the get methods to the value object
  }

  doc.elements.each("extensions/sql-query-method") { |method|  ⟵┐ Handles sql-
    name = getXMLAttr(method, "name")                              │ query XML
    valueObjName = getXMLAttr(method, "value-object")              │ elements
    valueObj = $valueObjs[valueObjName]
    if !valueObj
      raise "ERROR:  in sql-query-method [#{name}] " +
        "value-object [#{valueObjName}] not found"
    end
    m = FMethod.new(valueObj.table, name)
    m.valueObj = valueObj
    m.returnType = "java.util.Collection"
    loadParams(method, m)
    m.where = getXMLElemText(method, "where")                    ┌ Handles
  }                                                              │ finder-method
  doc.elements.each("extensions/finder-method") { |method|  ⟵┘ XML elements
    name = getXMLAttr(method, "name")
    tableName = getXMLAttr(method, "table")
    table = $tables[tableName]
    if !table
      raise "ERROR:  in finder-method [#{name}] " +
        "[table #{tableName}] not found"
    end
    m = FMethod.new(table, name)
    loadParams(method, m)
    m.ejbQL = getXMLElemText(method, "ejb-ql")                   ┌ Handles
  }                                                              │ custom-
                                                                 │ method XML
  doc.elements.each("extensions/custom-method") { |method|  ⟵┘ elements
    name = getXMLAttr(method, "name")
    tableName = getXMLAttr(method, "table")
    table = $tables[tableName]
    if !table
      raise "ERROR:  in custom-method [#{name}] " +
        "[table #{tableName}] not found"
    end
    m = FMethod.new(table, name)
    m.returnType = getXMLAttr(method, "return-type")
    loadParams(method, m)
    m.body = getXMLElemText(method, "body")
  }

end

def readSamples()      ⟵ Reads samples.xml, creating SampleRow, etc.
  $stderr.print "processing #{SAMPLES_FILE}...\n"              ┌ Reads the
  doc = REXML::Document.new( File.open(SAMPLES_FILE))          ⟵┘ samples file

  doc.elements.each("samples/row") { |row|      ⟵ Iterates through each row
    tableName = getXMLAttr(row, "table")
```

```
      table = $tables[tableName]
      if !table
        raise "ERROR:  table [#{tableName}] not found"
      end
      sampleRow = SampleRow.new(table)          ⟵— Creates the sample object

      row.elements.each("column"){ |column|     ⟵— Adds each column
        columnName = getXMLAttr(column, "name")
        col = table.columns[columnName]
        if !col
          raise "ERROR:  column [#{columnName}] not found"
        end
        value = getXMLAttr(column, "value")
        sampleColumn = SampleColumn.new(sampleRow,col,value)
      }
    }
end
```

C.1.2   ejbgenDefs.rb

The ejbgenDefs.rb file (listing C.2) contains the classes that will hold the data read by
the functions in ejbgenRead. The classes in this file are shown in chapter 10, figure 10.8.

Listing C.2   ejbgenDefs.rb

```
SQL_INTEGER = "intger"          ⟵— Constants
SQL_VARCHAR = "varchar"

JAVA_INTEGER = "Integer"
JAVA_STRING = "String"

DEF_DIR = "definitions/"
OUT_DIR = "output/"
TEMPLATE_DIR = "templates/"
SCHEMA_FILE = DEF_DIR + "schema.xml"
EXTENSIONS_FILE = DEF_DIR + "extensions.xml"
SAMPLES_FILE = DEF_DIR + "samples.xml"
SQL_TEMPLATE = TEMPLATE_DIR + "tables.sql.template"
ENTITY_TEMPLATE = TEMPLATE_DIR + "Entity.java.template"
ENTITY_HOME_TEMPLATE = TEMPLATE_DIR + "EntityHome.java.template"
ENTITY_BEAN_TEMPLATE = TEMPLATE_DIR + "EntityBean.java.template"
VALUE_TEMPLATE = TEMPLATE_DIR + "Value.java.template"
SS_TEMPLATE = TEMPLATE_DIR + "SS.java.template"
SS_HOME_TEMPLATE = TEMPLATE_DIR + "SSHome.java.template"
SS_BEAN_TEMPLATE = TEMPLATE_DIR + "SSBean.java.template"
EJB_JAR_TEMPLATE = TEMPLATE_DIR + "ejb-jar.xml.template"
JBOSS_XML_TEMPLATE = TEMPLATE_DIR + "jboss.xml.template"
JBOSS_CMP_TEMPLATE = TEMPLATE_DIR + "jbosscmp-jdbc.xml.template"
LIST_JSP_TEMPLATE = TEMPLATE_DIR + "List.jsp.template"
ADD_JSP_TEMPLATE = TEMPLATE_DIR + "Add.jsp.template"
UPDATE_JSP_TEMPLATE = TEMPLATE_DIR + "Update.jsp.template"
DELETE_JSP_TEMPLATE = TEMPLATE_DIR + "Delete.jsp.template"
```

```ruby
INDEX_JSP_TEMPLATE = TEMPLATE_DIR + "index.jsp.template"
CUSTOM_JSP_TEMPLATE = TEMPLATE_DIR + "Custom.jsp.template"
SS_FACTORY_TEMPLATE = TEMPLATE_DIR + "SSFactory.java.template"
TESTS_TEMPLATE = TEMPLATE_DIR + "Tests.java.template"
SQL_OUT_FILE = OUT_DIR + "tables.sql"
JAVA_OUT_DIR = OUT_DIR + "gen/"
TESTS_OUT_DIR = OUT_DIR + "tests/"
JSP_OUT_DIR = OUT_DIR + "jsp/"
XML_OUT_DIR = OUT_DIR + "META-INF/"
VALUE_SUFFIX = "Value"

$tables = {}       # Hash of all Table objects, hashed by table name
$table = nil       # current table used by ERB
$package = nil     # name of java package                            Globals
$jndiPrefix = nil  # prefix for bean jndi names
$valueObjs = {}    # Hash of all Value objects, hashed by value name
$valueObj = nil    # current value used by ERB
$sampleRows = []   # Array of all SampleRow objects

class Table                       ❶ The Table class, which holds
  attr_reader :name                 information about each table
  attr_reader :columns
  attr_reader :columnsArray
  attr_reader :referredBy
    attr_reader :hasSequence
  attr_reader :primaryKey
  attr_reader :valueObjs
  attr_reader :fmethods
  attr_reader :fmethodsArray

  def initialize( name )
      @name = name
    @columns = {}
    @referredBy = []
    @columnsArray = []
    @valueObjs = {}
    @fmethods = {}
    @fmethodsArray = []
    $tables[name] = self
    m = FMethod.new(self, "findAll")
    m.ejbQL = "SELECT OBJECT(o) FROM " + name + " o "
  end

  def addColumn( column )
    @columns[column.name] = column
    @columnsArray.push(column)
  end

  def addFMethod( fmethod )
    @fmethods[fmethod.name] = fmethod
    @fmethodsArray.push(fmethod)
  end

  def addForeignKey( fkCol, fkRefTable )
```

```ruby
    pk = nil
    fkRefTable.columnsArray.each { |col|
      if col.isPrimaryKey
        pk = col
        break
      end
    }
    if !pk
      raise "ERROR:  primary key not found for table [#{fkRefTable.name}] " +
        "referenced by [#{@name}][#{fkCol.name}]"
    end
    fkCol.references = pk
    fkRefTable.referredBy.push(fkCol)
  end

  def addSequence()
    @columnsArray.each { |column|
      if column.isPrimaryKey
        if !@primaryKey
          @primaryKey = column
        end
        if column.sqlType != SQL_INTEGER
          @hasSequence = FALSE
          break
        end
        if @hasSequence
          @hasSequence = FALSE
          break
        end
        @hasSequence = TRUE
      end
    }
  end

  def getSequenceName()
    "#{@name}_#{@primaryKey.name}_seq"
  end

  def downfirstName
    first = "" << @name[0]
    rest = @name[1..@name.length]
    first.downcase + rest
  end

end

class Column

  attr_reader :table
  attr_reader :sqlName
  attr_reader :name
  attr_reader :sqlType
  attr_reader :javaType
  attr_reader :charLength
```

❷ The Column class, which represents a column in a table

```ruby
    attr_writer :charLength
    attr_reader :isUnique
    attr_writer :isUnique
    attr_reader :isPrimaryKey
    attr_writer :isPrimaryKey
    attr_reader :isNotNull
    attr_writer :isNotNull
    attr_reader :references
    attr_writer :references

  def initialize( table, name )
    @table = table
    @sqlName = name
    @name = name
    table.addColumn(self)
  end

  def expandName()
    @name = @table.downfirstName + "_" + upfirstName
  end

  def setDatatype( sqlType )
    @sqlType = sqlType
    case sqlType
      # add mappings for additional datatypes here
      when SQL_INTEGER
        @javaType = JAVA_INTEGER
      when SQL_VARCHAR
        @javaType = JAVA_STRING
      else
        raise "ERROR:  invalid datatype [#{sqlType}] for column " +
          "[#{@name}] of table [#{@table.name}]"
    end
  end

  def upfirstName()
    first = "" << @name[0]
    rest = @name[1..@name.length]
    return first.upcase + rest
  end

  def stringConverter()
    return strConverter(@javaType)
  end
end

def strConverter( javaType )
  case javaType
    when JAVA_INTEGER
      return "Integer.valueOf"
    when JAVA_STRING
      return ""
    else
      raise "ERROR:  missing stringConverter for javaType [" + javaType + "]"
```

```
    end
  end

class FMethod                    ❸ FMethod, the wrapper
  attr_reader :name                   for a facade method
  attr_reader :table
  attr_reader :params
  attr_reader :returnType
  attr_writer :returnType
  attr_reader :valueObj
  attr_writer :valueObj
  attr_reader :where
  attr_writer :where
  attr_reader :ejbQL
  attr_writer :ejbQL
  attr_reader :body
  attr_writer :body

  def initialize( table, name )
    @table = table
    @name = name
    @params = []
    @returnType = "void"
    table.addFMethod(self)
  end
end

class MethodParam                ❹ The parameter
  attr_reader :name                   for a method call
  attr_reader :javaType
  attr_writer :javaType
  attr_reader :fmethod

  def initialize( fmethod, name )
    @fmethod = fmethod
    @name = name
    fmethod.params.push(self)
  end
end

class ValueObj                   ❺ ValueObj, which represents
  attr_reader :name                   a data transfer object
  attr_reader :table
  attr_reader :columns
  attr_reader :columnsArray
  attr_reader :isExtended

  def initialize( table, name )
    @table = table
    @name = name
    @columns = {}
    @columnsArray = []
    $valueObjs[name] = self
    table.valueObjs[name] = self
```

```
      @isExtended = FALSE
    end

    def addColumn( column )
      @columns[column.name] = column
      @columnsArray.push(column)
      if column.table != table
        @isExtended = TRUE
      end
    end

    def addGetMethods()
      m = FMethod.new(@table, "get" + @name)
      m.valueObj = self
      m.returnType = @name
      p = MethodParam.new(m,@table.primaryKey.name)
      p.javaType = @table.primaryKey.javaType
      m.where = @table.name + "." + @table.primaryKey.name + " = ? "
      m = FMethod.new(@table, "getAll" + @name)
      m.valueObj = self
      m.returnType = "java.util.Collection"
    end

    def addCUDMethods()
      m = FMethod.new(@table, "add")
      m.returnType = @table.primaryKey.javaType
      p = MethodParam.new(m, "value")
      p.javaType = @name
      m = FMethod.new(@table, "update")
      p = MethodParam.new(m, "value")
      p.javaType = @name
      m = FMethod.new(@table, "delete")
      p = MethodParam.new(m, @table.primaryKey.name)
      p.javaType = @table.primaryKey.javaType
    end

  end

class SampleRow            ❻  A row of sample data

  attr_reader :table
  attr_reader :columns

  def initialize( table )
    @table = table
    @columns = []
    $sampleRows.push(self)
  end
end

class SampleColumn         ❼  A column of sample data
  attr_reader :row
  attr_reader :column
  attr_reader :value

  def initialize( row, column, value )
```

```
    @row = row
    @column = column
    @value = value
    row.columns.push(self)
  end
end
```

■

1 The `Table` class models a table that we are going to build both as SQL and as EJB entity objects. The object includes the name of the table, the columns, the sequence, the primary key, the value objects, and the methods.

2 The `Column` class models a field within a table. The `Column` object contains a reference to its table, as well as the column name, the type, the length of characters (if this is a string), and the attribute of the field, such as the unique, primary key and not null attributes.

3 The `FMethod` class represents a facade method, such as `add`, `update`, `delete`, `get`, and `getAll`.

4 `MethodParam` is a structure class that handles storing the name and type of the arguments on a method.

5 `ValueObj` models the value object that handles data transfer across the facade interface. This object contains the name of the value object as well as the table to which it links and the columns of that table.

6 `SampleRow` models a row of sample data. A row of sample data contains the table it refers to and several columns of data. Each column is modeled by a `SampleColumn` object.

7 The `SampleColumn` object represents a single sample data value. The row refers to this object's `SampleRow` object. `column` is a reference to the `Column` object, and `value` is the value of data.

C.1.3   ejbgen.rb

The ejbgen.rb file (listing C.3) is the main entry point for the generator. It uses the functions and classes defined in the reader and definition files to read the three input files, store the input in memory, and then invoke a series of templates. These templates are then used to create the content of the output files.

Listing C.3   ejbgen.rb

```
require 'rexml/document'
require 'erb/erb'                                          Shows the
                                                           simple ERb
require 'ejbgenDefs'                                        template
require 'ejbgenRead'                                    ❶  processor

  def processTemplate( templateName, outfileName )
    $stderr.print "generating #{outfileName} using #{templateName}\n"
```

```ruby
  begin
    templateFile = File.new( templateName )
    erbScript = templateFile.read
    templateFile.close
  rescue
    print "Could not open #{templateName}\n"
    exit
  end

  erb = ERb.new(erbScript)
  erbResult = erb.result

  begin
    outfile = File.open( outfileName, "w" )
    outfile.write( erbResult )
    outfile.close
  rescue
    print "Could not write to #{outfileName}\n"
    exit
  end
end

readSchema()

processTemplate(SQL_TEMPLATE, SQL_OUT_FILE)

readExtensions()

readSamples()

$tables.values.each { |table|
  $table = table
  processTemplate(ENTITY_TEMPLATE, JAVA_OUT_DIR + table.name +
"Entity.java")
  processTemplate(ENTITY_HOME_TEMPLATE, JAVA_OUT_DIR + table.name
+"EntityHome.java")
  processTemplate(ENTITY_BEAN_TEMPLATE, JAVA_OUT_DIR + table.name
+"EntityBean.java")

  table.valueObjs.values.each{ |valueObj|
    $valueObj = valueObj
    processTemplate(VALUE_TEMPLATE, JAVA_OUT_DIR + valueObj.name + ".java")
    processTemplate(LIST_JSP_TEMPLATE, JSP_OUT_DIR + valueObj.name +
"List.jsp")
  }

  processTemplate(SS_TEMPLATE, JAVA_OUT_DIR + table.name + "SS.java")
  processTemplate(SS_HOME_TEMPLATE, JAVA_OUT_DIR + table.name
+"SSHome.java")
  processTemplate(SS_BEAN_TEMPLATE, JAVA_OUT_DIR + table.name
+"SSBean.java")
  processTemplate(ADD_JSP_TEMPLATE, JSP_OUT_DIR + table.name + "Add.jsp")
  processTemplate(UPDATE_JSP_TEMPLATE, JSP_OUT_DIR + table.name +
"Update.jsp")
  processTemplate(DELETE_JSP_TEMPLATE, JSP_OUT_DIR + table.name +
"Delete.jsp")
```

Reads the template

Runs the template ERb

Outputs the result of the template

❷ **Iterates through tables**

❸ **Iterates through value objects**

```
     table.fmethodsArray.each{ |fmethod|                    ④  Iterates through
       next if !fmethod.body                                    facade methods
       $fmethod = fmethod
       processTemplate(CUSTOM_JSP_TEMPLATE,
         JSP_OUT_DIR + table.name + fmethod.name + "Custom.jsp")
     }
   }                                                        Builds the single
                                                            item deliverables  ⑤
   processTemplate(INDEX_JSP_TEMPLATE, JSP_OUT_DIR + "index.jsp")    ◁

   processTemplate(SS_FACTORY_TEMPLATE, JAVA_OUT_DIR + "SSFactory.java")

   processTemplate(EJB_JAR_TEMPLATE, XML_OUT_DIR + "ejb-jar.xml")
   processTemplate(JBOSS_XML_TEMPLATE, XML_OUT_DIR + "jboss.xml")
   processTemplate(JBOSS_CMP_TEMPLATE, XML_OUT_DIR + "jbosscmp-jdbc.xml")

   processTemplate(TESTS_TEMPLATE, TESTS_OUT_DIR + "Tests.java")
```

❶ `processTemplate` takes the filename of a template and the filename of the output file. It first reads the template, then it runs the template and writes the output to the output filename.

❷ The first loop goes over all of the tables and builds the entity and stateless session files.

❸ Next the code loops over the value objects within each table and builds all of the value object files.

❹ The last step of processing each table is to iterate over the stateless session facade methods and build JSPs for them.

❺ At the end of the process, we build the index of all the pages, the stateless session factory, the deployment descriptors, and the sample data loader.

C.2   THE ENTITY TEMPLATES

We use three entity templates. These templates create the interface, bean, and home files. The template for the home file is available on the book's web site.

C.2.1   The Entity.java.template

The template in listing C.4 is used to build the Entity objects for each table.

Listing C.4   Entity.java.template

```
// <%= $table.name %>.java

package <%= $package %>;

import javax.ejb.EJBLocalObject;
import javax.ejb.EJBException;
import <%= $package %>.*;

public interface <%= $table.name %> extends EJBLocalObject {
```

```
<% $table.columnsArray.each{ |column|
%>  public <%= column.javaType %> get<%= column.upfirstName %>() throws EJ
BException;
   public void set<%= column.upfirstName %>(<%= column.javaType %> <%= colu
mn.name %>) throws EJBException;

<%  }
%>
}
```

This is the template's output for the Book table:

```
// BookEntity.java

package gen;

import javax.ejb.EJBLocalObject;
import javax.ejb.EJBException;
import gen.*;

public interface BookEntity extends EJBLocalObject {
  public Integer getBookID() throws EJBException;
  public void setBookID(Integer bookID) throws EJBException;
  public String getTitle() throws EJBException;
  public void setTitle(String title) throws EJBException;
  public String getISBN() throws EJBException;
  public void setISBN(String ISBN) throws EJBException;
  public Integer getAuthorID() throws EJBException;
  public void setAuthorID(Integer authorID) throws EJBException;
  public Integer getPublisherID() throws EJBException;
  public void setPublisherID(Integer publisherID) throws EJBException;
  public Integer getStatus() throws EJBException;
  public void setStatus(Integer status) throws EJBException;
  public Integer getNumCopies() throws EJBException;
  public void setNumCopies(Integer numCopies) throws EJBException;

}
```

C.2.2   The EntityBean.java.template

The template in listing C.5 is used to build the beans for each of the tables.

Listing C.5   EntityBean.java.template

```
// <%= $table.name %> EntityBean.java

package <%= $package %>;

import javax.ejb.EntityBean;
import javax.ejb.EntityContext;
import javax.ejb.EJBException;
import jutil.Sequence;
import javax.naming.InitialContext;

public abstract class <%= $table.name %> implements EntityBean {
```

```
    transient private EntityContext ctx;

  public static <%= $table.name %> getHome(){
    try {
      InitialContext jndiContext = new InitialContext();
      Object ref =
        jndiContext.lookup("<%= $package %>/<%= $table.name %>");
      <%= $table.name %> home = (<%= $table.name %>)ref;
      return home;
    }catch (Exception e){
      throw new EJBException("<%= $table.name %>.getHome() failed: " + e.g
etMessage());
    }
  }

  //====================================================================
  public Integer ejbCreate(

<%  first = TRUE

  $table.columnsArray.each{ |column|
%>    <% if !first %>,<% end %><%= column.javaType %> <%= column.name %>

<%    first = FALSE
  }
%>    )
  {

<%  $table.columnsArray.each{ |column|
    if column.isPrimaryKey && !column.references && column.javaType==JAVA_
INTEGER
%>    set<%= column.upfirstName %>(Sequence.next("<%= $table.getSequenceNa
me %>"));

<%    else
%>    set<%= column.upfirstName %>(<%= column.name %>);

<%    end
  }
%>
    return null;
  }

  //====================================================================
  public void ejbPostCreate(

<%  first = TRUE

  $table.columnsArray.each{ |column|
%>    <% if !first %>,<% end %><%= column.javaType %> <%= column.name %>

<%    first = FALSE
  }
%>    )
  {
    // set CMR fields here
  }
```

```
    //=================================================================
<%  $table.columnsArray.each{ |column|
%>   public abstract <%= column.javaType %> get<%= column.upfirstName %>();
    public abstract void set<%= column.upfirstName %>(<%= column.javaType %>
 <%= column.name %>);
<%  }
%>
    public void ejbRemove() {}
    public void ejbActivate() {}
    public void ejbPassivate() {}
    public void setEntityContext(EntityContext ctx) { this.ctx = ctx; }
    public void unsetEntityContext() { this.ctx = null; }
    public void ejbLoad() {}
    public void ejbStore() {}
}
```

This is the bean created by the template for the Book table:

```
// BookEntityBean.java

package gen;

import javax.ejb.EntityBean;
import javax.ejb.EntityContext;
import javax.ejb.EJBException;
import jutil.Sequence;
import javax.naming.InitialContext;

public abstract class BookEntityBean implements EntityBean {
  transient private EntityContext ctx;

  public static BookEntityHome getHome(){
    try {
      InitialContext jndiContext = new InitialContext();
      Object ref =
        jndiContext.lookup("gen/BookEntity");
      BookEntityHome home = (BookEntityHome)ref;
      return home;
    }catch (Exception e){
      throw new EJBException("BookEntityBean.getHome() failed: " +
e.getMessage());
    }
  }

  //=================================================================
  public Integer ejbCreate(
    Integer bookID
    ,String title
    ,String ISBN
    ,Integer authorID
    ,Integer publisherID
    ,Integer status
    ,Integer numCopies
```

```
      )
    {
      setBookID(Sequence.next("Book_bookID_seq"));
      setTitle(title);
      setISBN(ISBN);
      setAuthorID(authorID);
      setPublisherID(publisherID);
      setStatus(status);
      setNumCopies(numCopies);

      return null;
    }

    //=====================================================================
    public void ejbPostCreate(
      Integer bookID
      ,String title
      ,String ISBN
      ,Integer authorID
      ,Integer publisherID
      ,Integer status
      ,Integer numCopies
      )
    {
      // set CMR fields here
    }

    //=====================================================================
    public abstract Integer getBookID();
    public abstract void setBookID(Integer bookID);
    public abstract String getTitle();
    public abstract void setTitle(String title);
    public abstract String getISBN();
    public abstract void setISBN(String ISBN);
    public abstract Integer getAuthorID();
    public abstract void setAuthorID(Integer authorID);
    public abstract Integer getPublisherID();
    public abstract void setPublisherID(Integer publisherID);
    public abstract Integer getStatus();
    public abstract void setStatus(Integer status);
    public abstract Integer getNumCopies();
    public abstract void setNumCopies(Integer numCopies);

    public void ejbRemove() {}
    public void ejbActivate() {}
    public void ejbPassivate() {}
    public void setEntityContext(EntityContext ctx) { this.ctx = ctx; }
    public void unsetEntityContext() { this.ctx = null; }
    public void ejbLoad() {}
    public void ejbStore() {}
}
```

C.3 THE JSP TEMPLATES

The EJB generator also builds JSP files to test the generated classes. This section shows examples of only one of the JSP templates; the full collection is available on www.code-generationinaction.com.

C.3.1 The Add.jsp.template

The Add template (listing C.6) builds JSP pages that use the beans to add new records to the database.

Listing C.6   Add.jsp.template

```
<%%@ page language="java" %%>
<%%@ page import="<%= $package %>.*" %%>
<%%@ page import="java.util.*" %%>

<%%
  <%= $table.name %> ssb =
    SSFactory.create<%= $table.name %>();

  if(request.getParameter("doSubmit") != null){
    <%= $table.name %> val = new <%= $table.name %>();

<%  $table.columnsArray.each{ |column|
    next if column.isPrimaryKey
%>    val.set<%= column.upfirstName %>(request.getParameter("<%= column.na
me %>").equals("") ? null : <%= column.stringConverter %>(request.getParam
eter("<%= column.name %>")));

<%  }
%>
    ssb.add(val);
    ssb.remove();
%%>
    <jsp:forward page="<%= $table.name %>.jsp" />
<%%
  }
%%>
<head>
<title>Add <%= $table.name %></title>
</head>
<body>
<h1>Add <%= $table.name %></h1>
<form>
<table border=0>

<%  $table.columnsArray.each{ |column|
%><tr>
  <td><%= column.name %></td>
  <td>

<%    if column.isPrimaryKey
%>     
```

```
<%    else
%>  <input type=text name=<%= column.name %>>
<%    end
%>
  <td>
  <%= column.sqlType %>
  <% if column.charLength %>(<%= column.charLength %>)<% end %>
  <% if column.isUnique %><% end %>
  <% if column.isNotNull %> null<% end %>
  <% if column.references %> <a href="<%= column.references.table.name %>.
jsp"><%= column.references.table.name %></a><% end %>
  </td>
</tr>

<%  }
%>
</table>
<input type="submit" name="doSubmit">
</form>
</body>
</html>
<%%
  ssb.remove();
%%>
```

Figure C.1 shows the output of the Add template for the Book table. We kept the HTML simple so that the example would be short, but keep in mind that these are just test pages. The production pages are built by a different mechanism, with different mappings between pages and database entities.

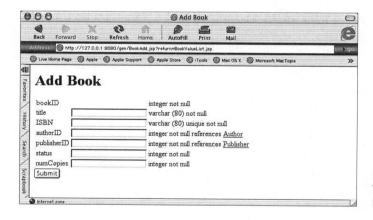

**Figure C.1
The generated Add
Book test page**

C.4 THE DEPLOYMENT DESCRIPTOR TEMPLATES

To actually run the beans on the application server, you need several deployment descriptors. In this section, we show one of the templates for the deployment descriptors. The others are in the complete code package available on the www.codegenerationinaction.com web site.

C.4.1 jboss.xml.template

Listing C.7 contains the template for the JBoss descriptor file. The descriptor contains references to each of the session and entity classes in the compiled JAR file.

Listing C.7 jboss.xml.template

```
<?xml version="1.0" encoding="UTF-8"?>
<jboss>
  <enterprise-beans>

<%  $tables.values.each { |table|
%>
    <entity>
      <ejb-name><%= table.name %></ejb-name>
      <local-jndi-name><%= $package %>/<%= table.name %></local-jndi-name>
    </entity>
    <session>
      <ejb-name><%= table.name %></ejb-name>
      <jndi-name><%= $package %>/<%= table.name %></jndi-name>
    </session>

<%  }
%>
  </enterprise-beans>
</jboss>
```

The output of the template JBoss deployment descriptor template is shown here:

```
<?xml version="1.0" encoding="UTF-8"?>
<jboss>
  <enterprise-beans>

    <entity>
      <ejb-name>BookEntityEJB</ejb-name>
      <local-jndi-name>gen/BookEntity</local-jndi-name>
    </entity>
    <session>
      <ejb-name>BookSS</ejb-name>
      <jndi-name>gen/BookSS</jndi-name>
    </session>

    <entity>
      <ejb-name>AuthorEntityEJB</ejb-name>
      <local-jndi-name>gen/AuthorEntity</local-jndi-name>
    </entity>
    <session>
```

```
      <ejb-name>AuthorSS</ejb-name>
      <jndi-name>gen/AuthorSS</jndi-name>
    </session>

    <entity>
      <ejb-name>PublisherEntityEJB</ejb-name>
      <local-jndi-name>gen/PublisherEntity</local-jndi-name>
    </entity>
    <session>
      <ejb-name>PublisherSS</ejb-name>
      <jndi-name>gen/PublisherSS</jndi-name>
    </session>

  </enterprise-beans>
</jboss>
```

C.5   THE SQL TEMPLATE

The generator creates SQL for the tables, sequence generators, and relationships within
the database. The template in the case study generator is designed to build SQL for the
Postgres database. Other database engines require slightly altered syntax.

C.5.1   The tables.sql.template

The template for building PostgreSQL code is shown in listing C.8.

Listing C.8   tables.sql.template

```
<%
  $tables.values.each{ |table|
%>
  drop table <%= table.name %>;

  create table <%= table.name %> (

<%    first = TRUE

    table.columnsArray.each{ |column|
%>   <% if !first %>,<% end %><%= column.name %> <%= column.sqlType %><%
if column.charLength %>(<%= column.charLength %>)<% end %> <% if column.is
NotNull %> null <% end %><% if column.isPrimaryKey %> key <% end %><% if c
olumn.isUnique %> <% end %>

<%       first = FALSE
    }
%>  );

  grant all on <%= table.name %> to public;

<%    if table.hasSequence
%>
  drop sequence <%= table.getSequenceName %>;

  create sequence <%= table.getSequenceName %> start 100;
```

```
      grant all on <%= table.getSequenceName %> to public;
<%    end
  }

  $tables.values.each { |table|
    table.columnsArray.each{ |column|
      next if !column.references
%>
  alter table <%= table.name %>
    add constraint <%= table.name %>_<%= column.name %>
    foreign key (<%= column.name %>)
    references <%= column.references.table.name %> (<%= column.references.
name %>);

<%    }
  }
%>
```

Here's the output of the SQL template:

```
drop table Book;

create table Book (
  bookID integer not null primary key
  ,title varchar(80) not null
  ,ISBN varchar(80) not null unique
  ,authorID integer not null
  ,publisherID integer not null
  ,status integer not null
  ,numCopies integer not null
);

grant all on Book to public;

drop sequence Book_bookID_seq;

create sequence Book_bookID_seq start 100;

grant all on Book_bookID_seq to public;

drop table Author;

create table Author (
  authorID integer not null primary key
  ,name varchar(80) not null unique
  ,penName varchar(80)
);

grant all on Author to public;

drop sequence Author_authorID_seq;

create sequence Author_authorID_seq start 100;

grant all on Author_authorID_seq to public;

drop table Publisher;
```

```
create table Publisher (
  publisherID integer not null primary key
  ,name varchar(80) not null unique
);

grant all on Publisher to public;

drop sequence Publisher_publisherID_seq;

create sequence Publisher_publisherID_seq start 100;

grant all on Publisher_publisherID_seq to public;

alter table Book
  add constraint Book_authorID
  foreign key (authorID)
  references Author (authorID);

alter table Book
  add constraint Book_publisherID
  foreign key (publisherID)
  references Publisher (publisherID);
```

All of the other files required for the EJBGen generator are included on the source code package available at www.codegenerationinaction.com.

APPENDIX D

Integrating code generation into your IDE

Writing a code generator can be difficult—but convincing your fellow engineers to use the generator can be even more difficult. The key to successfully deploying your generator is to make it as *simple* as possible to use. One technique is to use it to integrate the code generator into the tool you utilize every day: your integrated development environment (IDE).

In this appendix, we discuss how you can integrate tools into a number of popular IDEs.

D.1 INTEGRATION METHODS

Two methods are fairly common across all IDEs: *external tool invocation* and *filtering*. In this section, we describe these methods in detail.

D.1.1 External tool invocation

In this model, the editor runs an external command line with various parameters. These parameters can include the name of the file currently being edited, among other options.

The external tool can be any command-line executable program, which includes Ruby scripts. The tool may or may not update the files that are currently being edited. Most of the IDEs either scan the current files after the tool exits or present an option for doing the scan. Figure D.1 shows the relationship between an external tool and an IDE.

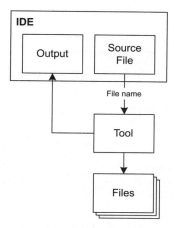

Figure D.1
The external tool invocation method

The tool is invoked by the IDE with the filename (or any other arguments) and it updates a number of files. Anything the tool prints to standard output is stored in the output window in the IDE, where the compiler messages are normally shown.

If the tool alters the source file, the IDE picks up the new version in the editor, as shown in figure D.2.

The external tool model is compatible with all of the generator models described in this book.

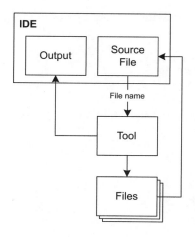

Figure D.2
The relationship between an external tool and an IDE where the input file is changed

An example Ruby tool

In this section, we show you how to define an external tool. We use the mymunger.rb Ruby file as the code for the tool. This simple script is shown here:

```
print "#{ARGV[0]}(1) : munged\n";     <── Prints information for the log

text = ""
File.open( ARGV[0] ) { |fh|            Reads the
  text = fh.read                       input file
}

File.open( ARGV[0], "w" ) { |fh|       Replaces the
  fh.print "Hi there!\n"               input file with
  fh.print text                        some new text
}
```

This is a simple Hello World–style code munger. It takes the original file and adds `Hi there!` as the first line of the file. This test should be enough to verify that your external tool is working properly, and it won't damage any files beyond repair.

D.1.2 Filtering

The second model is a filter that takes the contents you've selected in the editor and alters and replaces the text. This flow is shown in figure D.3.

This pattern is ideal for code munger scripts because the script gets its input from the IDE and simply needs to print new output to change the text within the selection.

An example Ruby filter

Let's use the myfilter.rb Ruby script to demonstrate the filter processing flow. The code for this script is shown here:

```
$stdin.each_line { |line|      Adds C++ style
  print "// #{line}"           comments to
}                              each line
```

This filter comments out the code coming in through standard output by adding C++ style comments to the beginning of each line.

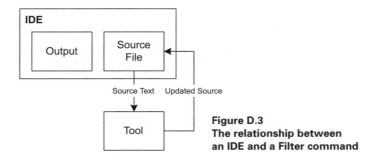

Figure D.3
The relationship between
an IDE and a Filter command

D.2 MSDEV FROM MICROSOFT

Microsoft's Developer Studio (MSDEV) supports external tool invocation natively and filtering through an extension. In this section, we illustrate both tool invocation and filtering.

D.2.1 External tool invocation

To begin, you select the Customize command from the Tools menu. This opens the dialog box shown in figure D.4, open to the Tools tab. As you can see, we created a new tool called "My Ruby Munger," which runs Ruby with the specified script file and on the current file. We specified the current file using $(FilePath). This dialog box also lets you specify the directory wherein you want the tool to run.

As you can see in figure D.4, we also enabled the Use Output Window check-box because we want MSDEV to put any of the tool's standard output into the output window.

We can now run the tool by choosing My Ruby Munger from the Tools menu.

D.2.2 Filtering

The MSDEV IDE does not have any support for filtering natively, but Microsoft does supply the code for a filter add-in with the MSDN (Microsoft Developers Network). Once you have compiled the add-in, add it to your development environment by issuing the Customize command from the Tools menu. You'll see the dialog box shown in figure D.5.

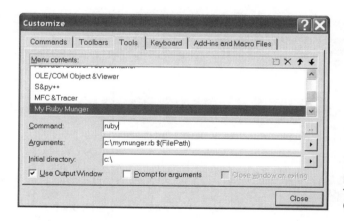

Figure D.4
The Tools tab of MSDEV's
Customize dialog box

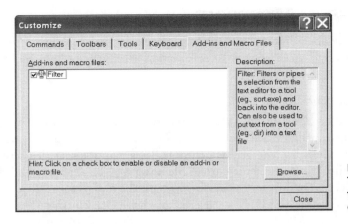

Figure D.5
The Add-ins and Macro Files tab of MSDEV's Customize dialog box

 You add the filter by using the Browse button on the Add-ins and Macro Files tab and choosing the filter.dll file that you compiled from the sample source code on the MSDN. Once you click the Close button, the Filter button appears on a floating toolbar by itself, as shown in figure D.6.

Figure D.6
The Filter toolbar button

Next, select some text in the editor and press the Filter button. You'll see the dialog box shown in figure D.7.

Here you can specify the name of the command line you want to run as the filter. (As you can see, we entered *ruby \myfilter.rb*.) Then, simply click the Apply button to run the filter on the current selection and replace it with the output from the filter.

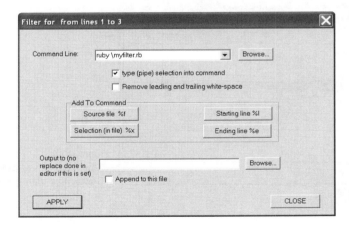

Figure D.7
The main dialog box for the Filter plug-in

D.3   ECLIPSE FROM IBM

IBM's Eclipse supports the external tool integration model only. In this section, we show you how to set up external tool invocation in Eclipse.

D.3.1   External tool invocation

The engineers at IBM must have spent a lot of time on external tools because they offer a lot of flexibility support for external tools. We only use a simple subset of that support with the Ruby code munger.

First, select the External Tools command from the Run menu to open the dialog box shown in figure D.8.

Next, select the Program category, and then click New to define a new tool. Type a name for your tool—in this case, use *My Ruby Munger*. At this point, specify the absolute path of the command that you want to run (e.g., c:\ruby\bin\ruby.exe), as well as the working directory and the arguments. The ${resource_loc} item in the arguments indicates where the pathname for the file you are currently editing should go in the command line. You also need to disable the option Run Tool In Background.

To ensure that the files are updated after the tool finishes running, click the Refresh tab and select the Refresh Resources After Running Tool checkbox, as shown in figure D.9.

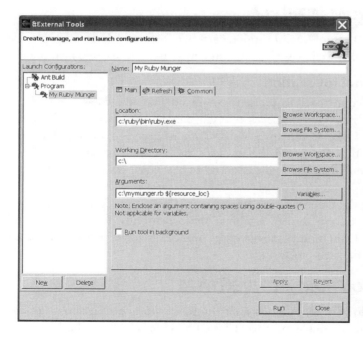

**Figure D.8
The External Tools
dialog box in Eclipse**

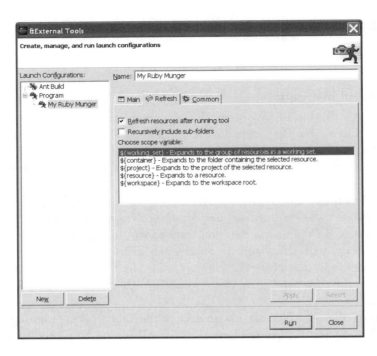

Figure D.9
The Refresh tab of the
External Tools dialog
box in Eclipse

D.4 IDEA FROM INTELLIJ

The IDEA IDE from IntelliJ supports external tools only; it does not provide a filtering capability. In this section, we'll show you how to use external tool invocation with IDEA.

D.4.1 External tool invocation

Start by selecting the IDE Options command from the Tools menu. Then select the External Tools category and click the Add button. This opens the dialog box shown in figure D.10. Once again, we used *My Ruby Munger* as the name for our tool. Then, we specified that Ruby is to be invoked with the first parameter as the script name and the second parameter as the $FilePath$, which is the path to the file we are currently editing.

Selecting the Open Console option tells IDEA to put any output generated by the tool into an output display. Enabling the Synchronize Files After Execution option ensures that if you modify the file in the munger it will be reloaded into the editor once the tool has finished processing.

D.5 KOMODO FROM ACTIVESTATE

The Komodo IDE for Windows and Linux supports both external tool and filtering models through a single interface. Let's take a look at both methods.

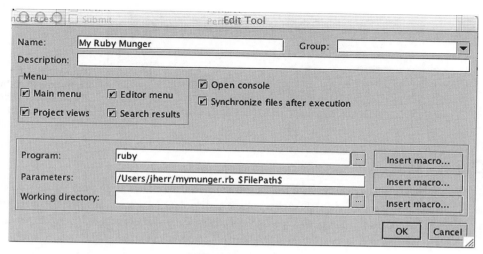

Figure D.10 The Add/Edit Tool dialog box in IDEA

D.5.1 External tool invocation

In Komodo, begin by pressing Ctrl+R or choosing Run Command from the Tools menu. You'll see the dialog box shown in figure D.11. As you can see, we have specified the `ruby` command (with the `%F` parameter) that will insert the pathname of the current file.

D.5.2 Filtering

The filtering model is also supported through the Run Command dialog box, shown in figure D.12. You enter the `ruby` command in the Run box. Then, select Insert Output and Pass Selection As Input to create the filter.

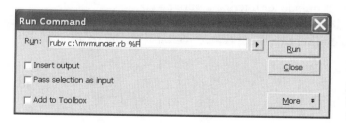

Figure D.11
Komodo's Run Command
dialog box

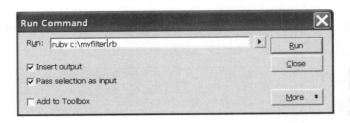

Figure D.12
Komodo's Run Command dialog box with the filter settings spcified

D.6   *VIM*

Vi-Improved (vim) is a fully customizable free editor that runs on all major platforms. Vim does not directly support external tools, though it does provide a robust scripting mechanism that allows you to create new commands that invoke external processes. Writing these commands is a simple process. For more information, check the Vim documentation at www.vim.org/docs.php.

D.6.1   Filtering

Vim allows for easy text filtering using an external command. To run an external filter, type a colon to get to the command prompt and then type a command using the following syntax:

```
[range]![command]
```

This command runs the entire current file through the Unix `sort` command:

```
%!sort
```

D.7   *EMACS*

Emacs is an editor of legendary power and complexity. If you are a long-term Emacs user, you will have your own workflow for the external command integration path. Let's look at the technique for filtering a buffer.

Begin by marking the region you wish to filter. Then, press Ctrl+U+Esc to run a shell command and replace the specified region with the results.

APPENDIX E

Simple templating

Text templating is a critical utility when developing a generator. However, you don't always need the most complex and feature-rich template tool. In this appendix, we examine some very simple text-template code in Ruby.

E.1 STRING FORMATTING

Ruby has its own text templating built in. It uses the double-quote string format, as shown in the following code:

```
name = "Jack"                          Initializes the
cost = "$20"                           data variables

str = "Dear #{name}, You owe us #{cost}"        ❶ Runs the formatting

print "#{str}\n"        ⟵ Prints the output
```

❶ Ruby supports the #{expression} syntax in the double-quoted string and specifies the results as text. In this case, the str variable is equal to "Dear Jack, You owe us $20" because we inserted the name and cost values inserted in the #{expression} sections.

E.1.1 Delayed string formatting

If you want to store a string format in a file, you have to force Ruby to evaluate it using the eval keyword, as shown here:

```
name = "Jack"
cost="$20"

format = 'Dear #{name}, You owe us #{cost}'        Formats as if it were
                                                    read from a file
```

323

```
str = eval( '"'+format+'"' )

print
"#{str}\n"
```

❶ Runs the string replacement code

❶ By using `eval` you force Ruby to run the `#{expression}` replacement syntax. You must add the quotes around the format string to properly evaluate the string. If you don't include the quotes, the string is evaluated as a Ruby statement.

E.2   REGULAR EXPRESSION TEMPLATES

Ruby is powerful enough to create a simple text-template syntax in a small amount of code with the use of regular expressions. This is demonstrated in the code shown here:

```
name = 'Jack'
cost = '$20'

template = 'Dear <name>, You owe us <cost>'    ⟵ Shows the template string

output = template    ⟵ Makes a copy of the template

output.gsub!( /<(.*?)>/ ) {
  eval( $1 )
}                                    ❶ Replaces the <variable> sections
                                       with the contents of the variable

print "#{output}\n"
```

❶ This code uses the global substitution regular expression function to replace all of the `<variable>` sections with the variable's value. Each time a `<variable>` item is found, the block is evaluated. The name of the variable is in `$1` because of the grouping in the regular expression. Using the `eval` keyword, you get the value of the variable with the name specified by `$1`. The result of the evaluation is returned from the block, which substitutes the `<variable>` text with the value from the block.

E.2.1   Regular expression templates with ERb syntax

The following code shows the same technique but uses the ERb syntax for expression replacement:

```
name = 'Jack'
cost = '$20'

template = 'Dear <%= name %>, You owe us <%= cost %>'    ⟵ New
                                                            template

output = template
output.gsub!( /<%=\s*(.*?)\s*%>/ ) {    ⟵ Updated regular expression
  eval( $1 )
}

print "#{output}\n"
```

APPENDIX F

Patterns for regular expressions

This book demonstrates generators written using Ruby. We understand that for a number of reasons Ruby may not be your language of choice for writing a generator. Because regular expressions are such an instrumental part of code generation, this appendix shows how you can use regular expressions in a variety of languages.

F.1   THE EXAMPLES

Each language implements up to four of the following examples:

- *Checking a string*—In this example, we check the string `file.txt` to see if it has the .txt extension.

- *Reading key/value pairs*—This example reads the key and value pairs from the string `a:1;b:2;c:3`. The correct output is a = 1, b = 2, and c = 3.

- *Replacing tabs with commas*—This example turns the string `jack\td\ther-rington` into `jack,d,herrington`.

- *Replacing values in a format string*—This example parses the format string `"Dear <name>, You owe us <cost>"`, where `<name>` is Jack and `cost` is `$20`. The correct output is `Dear Jack, You owe us $20`.

We believe these four examples show a set of use cases sufficient for you to get a good feel for how each language handles regular expressions.

F.1.1 Ruby

The following code sections show the examples implemented in Ruby.

Checking a string

```ruby
if ( "file.txt" =~ /[.]txt$/ )        <— Checks string for .txt at the end
  print "File name matched\n"
else
  print "File name did not match\n"
end
```

Reading key/value pairs

```ruby
"a=1;b=2;c=3;".scan( /(.*?)=(.*?);/ ) { |key,value|    <— Scans a string
                                                          for the key/
  print "#{key} : #{value}\n"          <— Prints the pairs   value pairs

}
```

Replacing tabs with commas

```ruby
str = "jack\td\therrington".gsub( /\t/, "," )   <— Replace tabs
print "#{str}\n"                                    with commas
```

Replacing values in a format string

```ruby
str = "Dear <name>, You owe us <cost>"    <— Outputs format

str.gsub!( /<(.*?)>/ ) {                  <— Replaces <keys> with their values

  if ( $1 == "name" )
      "jack"
  elsif ( $1 == "cost" )      Returns the
      "$20"                   value of the
  else                        key
      ""

  end

}
print "#{str}\n"
```

F.1.2 Python

The following code sections show the examples implemented in Python.

Checking a string

```python
import re

str = "field.txt"                         <— Creates the example filename

if re.search( ".txt$", str ):             <— Checks the filename
                                             against the expression
        print "File name matched\n"
else:
        print "File name doesn't match\n"
```

```
import re

myre = re.compile( "(.*?)=(.*?);" )          ⟵  Creates the expression object

for item in myre.findall( "a=1;b=2;c=3;" ):      Finds and prints key/value
        print item[0], ":", item[1]              pairs in the string
```

Replacing tabs with commas

```
import re

print re.sub( "\t", ",", "jack\td\therrington" )   ⟵  Replaces tabs
                                                        with commas
```

Replacing values in a format string

```
import re

def rep( match ):
        name = match.group( 1 )
        if ( name == "name" ):          Returns the
                return "Jack"           value of any
        if ( name == "cost" ):          key
                return "$20"
        return ""                                    Replaces key
                                                     items in the
                                                     string using
                                                     rep()
print re.sub( "<(.*?)>", rep, "Dear <name>, You owe us <cost>." )   ⟵
```

F.1.3 Perl

The following code sections show the examples implemented in Perl.

Checking a string

```
if ( "file.txt" =~ /[.]txt$/ )      ⟵┐  Checks the file name against
{                                        the regular expression
  print "File name matched\n"
}
else
{
  print "File name did not match\n"
}
```

Reading key/value pairs

```
$input = "a=1;b=2;c=3;";        ⟵  Creates the data string
while( $input =~ /(.*?)=(.*?);/g )       ⟵┐  Runs the expression
{                                             across the data string
  print "$1 : $2\n";        ⟵┐
}                             Prints any
                             groups it finds
```

```
$str = "jack\td\therrington";
$str =~ s/\t/,/g;              <-- Replaces tabs with commas
print "$str\n";
```

```
sub value($)
{                              Returns the value
  my ( $key ) = @_;            for a particular key
  return 'Jack' if ( $key eq 'name' );
  return '$20' if ( $key eq 'cost' );
  return '';
}

$str = 'Dear <name>, You owe us <cost>';

$str =~ s/<(.*?)>/value($1)/eg;      <-- Scans and replaces
                                         keys with value()
print "$str\n";
```

F.1.4 Java

The following code sections show the examples implemented in Java. These examples use the java.util.regex library from the 1.4 release of the JDK.

```
import java.util.regex.*;

class Regex1
{
  public static void main( String args[] )
  {
    Pattern pat = Pattern.compile( "\\S*.txt$" );    <-- Creates the
                                                         expression object
    Matcher mat = pat.matcher( "file.txt" );         <-- Runs the object
    if ( mat.matches() ) {          <-- Checks for matches   against the string
      System.out.println( "File matches" );
    } else {
      System.out.println( "File does not match" );
    }
  }
}
```

```
import java.util.regex.*;

class Regex2
{
  public static void main( String args[] )
  {                                                        Creates the
                                                           expression object
    Pattern pat = Pattern.compile( "(.*?)=(.*?);" );  <-- Runs the object
    Matcher mat = pat.matcher( "a=1;b=2;c=3;" );      <-- against the string
```

```
     while( mat.find() )
     {
       System.out.println( mat.group(1) + " : " + mat.group( 2 ) );   ⟵
     }
   }
}
```
                                                                        Prints the
                                                                        groups

Replacing tabs with commas

```
import java.util.regex.*;

class Regex3
{
  public static void main( String args[] )
  {
    String out = new String( "jack\td\therrington" );   ⟵ Original string

    Pattern pat = Pattern.compile( "\\t" );   ⟵ Expression object

    out = (pat.matcher( out )).replaceAll( "," );   ⟵ Code that replaces
                                                       tabs with commas
    System.out.println( out );
  }
}
```

Replacing values in a format string

```
import java.util.regex.*;

class Regex4
{                                              Contains the
  public static void main( String args[] )    original string
  {
    String str = new String( "Dear <name>, You owe us <cost>" );   ⟵

    Pattern pat = Pattern.compile( "<(.*?)>" );   ⟵ Creates the
    Matcher mat = pat.matcher( str );      ⟵ Runs the   expression object
                                              initial match
    while( mat.find() )
    {
      String key = mat.group(1);

      if ( key.compareTo( "name" ) == 0 )
        str = mat.replaceFirst( "jack" );
      else if ( key.compareTo( "cost" ) == 0 )   Replaces the
        str = mat.replaceFirst( "\\$20" );        found group
      else
        str = mat.replaceFirst( "" );

      mat = pat.matcher( str );   ⟵ Reruns the match
    }

    System.out.println( str );
  }
}
```

F.1.5   C#

The following code sections show the examples implemented in C#.

Checking a string

```csharp
using System;
using System.Text.RegularExpressions;

class Regex1
{
  static void Main()
  {
    Regex r = new Regex( "[.]txt$" );                    ⟵┐ Creates the
                                                            expression object
    if ( r.Match( "file.txt" ).Success ) {           ⟵┐ Checks the object
      Console.WriteLine( "File name matched" );          against the string
    } else {
      Console.WriteLine( "File name did not match" );
    }
  }
}
```

Reading key/value pairs

```csharp
using System;
using System.Text.RegularExpressions;

class Regex2
{
  static void Main()
  {
    Regex r = new Regex( "(?<key>.*?)=(?<value>.*?);" );   ⟵ Creates the
                                                              expression
                                                              object
    MatchCollection matches = r.Matches( "a=1;b=2;c=3;" );  ⟵ Runs the
                                                              expression
    foreach ( Match match in matches )    ⟵┐ Loops through   against the
    {                                        matches found   string
      Console.WriteLine(
        match.Groups["key"] + " : " + match.Groups["value"]   Prints out key
      );                                                       and value groups
    }
  }
}
```

Replacing tabs with commas

```csharp
using System;
using System.Text.RegularExpressions;

class Regex3
{
  static void Main()
  {
```

```
        Regex r = new Regex( "\t" );          ←—  Creates the expression object
        String str = r.Replace( "jack\td\therrington", "," );    ←┐ Replaces tabs
        Console.WriteLine( str );                                  ┘ with commas
    }
}
```

Replacing values in a format string

```
using System;
using System.Text.RegularExpressions;

class Regex4
{
  public static String myEval( Match mat )                    Is called each time a
  {                                                           match is found; returns
    if ( mat.Groups[ "key" ].ToString() == "name" )          value inserted into text
      return "Jack";

    if ( mat.Groups[ "key" ].ToString() == "cost" )
      return "$20";

    return "";
  }

  static void Main()
  {                                                        Builds the regular
    Regex r = new Regex( "<(?<key>.*?)>" );      ←—┘       expression object

    String str = r.Replace(       ←—  Replaces keys dynamically
                    "Dear <name>, You owe us <cost>",
                    new MatchEvaluator( myEval ) );

    Console.WriteLine( str );
  }
}
```

F.1.6   C

The following code sections show two of the four examples implemented in C. We excluded the substitution examples because they were too large. This code uses the Perl Compatible Regular Expression library (`pcre`).

Checking a string

```
#include <stdio.h>
#include <pcre.h>

int main( int argc, char *argv[] )
{
  pcre *re;
  const char *error;
  int erroffset, rc, ovector[30];                          Compiles the
  char *str = "file.txt";                                  expression

  re = pcre_compile( "[.]txt$", 0, &error, &erroffset, NULL );    ←—┘
```

```
  rc = pcre_exec( re, NULL, str, strlen(str),        │ Runs the expression
     0, 0, ovector, sizeof(ovector)/sizeof(ovector[0]) );   │ against the text

  if ( rc > 0 )        <— Checks the result
    printf( "File name matches\n" );
  else
    printf( "File name does not match\n" );
  return 0;
}
```

Reading key/value pairs

```
#include <stdio.h>
#include <pcre.h>

int main( int argc, char *argv[] )
{
  pcre *re;
  const char *error;
  int erroffset, rc, ovector[30], start;
  char *str = "a=1;b=2;c=3;", *totalStr, *key, *value;

  re = pcre_compile( "(.*?)=(.*?);", 0, &error, &erroffset, NULL );   <—┐
                                                                    Compiles the
  start = 0;                                                         expression
  while ( 1 )
  {
    rc = pcre_exec( re, NULL, str, strlen(str),          │ Runs the
      start, 0, ovector, sizeof(ovector)/sizeof(ovector[0]) );   │ expression
                                                          │ on the text
    if ( rc < 1 ) break;

    totalStr = malloc( 255 );
    pcre_copy_substring( str, ovector, rc, 0, totalStr, 255 );   <—┐
    start += strlen( totalStr );                            Gets the full
                                                            found string
    key = malloc( 255 );
    pcre_copy_substring( str, ovector, rc, 1, key, 255 );    <—┐ Gets the
                                                              first group
    value = malloc( 255 );
    pcre_copy_substring( str, ovector, rc, 2, value, 255 );  <—┐ Get the
                                                              second group
    printf( "%s : %s\n", key, value );

    free( totalStr );
    free( key );
    free( value );
  }

  return 0;
}
```

index

C++ 14, 60
  #define 62
  as a generator 41
  DLL wrappers 266
  embedded
    documentation 138
  external language
    wrapper 268
  generating 95
  generating lookup tables 273
  generating RPC stubs 231
  lookup functions 271
  maintaining header files 264
  RPC mapping libraries 232
  unit testing 157
C++ language scanner
  CPPLanguageScanner 56
  LanguageClass 57
Castor 137
class implementation files 5
Class Wizard 124
ClassCreator 266
CMP 199
CMR 199
code generation 3, 8
  abstraction 15
  advantages 6
  agile development 12
  at its best 25
  building base classes 73
  building schema 8
  buy/build decision 23, 24
  C preprocessor 27
  cascading 10
  categorization 29
  code munger 29
  common 27
  comparison to hand-
    coding 6, 8
  compilers 27
  concerns 35
  consistency 15

database layer and business
  logic 8
debugging generated code 35
design decisions 16
design stability 25
development process 23
editing output code 35
engineering benefits 16
for code compliance 62
for code indices 62
for data marshalling 31
for desktop interface 99
for documentation 29
for inline SQL 30
for internationalization 62
for resource identifier
  usage 62
for unit tests 31
for user interface 31
for variable catalogues 62
for web forms 99
full domain language 33
infrastructure 19
initial case study 15
inline code expander 30
languages 40
maintenance 26
management benefits 17
managing change 12
mass changes 8, 15
mixed code 30
model driven 5
off the shelf 3
open source 23
overhead 25
partial class 31
productivity 7, 15
quality 8, 15
schedule impact 10
single point of knowledge 15
skills 38
sourcecode control 19

templates 16
tier generation 32
top ten rules 25
unit tests 8, 11
warnings 26
web robots 11
workflow 34
code generators 5
code munger
  design 29, 77
  developing templates 77
  development 77
  from a directory 63
  from a single file 63
  from standard input 63
  parsing input 77
  possible uses 62
CodeCharge 126, 229
compatibility layer 8
concerns 35
  database access 195
  embedded SQL 161
  general 35
  inflexiblity 37
  overwriting comments 36
  team acceptance 36
  unit tests 141
  unwillingness to change 35
  web services layer 232
configuration files
  firewall 269
consistency 16
cookies 154
CppUnit 157
CsUnit 158
CSV 71, 173–174, 189
CSV file i/o
  generating 173
cultural issues 26
customization 9
Cygwin 40

D

data access layer
  generation 32
  generation tools 229
data adapter generator 186
  architecture 186
  process flow 187
  role 186
data handling 31
  binary file i/o 187
  case study 173
  data adapter 186
database access 190
  ASP 215
  ASP.NET 218
  C# 218
  case study 199
  concerns 195
  from JavaDoc 227
  generation design tips 228
  JDBC 212
  Perl 220
  PHP 223
  terminology 193
  tools 194
  working with other
    generators 194
  XDoclet 227
database access classes 4–5, 7
database access layer 4, 7
database generation
  abstraction 191
  bad application
    semantics 195
  bad SQL 196
  benefits 191
  database 193
  database complexity 196
  database operation 193
  development cost 197
  entity 193
  field 193
  field definition 193
  for client/server 198
  for generic data storage 198

foreign key 193
  joy of coding 196
  nomenclature 193
  out of control code 195
  prerequisite skills 197
  primary key 193
  productivity benefits 191
  query 193
  query result 193
  relationship 193
  repetitive code 191
  row 193
  schema 193
  schema definition 193
  table 193
  table definition 10, 193
  transaction 193
  workflow 198
  working with other
    generators 194
database wizards 194
DataFactory 158
DataVision 263
DeKlarit 220
deployment descriptors 5
design time 15
development
  agile 17
development tools 20
Dialog Wizard 121
Dijkstra, Edsger 143
DLL wrapper generator 266
  architecture 267
  process flow 267
  role 267
  tools 268
DLLs
  generating wrappers 266
DocBook 137
Doclet 59, 137
  API 59, 95, 137
  CastorDoclet 137
  DocBookDoclet 137
  for code generation 137
  for DocBook 137

for HTML 137
  for XML 137
  JELDoclet 137
  JUnitDoclet 137
  XDoclet 137
documentation
  architectural 21
  case study 129
  end user 21
  generation 29
  maintenance 129
Doxygen 95, 127, 138
DTD 39

E

ecpg 171
EJB 140, 192
  books 211
  classes 5
  deployment issues 6
  generating 199
  performance issues 6
  session beans 6
EJB generation
  access layer architecture 199
  architecture 203
  case study 199
  deployment descriptors 202,
    204
  EJB options 199
  EJBs 204
  entities 200
  extensions 207
  implementation 209
  process flow 205
  resources 211
  role 202
  sample data 205
  sample data definition 208
  schema 200
  schema definition 206
  SQL 204
  system tests 210
  test JSPs 204
  tools 212

PHPUnit 158
PL/SQL 192
POD 127
POJO 212, 260
Poseidon 227
Postgres language scanner 54
    PostgresSQLScanner 54
PostgresPHPGenerator 225
PostgresSQL 60, 204
    official site 211
Pro*C 79, 159, 171
Proc-Blaster 229
processing flow
    ASP 217
    ASP.NET 219
    binary file reader/writer 189
    C 146
    C++ header from scratch 265
    C++ header with existing
      methods 266
    CSV reader 175
    data adapter 187
    DLL wrapper 267
    EJB 205
    external language
      wrapper 269
    firewall configuration 270
    Java equation 254
    JDBC 215
    JSP 108
    lookup function 272
    lookup table 274
    MFC 123
    MFC mixed-code
      architecture 125
    ordered test 152
    PerlDBI 222
    PerlSQL 164
    PHP 225
    report logic 262
    SOAP 249
    SQL documentation 131
    Swing 121
    test data 153

test robot 157
    XML-RPC 237
projects
    long 17
Python 39, 43
    as a generator 41
    unit testing 158
PyUnit 158

Q

Qt 37, 102

R

Rational Rose 5, 194
RDoc 138
RDTool 138
recoder 59
refactoring 158
regular expressions 38
    C 332
    C# 331
    patterns 332
    Perl 328
    Python 327
    Ruby 282, 326
Remote Procedure Call 13
    authorization 232
report logic generator 260
    alternative architecture 262
    architecture 261
    process flow 262
    role 260
    tools 263
reporting 260
request authorization 232
Rexml 44, 175
    attributes 45
    document 44
    each_element 44
    elements 44
    installing 44
rexml 41, 46, 71
RMI 4, 201

RPC. *See* Remote Procedure Call
Ruby 39, 42–43
    as a generator 41
    binary file i/o 189
    directory handling 65
    downloading 43
    embedded
      documentation 138
    object orientation 42
    readability 41
    reading standard input 66
    regular expressions 282
    unit testing 286
    windows installer 43

S

ScanDoc 138
schema 4, 7
Segue 142
self-documenting code 127
semantic capture 17
sequential unit tests generator
    architecture 151
    process flow 152
    roles 151
Simple Object Access
    Protocol 13
skills
    directory handling 40
    file handling 39–40
    parsing xml 39
    regular expressions 38
    text templates 38
SOAP 13, 129, 201, 230, 248
    apache site 249
    books 249
    stateless model 232
SOAP generation
    design tips 249
    tools 250
SOAP generator 248
    architecture 248
    process flow 249